The "Silent Majority" Speech

The "Silent Majority" Speech treats Richard Nixon's address of November 3, 1969, as a lens through which to examine the latter years of the Vietnam War and their significance to U.S. global power and American domestic life.

The book uses Nixon's speech – which introduced the policy of "Vietnamization" and cited the so-called bloodbath theory as a justification for continued U.S. involvement in Southeast Asia – as a fascinating moment around which to build an analysis of the last years of the war. For Nixon's strategy to be successful, he requested the support of what he called the "great silent majority," a term that continues to resonate in American political culture. Scott Laderman moves beyond the war's final years to address the administration's hypocritical exploitation of moral rhetoric and its stoking of social divisiveness to achieve policy aims. Laderman explores the antiwar and pro-war movements, the shattering of the liberal consensus, and the stirrings of the right-wing resurgence that would come to define American politics.

Supplemental primary sources make this book an ideal tool for introducing students to historical research. *The "Silent Majority" Speech* is critical reading for those studying American political history and U.S.–Asian/Southeast Asian relations.

Scott Laderman is a professor of history at the University of Minnesota, Duluth. His previous books include *Tours of Vietnam: War, Travel Guides, and Memory* (2009) and *Empire in Waves: A Political History of Surfing* (2014).

Critical Moments in American History

Edited by William Thomas Allison, Georgia Southern University

For more information about this series, please visit:
https://www.routledge.com

The "Silent Majority" Speech

Richard Nixon, the Vietnam War, and the Origins of the New Right

Scott Laderman

Routledge
Taylor & Francis Group

NEW YORK AND LONDON

First published 2020
by Routledge
52 Vanderbilt Avenue, New York, NY 10017

and by Routledge
2 Park Square, Milton Park, Abingdon, Oxon, OX14 4RN

Routledge is an imprint of the Taylor & Francis Group, an informa business

Library of Congress Cataloging-in-Publication Data
A catalog record for this title has been requested

ISBN: 978-0-415-34746-4 (hbk)
ISBN: 978-0-415-34749-5 (pbk)
ISBN: 978-1-315-22939-3 (ebk)

Typeset in Bembo and Helvetica Neue
by codeMantra

Contents

Series Introduction

Welcome to the Routledge *Critical Moments in American History* series. The purpose of this new series is to give students a window into the historian's craft through concise, readable books by leading scholars, who bring together the best scholarship and engaging primary sources to explore a critical moment in the American past. In discovering the principal points of the story in these books, gaining a sense of historiography, following a fresh trail of primary documents, and exploring suggested readings, students can then set out on their own journey, to debate the ideas presented, interpret primary sources, and reach their own conclusions – just like the historian.

A critical moment in history can be a range of things – a pivotal year, the pinnacle of a movement or trend, or an important event such as the passage of a piece of legislation, an election, a court decision, and a battle. It can be social, cultural, political, or economic. It can be heroic or tragic. Whatever they are, such moments are by definition "game changers," momentous changes in the pattern of the American fabric, and paradigm shifts in the American experience. Many of the critical moments explored in this series are familiar; some less so.

There is no ultimate list of critical moments in American history – any group of students, historians, or other scholars may come up with a different catalog of topics. These differences of view, however, are what make history itself and the study of history so important and so fascinating. Therein can be found the utility of historical inquiry – to explore, to challenge, to understand, and to realize the legacy of the past through its influence of the present. It is the hope of this series to help students realize this intrinsic value of our past and of studying our past.

William Thomas Allison
Georgia Southern University

Figures

Acknowledgments

My completion of this volume was made immensely easier because of the important research done by scholars before me. I wish to especially acknowledge the work of Jeffrey Kimball and David Schmitz, whose books on Nixon's Vietnam War offer a far fuller account than the one found in these pages. Not only did their findings influence my own thinking, but their footnotes saved me countless hours I would have otherwise had to spend searching through innumerable sources on my own.

The staff at the National Archives in College Park, Maryland, has consistently been helpful. And I cannot say thank you enough to the librarians – especially Kay Westergren, who was always quick to get me books through interlibrary loan – at the University of Minnesota, Duluth (UMD). I am grateful, too, to the College of Liberal Arts at UMD, which helped to fund the research that made The "Silent Majority" Speech possible.

At Routledge, I want to thank Genevieve Aoki, Dan Finaldi, Zoë Forbes, Margo Irvin, Eve Mayer, Ted Meyer, and Kimberley Smith for their interest in this book and their assistance in seeing it through to completion. My thanks also to series editor Bill Allison for the feedback and thumbs up. And my sincere appreciation to Derek Gottlieb for his work on the index.

As always, my deepest debt is owed to my wife Jill and my two daughters, Izzy and Sam. Their love and support made years of studying the Nixon administration tolerable.

A Brief Note on Language

Readers unversed in the nuances of the Vietnam War or the modern right-wing movement may be misled by their lexicons. In an effort to minimize that possibility, I want to comment on several widely used terms, some of which you will encounter in these pages.

Those who fought against the Americans (and, before them, the French) have often been called "the communists." I avoid that designation. Why? For two principal reasons. First, it is inaccurate. Many noncommunists also fought the Americans and their "anticommunist" allies, and use of *communists* erases these noncommunists' participation. And second, the moniker simply carries too much Cold War baggage. I have thus opted to use the term *revolutionaries*. The Vietnamese revolutionaries were indeed led by communists, but they were not exclusively communist, and those who were communists were often not communists in the most doctrinaire, Cold War sense.

There were no countries called North Vietnam and South Vietnam. Instead, there was a country called Vietnam that, in 1954, was temporarily divided at the seventeenth parallel into two nonstate zones. *North Vietnam* and *South Vietnam* have been used as shorthand for the governments that established their capitals in Hanoi and Saigon, the largest cities in the northern and southern zones, respectively. The government in Hanoi referred to Vietnam as the Democratic Republic of Vietnam (DRV); the government in Saigon referred to it as the Republic of Vietnam (RVN). Neither of these two governments recognized Vietnam as two separate states. While you will encounter *North Vietnam* and *South Vietnam* in *The "Silent Majority" Speech*, I want to underscore that these are merely terms of convenience.

Likewise, to think of the war as one between North Vietnam and South Vietnam – or, as American propaganda would have it, an invasion by North Vietnam of South Vietnam – is misleading. Apart from bombing campaigns and occasional covert operations, the American war was fought entirely in the south, and through the mid-1960s, most of its combatants were southerners. On one side were revolutionary insurgents, led by communists, who after 1960 referred to themselves as the National Liberation Front (NLF) and were later subsumed under the Provisional Revolutionary Government (PRG). The Americans and the Saigon government dismissed them as the *Viet Cong*, an appellation that could be roughly translated to "Vietnamese commie," which is clearly pejorative. When you see references to the Viet Cong (or VC, Cong, or Charlie), those are all references to the NLF. None of the revolutionaries during the war referred to themselves as the Viet Cong. For the sake of historical accuracy, I avoid that propaganda term.

I use *conservative* (or *conservatives*) as shorthand for the modern American right despite the fact that there was (and is) usually little that is conservative about it. The movement's partisans could often better be described as reactionaries.[1] But given how widely *conservative* is used in American political discourse, and how a different term might cause confusion, I have opted to use it in this book as well.

---

1 For more on the problematical nature of the term conservative, see, among others, Jeffrey P. Kimball, "The 'Conservative' Label Is a Misnomer," *History News Network*, February 18, 2018, at http://historynewsnetwork.org/article/168094 (accessed February 18, 2018); and Corey Robin, *The Reactionary Mind: Conservatism from Edmund Burke to Sarah Palin* (Oxford: Oxford University Press, 2011).

Timeline

January 9, 1913	Richard Nixon (RN) is born in Yorba Linda, California.
August 25, 1945	Vietnamese emperor Bao Dai abdicates the throne and hands power to the Viet Minh.
September 2, 1945	Ho Chi Minh proclaims the Democratic Republic of Vietnam (DRV) before hundreds of thousands of cheering supporters in Hanoi's Ba Dinh Square.
November 5, 1946	RN elected to the U.S. House of Representatives, defeating incumbent Democrat Jerry Voorhis in California's twelfth congressional district.
November 23, 1946	France attacks Haiphong, a port city, killing thousands of Vietnamese.
March 12, 1947	President Harry S. Truman delivers the "Truman Doctrine" speech to Congress, announcing that U.S. foreign policy would now be centered on countering Soviet expansionism.
March 8, 1949	The ostensibly independent "Associated State of Vietnam" is established by France and former emperor Bao Dai, with Bao Dai declaring himself head of state.
May 1, 1950	The United States begins openly providing aid to the French effort in Indochina.
November 4, 1952	Republican Dwight Eisenhower and RN, his vice presidential running mate, win U.S. presidential election.
May 7, 1954	Viet Minh forces defeat the French at Dien Bien Phu.
May 8, 1954	Geneva conference opens.
July 21, 1954	France, the Democratic Republic of Vietnam, and most of the major world powers sign the Geneva Accords; the United States and the State of Vietnam do not.
October 26, 1955	Following a fraudulent referendum, Ngo Dinh Diem proclaims the Republic of Vietnam (RVN, or "South Vietnam") with himself as president.
November 8, 1960	RN loses the U.S. presidential election to Democratic candidate John F. Kennedy.
December 20, 1960	National Liberation Front (NLF) is established.

January 20, 1961	Kennedy is inaugurated as president, shortly afterward accelerating the U.S. military escalation in Vietnam.
November 1, 1963	RVN president Ngo Dinh Diem is overthrown in an RVN military coup.
November 2, 1963	Ngo Dinh Diem and his brother, Ngo Dinh Nhu, are assassinated.
November 22, 1963	President John F. Kennedy is assassinated in Dallas, Texas.
August 2, 1964	USS *Maddox* is attacked by Vietnamese naval vessels in the Gulf of Tonkin.
August 4, 1964	USS *Turner Joy* is allegedly attacked in the Gulf of Tonkin.
August 7, 1964	Congress passes the Tonkin Gulf resolution with only two dissenting votes.
November 3, 1964	Lyndon B. Johnson, serving as president since Kennedy's assassination, defeats the Republican candidate Barry Goldwater in the U.S. presidential election.
March 8, 1965	First official U.S. combat troops enter Vietnam.
September 3, 1967	Nguyen Van Thieu is elected president of the RVN in a rigged election.
January 30, 1968	NLF and People's Army of Vietnam (PAVN) launch the Tet Offensive.
March 16, 1968	U.S. troops massacre hundreds of Vietnamese civilians at Son My (My Lai).
March 31, 1968	Lyndon B. Johnson announces that he will not seek reelection.
August 26–29, 1968	Democratic National Convention is held in Chicago, Illinois.
November 5, 1968	RN defeats the Democratic candidate Hubert Humphrey and third-party candidate George Wallace in the U.S. presidential election.
January 20, 1969	RN is inaugurated as president of the United States.
November 3, 1969	RN delivers the "silent majority" speech.
February 20, 1970	Henry Kissinger begins secret peace talks with the Vietnamese revolutionaries in Paris.
April 30, 1970	The United States invades Cambodia.
February 8, 1971	RVN military forces commence Operation Lam Son 719.
June 13, 1971	*New York Times* begins publishing the Pentagon Papers.
June 17, 1972	The "Plumbers" break into the Democratic National Committee headquarters in the Watergate complex in Washington, DC.
October 26, 1972	Henry Kissinger, following months of secret negotiations with the Vietnamese revolutionaries, announces that "peace is at hand."
December 18–29, 1972	The United States engages in massive bombing campaign in North Vietnam.
January 27, 1973	Paris Peace Accords is signed by the United States, the Democratic Republic of Vietnam, the Provisional Revolutionary Government (National Liberation Front), and the Republic of Vietnam.
August 9, 1974	RN resigns as president of the United States.
September 8, 1974	Gerald Ford issues RN a full and unconditional pardon for any crimes he may have committed while president.
April 30, 1975	War ends with PAVN/NLF capture of Saigon.
April 22, 1994	RN dies in New York City.

INTRODUCTION

Toward "Peace"

Richard Nixon had an unenviable task. It was 9:32 p.m. on November 3, 1969, and he had been president for less than a year. American opposition to the war in Vietnam was growing more pronounced by the week. Members of the armed forces were increasingly airing their opposition to U.S. policy, and millions of civilians had just participated in an antiwar moratorium. Another huge demonstration was scheduled for November 15. When the president sat down at his Oval Office desk, a motion-picture camera steadily recording his every utterance, he knew, therefore, that a lot was on the line. This speech would frame for the next three years his approach to the nation's most controversial issue. "Good evening, my fellow Americans," he began. "Tonight I want to talk to you on a subject of deep concern to all Americans and to many people in all parts of the world – the war in Vietnam."[1] And so he did. Nixon spent the next thirty-one minutes attempting to sell a frustrated, skeptical, and exhausted public on his vision for how to proceed in Southeast Asia.

We know this address today as the "silent majority" speech, so named because of Nixon's plea rather late in his remarks for the "great silent majority" of the American people to grant him their support in "end[ing] the war in a way that … could win the peace."[2] Nixon proved masterful in employing words and phrases that could alternatively inspire people's greatest hopes or inflame their deepest resentments. In this case, his invocation of a "great silent majority" – which carried with it an implication of a *silenced* majority – was an appeal to those millions of Americans who may not have liked the war in Vietnam but who disliked even more the hundreds of thousands of people, most of them young, who were anything but silent as they marched, rallied, wrote, sang, spoke, sat in, and otherwise demonstrated their opposition to U.S. foreign policy. This was a foreign policy that, Americans had been told for decades, essentially amounted to an expression of God's will for the human race. The United States was a force for good in the global battle against evil, the story went, including in the jungles of Southeast Asia. It seemed inconceivable to this "silent majority" that millions of their compatriots could possibly reject America's salvific mission.

But Nixon's November 3 address was significant for much more than a memorable phrase. In it, the president outlined how he would deliver the "honorable end to the war" he had pledged in his 1968 White House run.[3] Most notably, this meant "Vietnamization," a policy in which the United States would slowly pull its ground forces out of Vietnam while escalating the air war and increasing its training of the South Vietnamese military. And through what came to be known as the "bloodbath theory," Nixon presented what he claimed was a moral basis for ongoing U.S. intervention: the effort to stop the inevitable slaughter by the Vietnamese revolutionaries of those countless Vietnamese who were allied with or otherwise supported the United States. *The "Silent Majority" Speech* explores all of these facets of the speech, seeing Nixon's address as a critical moment on at least three principal levels.

First, by November 1969 the United States, after years of military escalation, had come to recognize that more boots on the ground had not in fact secured Washington's objectives for Vietnam. Nixon thus began a process of gradual troop withdrawal. This did not mean Nixon was abandoning the quest for victory. Rather, it meant attempting to end the war through other means on terms acceptable to the White House. Second, for a presidential administration that has come to be known for realpolitik – a sense that practical considerations drove its foreign policy – the nationwide address highlighted a moral argument by the president: a "precipitate withdrawal" from Vietnam would usher in a series of communist-perpetrated massacres that would become "the nightmare of the entire nation."[4] This, he said, the United States could not abide. Nixon may not have placed a great premium on the value of Vietnamese life – among other sordid episodes, his response to the genocide in Bangladesh, the American carpet bombing of Cambodia, and the atrocities that followed the U.S.-backed coup in Chile all suggest a lack of concern for the fate of Third World peoples –

but he did see political value in moral appeals. There could be benefits, in other words, to framing the war in humanitarian terms. This says something about Nixon as a politician, but it also says something about the centrality of "American exceptionalism" to a broader public with whom his appeals resonated. And third, Nixon helped to usher in the rise of the political right. The Nixon presidency was sandwiched between two important chapters in the story of the modern "conservative" movement. The first of these was the 1964 campaign of Republican presidential candidate Barry Goldwater. The second was the 1980 election of former actor and California governor Ronald Reagan. Nixon may have been distrusted by movement conservatives, but his contributions to their success, which are often underappreciated, were considerable.

Nixon's nationally televised speech, together with the larger moment in which it unfolded, tells us a great deal about the latter years of the Vietnam War and their significance for U.S. global power and domestic life. More than 72 million people tuned in to the president's address, which is three times greater than the number who watched his inauguration just months earlier, and the White House was flooded with approximately 400,000 letters, telegrams, and postcards in response.[5] By looking at both the speech and its context, we can develop an appreciation for the post–Lyndon B. Johnson years of the Vietnam War, including the significance of the antiwar and pro-war movements, the shattering of the liberal consensus, and the stirrings of the right-wing resurgence that, in the last decades of the twentieth century and the first decades of the twenty-first, would come to dominate and define American politics.

NOTES

1 Richard Nixon, "Address to the Nation on the War in Vietnam," November 3, 1969, in *Public Papers of the Presidents of the United States: Richard Nixon, 1969* (Washington, DC: Government Printing Office, 1971), 901.

2 Nixon, "Address to the Nation," 909.

3 Richard Nixon, "Address Accepting the Presidential Nomination at the Republican National Convention in Miami Beach, Florida," August 8, 1968, *The American Presidency Project*, at www.presidency.ucsb.edu/ws/?pid=25968 (accessed July 20, 2017).

4 Nixon, "Address to the Nation," 902.

5 Henry Rahmel to Herbert Klein, November 20, 1969, Folder: SP 3-56/Nation wide T.V. and Radio Address re: Vietnam at Wash. Hilton Hotel, November 3, 1969 (3 of 3), Box 106, Subject Files: Speeches (Ex), White House Central

Files [hereafter WHCF], Nixon Presidential Materials Staff [hereafter NPMS], National Archives II, College Park, MD [hereafter NA II]; Herbert G. Klein to Pope Hill, January 24, 1970, Folder: SP 3-56/Nationwide T.V. and Radio Address re: Vietnam at Wash. Hilton Hotel, November 3, 1969 (2 of 2), Box 106, Subject Files: Speeches (Gen), WHCF, NPMS, NA II. Klein added that in addition to the 400,000 individual correspondents, "hundreds of thousands of names were signed to petitions."

CHAPTER 1

Richard Nixon, the Cold War, and Southeast Asia

The Cold War made Richard Nixon. When he ran for Congress as a Republican from Whittier, California, in 1946, he had spent the previous decade practicing law, working for the Office of Price Administration, and serving in the U.S. Navy. His professional future looked bright. But that future took a public turn when World War II came to an end. In September 1945, just weeks after the Japanese surrender, Nixon received a letter from a banker in his Southern California hometown asking whether he would be willing to take on Representative Jerry Voorhis, the popular New Deal Democrat who held the state's expansive Twelfth District seat. The idea of public service appealed to the young lawyer. Nixon excitedly agreed. He would "tear Voorhis to pieces," he said.[1] How? By smearing him Red. Nixon would discover what a valuable tool red-baiting could be, and he used it to great effect.

Anticommunism was not new to the Cold War. The American financial and commercial establishment, which by 1945 oversaw the world's preeminent industrial economy, had long been hostile to communism, socialism, and anarchism, all of which threatened the nation's capitalist juggernaut. Even labor unionism, which was intended to provide workers with some semblance of power in their workplaces, was generally viewed hostilely. The antipathy of American elites grew as the twentieth century progressed. When Russia underwent a political revolution during World War I that overthrew Czar Nicholas II's detested regime, the Woodrow Wilson administration was initially jubilant. But after the provisional government that had replaced the czar was overthrown by the anticapitalist Bolsheviks, or communists, in late 1917, Washington grew angry. Bolshevism, President Wilson said, represented "the poison of disorder, the poison of revolt, the poison of chaos."[2] In addition to overseeing a "Red Scare" led by his attorney general, A. Mitchell Palmer, the president joined a number of allies – most significantly the British and French – in an ill-fated intervention in Russia from 1918 to 1920. The overseas campaign may have failed, but it underscored a growing American consensus in the halls of power: communism was unacceptable and had to be destroyed.

Still, the United States was at times forced to accommodate itself to its existence. The constitution offered some protection to domestic communists, who reached probably the height of their influence during the Great Depression of the 1930s, when the capitalist economy failed and approximately a quarter of the American workforce could not find jobs. And internationally, Washington learned, communists could serve as crucial allies in a global crisis. Such was the case with Joseph Stalin's Soviet Union during World War II when the Americans and the Soviets shared a common enemy in Nazi Germany. But with the end of the Second World War in 1945, a new epoch began. Washington enjoyed a monopoly of atomic weapons; it occupied Japan, half of Korea, and a substantial portion of Germany; and wartime production had laid the foundation for a capitalist golden age. The United States was the world's dominant economic and military power. It would be a couple of years before the Cold War was unambiguously established, but, even in those first months following the German and Japanese surrenders, rank anticommunism once more became acceptable. And Nixon exploited it.

His Democratic opponent in 1946 was not a communist. Indeed, he was despised by communists as a "red-baiter" and the sponsor of legislation in 1940 that forced communists to register with the federal government. But Nixon didn't care. "Fellow travelers" was a term used to refer to those sympathetic to the views of the Communist Party, and Washington's fellow travelers were "wild about" Voorhis, Nixon claimed. The young California lawyer did everything he could to tar him. Nixon made the incumbent look like a "Red dupe," wrote biographer John Farrell, in a classic case of guilt by association.[3] Nixon proved an expert at it. He trounced Voorhis at the ballot box, winning 56 percent of the vote. It was only a year since World War II ended, and Richard Milhous Nixon was going to Congress.

Once in Washington, the new representative from California only sharpened his attacks on the left. He joined the House Education and Labor Committee that crafted what became known as the Taft–Hartley Act of 1947, which seriously weakened the power of organized labor. He was assigned to the bipartisan Herter mission to Europe that would assess the need for massive U.S. foreign aid (i.e., the Marshall Plan); such aid, Nixon wrote of its utility in combating the Soviet

Union, would give the European people "food & shelter & security and a chance for freedom & peace they will [use to] resist the totalitarian pressure."[4] And he was granted a seat on the House Un-American Activities Committee (HUAC), which became the leading vehicle of the 1940s and 1950s for ferreting out communists, alleged communists, and those said to have communist sympathies. As a member of HUAC, Nixon helped to take down Alger Hiss, a former State Department official alleged to have been a Soviet spy, and he proved eager to go after New Dealers, Hollywood, and any others he saw as insufficiently hostile to the supposed communist conspiracy.

When Nixon decided to move beyond the House and run for the U.S. Senate in 1950 against actress, opera singer, and congresswoman Helen Gahagan Douglas, he smeared her much like he smeared Jerry Voorhis. Her voting record on "Un-American Activities and Internal Security," according to a "pink sheet" disseminated by the campaign, was virtually identical to that of Vito Marcantonio, a New York Democrat that the "pink sheet" called a "notorious Communist party-liner." In fact, Nixon himself had voted the same way as Marcantonio hundreds of times.[5] But that didn't matter. Nixon defeated Douglas by an even larger margin than he had Voorhis four years earlier; he won the Senate race by nearly twenty percentage points. Two years later he would appear as the vice presidential nominee on the Republican presidential ticket of Dwight Eisenhower. They won, and in 1953, at the age of 40, Nixon assumed the second highest office in the United States. By then, given his willingness to manipulate the facts, the Democrats had taken to calling him "Tricky Dick." His massaging of reality was only beginning.

★★★★★

Domestic anticommunism was one thing, but U.S. foreign policy was another. It was in Nixon's capacity as vice president that he first began to seriously address the violence, politics, and uncertain future of Vietnam, which in 1953 was more than seven years into a bloody anticolonial conflict. Until World War II, when imperial Japanese forces occupied much of China and Southeast Asia, Vietnam had been a relatively sleepy backwater of the French empire, which had created a large colony in what is today Vietnam, Laos, and Cambodia. This colony – or, more accurately, this grouping of colonial territories – was given the name French Indochina by the government in Paris. France, like most of the major global powers, had set out in the nineteenth century to colonize portions of Africa and Asia. This followed the colonial conquests of the Spanish, Portuguese, British, French, and Dutch in earlier centuries, including the multinational colonization of North America that, following an eighteenth-century anticolonial war against the British, culminated in the creation of the United States. With complex histories that feature competing governments, private individuals, and corporate entities, parsing the detailed particulars of colonization worldwide is an enormously complicated undertaking. But, in Southeast Asia, the Dutch (Indonesia), the British (Malaysia, Singapore, Burma, and Brunei), the Portuguese (East Timor), the Spanish (the Philippines until 1898), the Americans (the Philippines after 1898), and the French (Vietnam, Cambodia, and Laos) all participated in the imperial race.

Vietnam's experience with French colonialism was not its first. As far back as the second century BCE, the Vietnamese people had suffered the domination of their neighbor to the north, living for over a thousand years under Chinese rule. It was not until 938 that they successfully threw off the Chinese yoke. Apart from a relatively brief period of further Chinese occupation in the fifteenth century, the Vietnamese were able to maintain their sovereignty and continue their own creeping conquest of southern territory until the mid-nineteenth century, when they began to face gradual French colonization. This was not, however, the first Vietnamese encounter with Europeans. French and other explorers, merchants, and missionaries had begun making their way to Vietnam in the sixteenth century. They sought riches, engaged in trade, and proselytized in the name of Christianity. While Vietnamese were fiercely protective of their independence and cultural patrimony, they were also politically divided, with deep frustrations over corruption, inequities in land distribution, taxation, and the often unjust treatment of ethnic minorities.[6] Foreigners exploited this discontent. In the late 1850s, France began military hostilities against the Vietnamese imperial leadership, and in 1862 it acquired its first Vietnamese colony, Cochin China, in the southern third of the country. By 1884 the government in Paris controlled all of Vietnam.

The French colonization inspired local hostility and countless acts of resistance. Vietnamese drew on their proud, centuries-long history of rebellion in creatively crafting their response to French domination. But, in what would later prove an ironic turn, they also looked to the United States – which had its own history of anti-European rebellion – as a model for their national ambitions.[7] Phan Boi Chau, for example, one of the most prominent Vietnamese intellectuals, poets, and revolutionaries of the late nineteenth and early twentieth centuries, extolled "the genius of [George] Washington" in uniting eighteenth-century American patriots and defeating the British. "Venerate Washington who served as commander-in-chief," he wrote. "Follow the example of Washington."[8]

No individual was more influential in organizing resistance to French colonialism, however, than the man known today as Ho Chi Minh. Ho, after whom Vietnam's largest city, the former Saigon, is today named, spent decades agitating for Vietnamese liberation. He, like Phan Boi Chau, looked to the United States as a model and potential ally. Ho had become active in left-wing politics while living in France from 1919 to 1923 – he was a founding member of the French Communist Party in 1920 – and he joined with other Vietnamese nationalists in seeking the independence of his ancestral homeland. During the Versailles peace conference following World War I, Ho, operating under the name Nguyen Ai Quoc ("Nguyen the Patriot"), wrote to the American representative at the conference, Secretary of State Robert Lansing. President Woodrow Wilson had recognized the right of self-determination in his Fourteen Points speech in 1918, and Ho and his fellow Vietnamese revolutionaries took this call seriously. They sought greater rights for the Vietnamese people until "the principle of national self-determination [passed] from ideal to reality."[9] But, despite its consonance with American political rhetoric, their plea fell on deaf ears. The United States never responded to their entreaties, and French colonialism continued.

It took World War II to finally bring about change. Germany had invaded France in 1940, ushering in four years of collaborationist rule and Nazi occupation. Germany's Asian ally Japan, which had decades earlier colonized Korea, Taiwan, and the Ryukyu Islands and in 1931 occupied the Chinese region of Manchuria, took over much of Southeast Asia, including French Indochina, in the early 1940s. The French collaborationist government, popularly known as Vichy France, offered virtually no resistance; indeed, it continued to administer Vietnam under Japanese control. The Vietnamese now faced two occupying powers: France, which they had been opposing for decades, and Japan, which spoke of liberating Asia from European colonization but in fact proved just another colonial oppressor. A militant resistance group formed in response. Founded in 1941, the Viet Nam Doc Lap Dong Minh Hoi, or Viet Minh, was a coalition led by the Indochinese Communist Party to resist French colonial rule and Japanese wartime occupation. It rescued American pilots, engaged in sabotage operations, gathered intelligence, and established a working relationship with the U.S. Office of Strategic Services, which was the predecessor of the Central Intelligence Agency (CIA).

For Ho and the communists, who saw the United States as a model for their own revolutionary aspirations, this alliance with Washington made sense. Indeed, when Ho drafted the Vietnamese Declaration of Independence following the Japanese surrender in August 1945, he modeled its introduction on America's own founding document. "All men are created equal. They are endowed by their Creator with certain unalienable rights: among these are Life, Liberty, and the pursuit of Happiness," it began.[10] The declaration's public reading before hundreds of thousands of supporters in Hanoi's Ba Dinh Square on September 2 was met with ecstatic cheers. But this ecstasy over the creation of the Democratic Republic of Vietnam would be short-lived. Although the Vietnamese declaration had also been inspired by the French Declaration of the Rights of Man and of the Citizen, France did not wish to see its former colony independent. Rather, the French government wanted to reconquer Vietnam and restore the grandeur of the diminished French empire. This flew in the face of the self-determination talk that marked the 1941 Atlantic Charter, the 1942 Declaration by United Nations, and the 1945 UN Charter, but this would hardly be the first time that great-power rhetoric failed to match lived reality. France, while severely weakened by World War II, still had influential champions in Washington. It was thus assisted by the United States in the effort to restore its Vietnamese colony.

Washington may have been reluctant to support French colonialism in the 1940s, but it nevertheless provided crucial early assistance.[11] In late 1945, at least eight U.S. troopships – and possibly as many as twelve – that had been tasked with bringing American military personnel home from Europe were ordered to instead deliver U.S.-armed French troops and Foreign Legionnaires from France to Vietnam. This generated outrage among the enlisted crewmen of the U.S. Merchant Marine aboard these ships. They sent a protest letter to the War Shipping Administration in Washington, cabled President Harry Truman and Senator Robert Wagner about their opposition to "further[ing] the imperialist policies of foreign governments," and drafted a resolution condemning the U.S. government for assisting in the "subjugat[ion of] the native population."[12] This was the beginning of the American antiwar movement – a beginning, significantly, that emanated from those tasked with carrying out military orders – though it seemed to make little difference. U.S. support for France continued, though in somewhat muted form.

American policymakers faced a dilemma. On the one hand, the United States had long professed support for the right of self-determination. On the other, however, Washington sought the elimination of "Communist influence in Indochina" and the association of its people with the "western powers," especially France, according to a 1948 State Department review of policy. The problem, according to the State Department, was that Ho Chi Minh, who was a communist, "probably is now supported by a considerable majority of the Vietnamese people," and these people have "stubbornly resisted the reestablishment of French authority."[13] So what was the United States to do? Honoring the principle of self-determination would mean allowing the creation of an independent communist government in Vietnam. By 1948, however, such a notion was essentially verboten. Communism was something that enslaved free peoples, the United States claimed. It was not something that people were supposed to freely choose. Thus the dilemma for Washington. The Cold War, and its attendant ideology, had arrived.

While American policymakers had been hostile to communism for decades, this hostility intensified following the end of World War II. The Soviet Union found itself transformed in American political culture from a wartime ally of the United States against Nazi tyranny into the nation's principal enemy and an existential threat to modern civilization. With the onset of what journalist Walter Lippmann called America's "cold war" with the Soviet communists, just about everything began to be interpreted through an anticommunist lens.[14] Labor radicalism was communist subversion. Critical Hollywood films were communist propaganda. Political dissent was a communist plot. And anticolonial struggles, such as the one in Vietnam, were communist conspiracies. Reality was in fact far more complex than such Cold War reductionism allowed, but the Cold War was about absolutes: good and evil, lightness and darkness, freedom and totalitarianism. Complexity and nuance had no place in America's new existential struggle.

If these first years of the Cold War saw a deepening of domestic repression and an increasingly paranoid view of international affairs, several developments in the late 1940s and early 1950s helped to seal Vietnam's fate. In August 1949, the Soviet Union successfully detonated an atomic bomb, ending the U.S. nuclear monopoly. Approximately a month later, the Chinese communists defeated the Kuomintang in that country's long civil war. Then, in June 1950, the Democratic People's Republic of Korea (North Korea) launched an offensive across the thirty-eighth parallel into the southern, formerly U.S.-occupied half of the Korean Peninsula. The armed forces of the Republic of Korea (South Korea) quickly collapsed. This was interpreted by Washington as evidence of communism's global march.

How Washington should respond was clear. According to NSC-68, a top-secret U.S. policy paper drafted in April 1950 that served as an ideological blueprint for the emergent Cold War, the success of communism anywhere was a threat to "freedom" everywhere.

The revolutionary fight against French colonialism in Vietnam, which was led by communists, suddenly took on new urgency. What had been viewed by many as a nationalist campaign against the waning vestiges of European imperial power was transformed, under U.S. Cold War ideology, into a clear-cut case of global communist subversion. The Viet Minh, which had been allied with the United States during World War II, were now seen unambiguously as puppets of Soviet totalitarianism, and the free world's survival depended on their defeat. Fortunately, according to Washington, France was leading the good fight. It was incumbent on the Harry Truman administration to lend a hand. So it did. In 1950, following several years of bloody warfare between France and the Viet Minh, the United States began to substantially increase its support for the French campaign. This meant the provision of massive amounts of military aid – so much, in fact, that by 1954, when the French were finally defeated by the Viet Minh, the United States was paying for roughly 80 percent of France's war costs.

This period of increased U.S. support coincided with Nixon's elevation to the vice presidency in January 1953. At the time, Nixon had little policy experience with U.S. foreign relations, and he had no substantive experience with Southeast Asia. What he did have were deep anticommunist convictions and an abiding faith in the justice of America's Cold War mission. President Eisenhower wanted to provide Nixon with firsthand experience abroad, so he sent his vice president on a tour of New Zealand and Australia, Asia, and the Middle East that fall (Figure 1.1). It was during this two-month trip that Nixon first stepped foot in Vietnam. While there, he observed a French attack near the border with China and privately concluded, according to biographer John Farrell, that "France's effort to retain its Southeast Asia colonies was doomed by arrogance and a fatal underestimation of the power of nationalism."[15]

Nixon was certainly not alone in this conviction. U.S. diplomat George Kennan, for example, felt similarly.[16] Yet the problem, Nixon assumed, was not in the great-power intervention itself; rather, it was in its motivation and sponsor. If France was inspired by imperial concerns or could not escape the baggage of its colonial past, the United States, the vice president believed, was different. Nixon subscribed, like most of his compatriots, to the notion of American exceptionalism. Under this ideological belief, the United States was unlike other great powers. Whereas *they* intervened for reasons of self-interest, *we* did so selflessly. Washington was a unique global force for good, according to this logic, seeking to bring "freedom" to people around the world – even if, as it so

Figure 1.1 As vice president during much of the 1950s, Richard Nixon received a
firsthand introduction to the war and political unrest in Vietnam, which
he viewed through a Cold War lens. Here, Nixon and President Dwight
Eisenhower appear together in the Oval Office in August 1954.
Everett Collection Historical/Alamy Stock Photo.

often did, "freedom" meant support for imperial actors, military regimes,
and right-wing dictators.[17] A deep anticommunist, Nixon believed the
situation in Vietnam could be resolved with American assistance.

He promised his French hosts when touring the country, "You
shall not fight unaided," and he publicly celebrated their effort.[18]
Nixon even compared France's war in Vietnam with that country's
eighteenth-century contribution to American independence. Only
now, it seemed, the imperial power had become the liberator. "What
is at stake in this war is fundamentally the freedom and independence of Southeast Asia," he said. "If the Communists should win in
Indo-China, independence would be lost to this whole part of the
world."[19]

And independence, according to Nixon, was incompatible with communism. "You must destroy the Communists on your soil," he told Bao Dai, the former Vietnamese emperor who collaborated with Japan during World War II and, at the time of Nixon's 1953 visit, was serving as chief of state of the wildly unpopular government established by the French. "[Y]ou cannot do that without powerful allies and first of all without the presence of the French Expeditionary Corps."[20] Vietnamese independence, Nixon told a dinner audience a couple of nights later, was only possible with a Vietnamese state that existed within the French Union. "French aid is indispensable to Vietnam," he said, and victory would result "only if Frenchmen and Vietnamese fight together and remain united." A French loss in Indochina would do incalculable harm, he believed. Suggesting that the Viet Minh were international aggressors doing the bidding of a monolithic communist enemy, Nixon associated a Viet Minh victory over France – or even a negotiated settlement – with "foreign bondage" for the Vietnamese people.[21]

Nixon, like most other American policymakers, could not conceive of the unrest in Vietnam outside of a Cold War framework. The Viet Minh could *not* be patriots seeking independence just as Americans once had; rather, they *had* to be tools of the international communist conspiracy. This was reinforced in a speech he delivered over national television and radio shortly after his return to the United States. It was Nixon's first major foreign policy address.[22] Speaking of his recent visit to Asia, Nixon framed the Cold War – and the Indochina conflict – in zero-sum terms. There were 540 million people in "the free nations" and 800 million on "the Communist side," he said. That left 600 million people around the world who were "uncommitted," and most of them were in the countries he just visited. The war in Indochina, together with the wars in Korea and Malaya and the "revolutions" and "subversion" that had been stirred up elsewhere, was evidence of the communists' "all-out effort" to win them over. If the communists were to persevere in Asia, he said, "the balance of power in the world in people and resources will be on their side, and the free world eventually will be forced to its knees."[23] This could not be allowed to happen. U.S. support to France was thus imperative.

The fall of Indochina, Nixon suggested in foreshadowing the "domino theory" the president articulated a few months later, could lead to the fall of Thailand, Malaya, and Indonesia.[24] This, President Eisenhower explained in an April 1954 news conference, was because the countries of Southeast Asia were like dominoes stacked up from end to end.

President Dwight Eisenhower's News Conference: April 7, 1954

President Dwight Eisenhower first publicly articulated what came to be known as the "domino theory" in a news conference in April 1954. Below are excerpts:

Q. *Robert Richards, Copley Press*: Mr. President, would you mind commenting on the strategic importance of Indochina to the free world? I think there has been, across the country, some lack of understanding on just what it means to us.

The President. You have, of course, both the specific and the general when you talk about such things.

First of all, you have the specific value of a locality in its production of materials that the world needs.

Then you have the possibility that many human beings pass under a dictatorship that is inimical to the free world.

Finally, you have broader considerations that might follow what you would call the "falling domino" principle. You have a row of dominoes set up, you knock over the first one, and what will happen to the last one is the certainty that it will go over very quickly. So you could have a beginning of a disintegration that would have the most profound influences.

Now, with respect to the first one, two of the items from this particular area that the world uses are tin and tungsten. They are very important. There are others, of course, the rubber plantations and so on.

Then with respect to more people passing under this domination, Asia, after all, has already lost some 450 million of its peoples to the Communist dictatorship, and we simply can't afford greater losses.

But when we come to the possible sequence of events, the loss of Indochina, of Burma, of Thailand, of the Peninsula, and Indonesia following, now you begin to talk about areas that not only multiply the disadvantages that you would suffer through loss of materials, sources of materials, but now you are talking really about millions and millions and millions of people.

Finally, the geographical position achieved thereby does many things. It turns the so-called island defensive chain of Japan, Formosa, of the Philippines and to the southward; it moves in to threaten Australia and New Zealand.

It takes away, in its economic aspects, that region that Japan must have as a trading area or Japan, in turn, will have only one place in the world to go – that is, toward the Communist areas in order to live.

So, the possible consequences of the loss are just incalculable to the free world.

Source: *Public Papers of the Presidents of the United States: Dwight D. Eisenhower, 1954* (Washington, DC: Government Printing Office, 1960), 382–383.

If one fell, it would knock over the next, and soon enough they all would fall over.[25] The objective for the United States, therefore, was to ensure that the first domino – Vietnam – not fall. For if it did, according to Nixon, "[i]f this whole part of Southeast Asia goes under Communist domination or Communist influence, Japan, who trades and must trade with this area in order to exist, must inevitably be oriented toward the Communist regime." The United States occupied Japan for years following World War II, and it was crucial to Washington's strategic vision for Asia. Nixon therefore stressed the imperative of continued U.S. support for the French and their Vietnamese allies in the fight against the Viet Minh, which he called the "forces of Communist colonialism which would enslave them."[26]

There was no room in this struggle for hesitation or half measures. The people of Asia "want independence," Nixon said. "They want economic progress. They want peace. They want freedom of choice as to their culture, religion, and their economic systems. And they want fundamental recognition of their equal dignity as human beings." Communism would deny them all of these, according to the vice president, for communism "runs counter to human nature" and "goes against all the fundamental desires of the people of Asia. Instead of independence it has brought colonial imperialism and slavery. Instead of economic progress it has brought poverty. Instead of peace it has brought war." Americans understood this. But, Nixon worried, "there are millions of people in this area of the world [Asia and the Middle East] who honestly believe in their hearts that the United States is just as great a threat to the peace of the world as is the Soviet Union and Communist China. And they believe that we may use our military power aggressively, just as quickly as will the Communists."[27]

Yet American intentions were always noble, and American force was never aggressive. It was "only for defense and peace."[28] Or so assumed Nixon in a reflection of the Cold War ideology to which he and millions of his compatriots subscribed. For the Vietnamese revolutionaries fighting for an independent Vietnam, things may have looked different. But American might was righteous, Nixon believed, and this conviction fueled his Cold War militance.

Unfortunately for the United States, ideology was not enough. The war had been going badly for France, and by early April 1954, there were concerns that Paris might give up. A French withdrawal, Nixon told the *New York Times* under the condition that he not be identified, would lead to a communist-dominated Indochina within weeks. In such a case, Washington would have to send in American troops. "The situation in Southeast Asia is currently the most important issue facing the United States," he said. "It relates to a war we might have to fight in the future and that we might lose." But the Eisenhower administration had no choice, he claimed. "The United States, as the leader of the free world, cannot afford further retreat in Asia."[29] A major problem, as he saw it, was that the Vietnamese "lack the ability to conduct a war by themselves or govern themselves."[30] Such statements, which seem jarring to readers in the twenty-first century, reflected the racist paternalism with which white American policymakers viewed Asians and other people of color in the 1950s. The Indochinese, Nixon claimed, lacked "the will to fight." What this might have suggested to those unencumbered by either racism or Cold War ideology was the utter lack of popularity of the French imperial cause among Vietnamese, Cambodians, and Laotians. And no wonder. In the wake of World War II, oppressed peoples worldwide were attempting to throw off the colonial system. They were not welcoming it. But Nixon apparently did not see it that way. "It is not a war to perpetuate French colonialism but to resist extension of Chinese communism," he told an audience in Cincinnati.[31] For him, the war in Vietnam was "a war of aggression by the Communist conspiracy against all the free nations," and the problem was that the French had "tired of the war" and "been slow in training the native soldiers."[32]

Moreover, the vice president suggested, the Vietnamese lacked capable leaders. "Indo-China needs a Syngman Rhee," he maintained, referring to the authoritarian president of the U.S.-backed Republic of Korea (South Korea).[33] Though he did not realize it at the time, Nixon got his wish a few weeks later. In May, Bao Dai appointed Ngo Dinh Diem premier of the State of Vietnam, the nominally independent Vietnamese entity that had been created as a "puppet regime" by the French in 1949.[34] Diem would go on to dominate South Vietnamese politics until he was overthrown in a U.S.-backed coup in 1963. His initial 1954 appointment came too late for Paris, however. Days earlier, on May 7, the French had succumbed to the Viet Minh following a drawn-out battle at Dien Bien Phu, an isolated outpost in northwest Vietnam near the border with Laos. While the French retained considerable strength in the south, their rule effectively came to an end. What remained, however, were the negotiations to determine the terms of the French withdrawal and the political future of Vietnam.

Those negotiations unfolded at a multinational conference in the Swiss city of Geneva. The proceedings in Geneva brought together the two principal belligerents – France and the Democratic Republic of Vietnam (DRV), which oversaw the Viet Minh armed forces – as well as the major world powers: the United States, the United Kingdom (Great Britain), the Soviet Union, and the People's Republic of China. There were also delegations from the Kingdom of Cambodia and the Kingdom of Laos, which reached their own agreements with France, and from the State of Vietnam.

By all accounts, the DRV participated in the conference from a position of relative strength. By early May, the Viet Minh had struck French imperialism an enormous blow, and the revolutionaries enjoyed the popular support of most Vietnamese. If a "free election" were held in Indochina, the U.S. Joint Chiefs of Staff had concluded in March, it was "almost certain" that the communists would win.[35] President Eisenhower was even more categorical. "I have never talked or corresponded with a person knowledgeable in Indochinese affairs," he wrote in his memoirs, "who did not agree that had elections been held as of the time of the fighting, possibly 80 per cent of the population would have voted for the Communist Ho Chi Minh as their leader rather than Chief of State Bao Dai."[36]

Still, the victorious DRV did not secure an immediate French withdrawal.

The final declaration of the conference, which concluded in July, did recognize the independence, unity, and territorial integrity of Vietnam. However, it prevented the DRV from promptly exercising authority

Final Declaration of the Geneva Conference, July 21, 1954

Excerpts from the Final Declaration of the Geneva Conference:

1. The Conference takes note of the agreements ending hostilities in Cambodia, Laos, and Viet-Nam and organizing international control and the supervision of the execution of the provisions of these agreements.
2. The Conference expresses satisfaction at the ending of hostilities in Cambodia, Laos, and Viet-Nam. The Conference expresses its conviction that the execution of the provisions set out in the present declaration and in the agreements on the cessation of hostilities will permit Cambodia, Laos, and Viet-Nam henceforth to play their part, in full independence and sovereignty, in the peaceful community of nations.

3. [...]
4. The Conference takes note of the clauses in the agreement on the cessation of hostilities in Viet-Nam prohibiting the introduction into Viet-Nam of foreign troops and military personnel as well as of all kinds of arms and munitions....
5. The Conference takes note of the clauses in the agreement on the cessation of hostilities in Viet-Nam to the effect that no military base at the disposition of a foreign state may be established in the regrouping zones of the two parties, the latter having the obligation to see that the zones allotted to them shall not constitute part of any military alliance and shall not be utilized for the resumption of hostilities or in the service of an aggressive policy....
6. The Conference recognizes that the essential purpose of the agreement relating to Viet-Nam is to settle military questions with a view to ending hostilities and that the military demarcation line should not in any way be interpreted as constituting a political or territorial boundary. The Conference expresses its conviction that the execution of the provisions set out in the present declaration and in the agreement on the cessation of hostilities creates the necessary basis for the achievement in the near future of a political settlement in Viet-Nam.
7. The Conference declares that, so far as Viet-Nam is concerned, the settlement of political problems, effected on the basis of respect for the principles of independence, unity, and territorial integrity, shall permit the Vietnamese people to enjoy the fundamental freedoms, guaranteed by democratic institutions established as a result of free general elections by secret ballot.

    In order to insure that sufficient progress in the restoration of peace has been made, and that all the necessary conditions obtain for free expression of the national will, general elections shall be held in July 1956, under the supervision of an international commission composed of representatives of the member states of the International Supervisory Commission referred to in the agreement on the cessation of hostilities. Consultations will be held on this subject between the competent representative authorities of the two zones from April 20, 1955, onwards.
8. The provisions of the agreements on the cessation of hostilities intended to insure the protection of individuals and of property must be most strictly applied and must, in particular, allow every one in Viet-Nam to decide freely in which zone he wishes to live.
9. The competent representative authorities of the northern and southern zones of Viet-Nam, as well as the authorities of Laos and Cambodia, must not permit any individual or collective reprisals

against persons who have collaborated in any way with one of the parties during the war, or against members of such persons' families.

10. The Conference takes note of the declaration of the French Government to the effect that it is ready to withdraw its troops from the territory of Cambodia, Laos, and Viet-Nam, at the request of the governments concerned and within a period which shall be fixed by agreement between the parties except in the cases where, by agreement between the two parties, a certain number of French troops shall remain at specified points and for a specified time.

11. The Conference takes note of the declaration of the French Government to the effect that for the settlement of all the problems connected with the reestablishment and consolidation of peace in Cambodia, Laos, and Viet-Nam, the French Government will proceed from the principle of respect for the independence and sovereignty, unity, and territorial integrity of Cambodia, Laos, and Viet-Nam.

12. In their relations with Cambodia, Laos, and Viet-Nam, each member of the Geneva Conference undertakes to respect the sovereignty, the independence, the unity, and the territorial integrity of the above-mentioned states, and to refrain from any interference in their internal affairs.

13. The members of the Conference agree to consult one another on any question which may be referred to them by the International Supervisory Commission, in order to study such measures as may prove necessary to insure that the agreements on the cessation of hostilities in Cambodia, Laos, and Viet-Nam are respected.

Source: *Department of State Bulletin* 31:788 (August 2, 1954): 164.

nationwide. Instead, the accords called for a temporary division of the country at the seventeenth parallel and the creation of two "regrouping zones" – one in the north for the People's Army of Vietnam (i.e., the Viet Minh) and the other in the south for the "forces of the French Union." This was done to facilitate the separation of the competing militaries and pave the way for the French exit.[37] The final declaration was unambiguous, however, that the "military demarcation line" bisecting the nation was "provisional and should not in any way be interpreted as constituting a political or territorial boundary."[38] That language was crucial in light of later American claims that the Geneva Accords created two "countries." They did not. On the contrary, the accords recognized Vietnam as one country that was being only temporarily partitioned; it was to be reunified in 1956 following the two-year period designated for the French withdrawal, with "general elections" to determine the new government.

The declaration, coming a day after France and the DRV reached a bilateral ceasefire agreement, reflected the official consensus of the participants in the Geneva conference, including the war's two principal belligerents. Ominously, however, Bao Dai's French-backed State of Vietnam, which had largely been ignored by the French during the proceedings, indicated its refusal to abide by the accords. The United States also expressed reservations, though it did openly pledge to "refrain from the threat or the use of force to disturb them."[39] That pledge would shortly be abandoned.

The Geneva Accords marked the effective end of French colonialism in Vietnam. For the two years prior to Vietnam's promised reunification, the DRV exercised authority over the northern zone, confident that the 1956 elections would usher the revolutionary leadership into power. France maintained official jurisdiction over the southern zone. Concerned, however, with effectuating their planned withdrawal, the French essentially ceded authority to the State of Vietnam. It quickly became clear that the onetime puppet government, particularly under Ngo Dinh Diem, had no interest in honoring accords to which it had not agreed. This portended future unrest.

So, too, did the rocky politics of the south. Diem, who held nationalist ambitions, engineered the ouster of Bao Dai in a fraudulent 1955 referendum that the U.S. ambassador in Saigon quietly characterized as a "travesty on democratic procedures."[40] The referendum, for which Diem claimed an improbable 98 percent of the vote, elevated the prime minister – that is, Diem – to the presidency of a newly declared "Republic of Vietnam" (RVN). From this new perch, Diem undertook a brutal campaign to crush his political opponents, consolidate his power, and pursue his own vision for a Vietnamese state. Washington, while initially dubious of Diem's ability to succeed, became only too happy to offer its support once he appeared to have neutralized his most significant competitors.[41] Its reasoning was obvious. Like the United States, Diem despised communists. Moreover, he had developed relationships with several influential Americans while earlier living in self-imposed exile in New Jersey, and, as a Catholic, he seemed relatable to American officials.[42]

The Eisenhower administration was prepared to do whatever it took to destroy the Vietnamese revolutionaries. Diem became its preferred instrument.

While the RVN president was not an American puppet – he often refused U.S. advice and stubbornly held to his own preferences – Diem's government became almost wholly dependent on U.S. financial and military aid. He became the face, albeit a brutal and authoritarian one, of the American campaign for "freedom" in Vietnam. Together, Diem and Washington would ignore the 1956 elections called for in the Geneva Accords and would pursue their shared anticommunist vision. They did not always see eye to eye, however. As a Vietnamese nationalist, Diem did not recognize the division of Vietnam into two separate states. On the contrary, he, like the revolutionaries in Hanoi, believed Vietnam to be a single nation, though one temporarily divided, and he of course departed from his revolutionary compatriots by believing that he should lead it. The United States did not agree with this one-state consensus. Seeing the reclamation of the north as a hopeless cause, Washington ultimately sought to create a separate, anticommunist Vietnamese state below the seventeenth parallel. Despite this fundamental disagreement on the nature of Vietnamese nationalism, however, Washington went all in for Diem.

And Nixon was there to support him. In July 1956, two years after the Geneva Accords were signed and when its promised elections were supposed to be held, Nixon visited Saigon, where he met privately with Diem and became the first guest speaker ever invited to appear before the Vietnamese National Constituent Assembly. "[T]he militant march of communism had been halted," he told the southern legislators. "I do not exaggerate when I say that your friends everywhere have derived great inspiration from the successes which have marked the first two years of President Ngo Dinh Diem's Administration." Wishing to underscore the U.S. commitment to Diem, Nixon shared a letter from President Eisenhower extolling Diem's "devotion, ... courage, and determination." The American vice president told the Vietnamese assembly: "It is because of the importance which the American Government attaches to this leadership that I have come on President Eisenhower's behalf to extend to your President on his second anniversary in office the warmest congratulations and good wishes of the American Government and American people."[43]

Not surprisingly for someone so steeped in Cold War ideology, Nixon viewed the situation in Vietnam almost entirely through a Cold

War lens. It was, for American policymakers, yet one more place that communists sought to conquer. To combat this possibility, the United States had to be prepared to fight. "[T]he least chance for war and the best chance for peace will be created through following a policy of strength and firmness with the door always open to negotiation but never to appeasement," Nixon had told a group of school administrators in Ohio a year earlier.[44] Yet, he believed, the communists were wily, professing benevolent intentions while encouraging American complacency. This particularly jeopardized areas such as Southeast Asia. The so-called Third World must not be fooled by the "salesmen of slavery [who] have tried to win over the neutral nations by advocating peace, economic progress, independence, and equality for all peoples," Nixon warned in 1956.[45] America's enemies in fact desired none of these things. "Communism is totally opposed to all that we believe and cherish," he said.[46]

The threat, the vice president suggested later, was particularly acute in Asia and Latin America. In 1960, with Eisenhower's second term coming to an end, Nixon ran as the Republican candidate for president against John F. Kennedy. He lost. In the wake of that defeat, he worried about the American commitment to defeating communism worldwide. "If the smaller nations get the idea that we don't consider them important enough to fight for and that the Communists do, they will go down the Communist line like a row of dominoes," Nixon predicted.[47] This had obvious implications for Vietnam, which Washington saw as threatened by communist imperialism, not legitimate revolutionary nationalism. Diem had spent the second half of the 1950s attempting to destroy his perceived enemies in South Vietnam, but as the new decade began, it was apparent that his repression had backfired. Peasants – undirected by the Communist Party – were beginning to violently confront his regime.[48] Southern revolutionaries lobbied Hanoi to authorize "armed struggle" – not just "political struggle" – against the Saigon government, and in 1960 the National Liberation Front (NLF) was born.[49]

The NLF sought the overthrow of what its founding program called "the camouflaged colonial regime of the American imperialists and the dictatorial power of Ngo Dinh Diem, servant of the Americans," as well as the creation, it claimed, of a democratic government, an improvement in the standard of living, the institution of land reform, a "neutral" foreign policy, and what the organization termed "the dearest desire of all our compatriots throughout the country": the reunification of Vietnam.[50]

Program of the National Liberation Front of South Vietnam

Excerpts from the founding program of the National Liberation Front (NLF) of South Vietnam, which was issued following the NLF's creation in December 1960:

I.   Overthrow the camouflaged colonial regime of the American imperialists and the dictatorial power of Ngo Dinh Diem, servant of the Americans, and institute a government of national democratic union.

II. Institute a largely liberal and democratic regime.

III. Establish an independent and sovereign economy, and improve the living conditions of the people.

IV. Reduce land rent; implement agrarian reform with the aim of providing land to the tillers.

V.   Develop a national and democratic culture and education.

VI. Create a national army devoted to the defense of the Fatherland and the people.

VII. Guarantee equality between the various minorities and between the two sexes; protect the legitimate interest of foreign citizens established in Viet-Nam and of Vietnamese citizens residing abroad.

VIII. Promote a foreign policy of peace and neutrality.

IX. Re-establish normal relations between the two zones, and prepare for the peaceful reunification of the country.

X.   Struggle against all aggressive war; actively defend universal peace.

Source: Reproduced in Edward S. Miller, ed., *The Vietnam War: A Documentary Reader* (Malden, MA: Wiley Blackwell, 2016), 75–80.

While guided by Hanoi, the NLF was not exclusively communist. Its membership was open to all who opposed Diem and his American benefactors, and its leadership included several noncommunists.

Washington and Saigon attempted to dismiss the group as unpopular, unrepresentative, and a blatant instrument of northern aggression against the south. They dubbed the southern insurgents "Viet Cong" – a derisive propaganda term that dates to the mid-1950s and is akin to the English-language epithet "commie." The situation in Vietnam, insisted Secretary of State Dean Rusk, was in fact unambiguous: "the Communist regime in North Viet-Nam" was attempting "to destroy the Republic of Viet-Nam and subjugate its peoples." This was unacceptable. "The independence and territorial integrity of that free country is of major and serious concern not only to the people of Viet-Nam and their immediate neighbors but also to all other free nations," he said.[51] Rusk was a Democrat and Nixon a Republican, but both men, like their respective parties, subscribed to a consensus view of the Cold War and the burgeoning Vietnamese insurgency. The revolutionaries, both north and south, were aggressors doing the bidding of the international communist conspiracy, they believed. To save the free world, the NLF and its patrons had to be crushed.

The problem with this view was what one scholar called its "fragility."[52] The notion that the southern revolution was simply a case of "North Viet-Nam's effort to conquer South Viet-Nam," as a State Department white paper put it, was mistaken.[53] It may have been convenient for policymakers to assert this view publicly, and it remained the official U.S. position, but it was "not wholly compelling," Defense Department analysts privately conceded.[54] Walt W. Rostow, President Kennedy's top advisor for Vietnam, told Secretary of State Rusk in July 1961, "As I see it, the purpose of raising the Viet-Nam issue as a case of aggression is either to induce effective international action or to free our hands and our consciences for whatever we have to do."[55]

And what they had to do – or at least what they did – was to increase the number of U.S. military personnel in the country. Thus began in 1961 the concerted American effort to achieve militarily what it could not achieve politically: a legitimate South Vietnamese state. The inherent challenge for Washington was its pursuit of an unpopular cause: the artificial division of the Vietnamese nation with the support of a leader, Diem, who was far less popular than the revolutionaries. This became glaringly apparent as the insurgency grew. And as the insurgency grew, so did the number of American troops sent to Vietnam. From fewer than 1,000 in early 1961, they increased to more than 16,000 by 1963. The U.S. personnel were there, the Kennedy administration claimed, to advise the armed forces of the Republic of Vietnam; they were not combat troops. But to Vietnamese and Americans alike, the distinction was not always obvious. In the two years following Kennedy's 1961 inauguration, the Americans increasingly engaged in hostile activities, and they were being killed in growing numbers. Only one American advisor had died in combat prior to the inauguration. But "now," historian William Turley noted, "deaths and casualties occurred regularly."[56] Yet this was no time for retreat, Nixon and other anticommunists maintained. The revolutionaries posed an existential threat, and they had to be defeated.

Just how to defeat them was a mystery, however. Increasing the number of U.S. advisors did not appear to have an appreciable effect on the insurgency's resilience. And for Diem, the political situation in South Vietnam grew worse. In 1963, an organized movement of Buddhists who had grown to detest Diem's rule received international media attention when one of their number, Thich Quang Duc, burned himself to death on a Saigon street. It was a brutal display of political opposition. A graphic image of the incident taken by Associated Press photographer Malcolm Browne appeared in newspapers worldwide. The Kennedy administration recognized the growing political crisis that surrounded the RVN president. It faced a serious choice. It could continue to support Diem, though such support would be difficult to sustain unless Diem made changes that Washington considered necessary. Foremost among these was firing his brother and closest advisor, Ngo Dinh Nhu, who was widely despised for his service as head of the secret police. Or the administration could assent to a coup by Diem's own armed forces, much of the leadership of which had turned against the RVN president. Kennedy initially pursued the former option, though without success. Diem stubbornly refused to heed the Americans' advice. The White House then secretly agreed to the latter.

The coup began in late October 1963. By November 1, it had succeeded. Diem and Nhu were overthrown and killed. Three weeks later, an assassin's bullet felled President Kennedy in Dallas, forcing his vice president, former Senate Majority Leader Lyndon B. Johnson, to assume charge of U.S. policy amid the political chaos and violence in Vietnam. Johnson quickly sent his secretary of defense, Robert S. McNamara, to Southeast Asia. McNamara's report upon returning to Washington made for sober reading. "The situation is very disturbing," he told the president. "Current trends, unless reversed in the next 2–3 months, will lead to neutralization at best and more likely to a Communist-controlled state."[57] U.S. officials in Vietnam, he revealed, were not coordinating policy effectively, the NLF was growing even stronger, and the Republic of Vietnam lacked a stable government – in the sixteen months following the coup against Diem, more than a dozen aspirants rotated through the presidential palace.[58]

Some political leaders in Washington advised against U.S. escalation. Indeed, the change in administrations presented an opportunity for an early withdrawal. But Johnson chose war. "I am not going to lose Vietnam," he insisted. "I am not going to be the President who saw Southeast Asia go the way China went."[59] His decision only heightened the American dilemma. Lacking an effective political strategy for defeating the Vietnamese revolution, the president opted to pursue victory on the battlefield; he poured in hundreds of thousands of troops, hoping that each new escalation would result in the insurgents' defeat. In 1969, when Johnson finally left the White House, more than 550,000 U.S. military personnel were serving in the country. Nothing they did seemed to work. For years U.S. officials had privately lamented that the prognosis was grim, but their public statements often suggested the exact opposite. William Westmoreland, for example, the commander of U.S. forces in Vietnam, told the press in November 1967 that American troops were "grinding down the enemy." There was "some light at the end of the tunnel," he assured his deputy.[60] "Light at the end of the tunnel?" Johnson later scoffed to his press secretary, Bill Moyers. "Hell, we don't even have a tunnel. We don't even know where the tunnel is."[61]

The optimistic façade, which fewer and fewer Americans took seriously, essentially crumbled in 1968. In January of that year, the Vietnamese revolutionaries launched what came to be known as the Tet Offensive, a coordinated military assault during the lunar new-year holiday against nearly every major population center in South Vietnam.

The Tet Offensive and the "Credibility Gap"

The Tet Offensive only deepened the American public's decreasing faith in U.S. officials. For months prior to January 1968, when the Tet Offensive began, American leaders, both civilian and military, had been speaking in optimistic terms about U.S. progress in the war. "We have reached an important point when the end begins to come into view," General William Westmoreland, the commander of U.S. forces in Vietnam, said in an address before the National Press Club in November 1967.[1] U.S. ambassador in Saigon Ellsworth Bunker, throwing a New Year's Eve party to mark the arrival of 1968, invited his guests to come "see the light at the end of the tunnel."[2] Yet the Tet Offensive demonstrated to an exhausted public that there was no such light. The war was not almost over, and the Vietnamese revolutionaries were hardly on the verge of defeat. The offensive thus contributed to the American public's growing skepticism about what American officials told them. Distrust prevailed – and with good reason, as U.S. policymakers were, in private, deeply pessimistic about an American victory. They had indeed been dishonest with the American public.

1 Nick Turse, *Kill Anything That Moves: The Real American War in Vietnam* (New York: Metropolitan Books, 2013), 99.
2 Marilyn B. Young, *The Vietnam Wars, 1945–1990* (New York: HarperPerennial, 1991), 216.

Although the United States and its RVN allies successfully repelled it, the simple fact that the revolutionaries could launch such a massive offensive put the lie to the notion that they were on the verge of defeat. Much of the public had already been tiring of the war, participating in antiwar activities in growing numbers. For a great many of those influential Americans who continued to give Washington the benefit of the doubt, the Tet Offensive was the last straw. Walter Cronkite, the CBS newscaster who was said to be the most trusted man in America, summed up his views in the offensive's wake. "To say that we are closer to victory today is to believe, in the face of the evidence, the optimists who have been wrong in the past," he pronounced over the nation's airwaves. "To suggest that we are on the edge of defeat is to yield to unreasonable pessimism. To say that we are mired in stalemate seems the only realistic, yet unsatisfactory, conclusion."[62] Johnson seemed deflated. "[I]f he had lost Walter Cronkite he had lost Mr. Average Citizen," the president reportedly told Moyers.[63]

By early 1968, just months before that year's presidential election, it had come to this: "stalemate." The word stung in a nation that long celebrated its victory culture.[64] Is this the best that Americans could hope for?

Richard Nixon watched these developments with concern. He spent the years through late 1967 largely supportive of the escalation in Vietnam. Always a political opportunist, however, he made a point of placing some daylight between himself and the Democrats in charge. As Kennedy and then Johnson gradually sent more and more American troops to Southeast Asia, Nixon advocated different numbers and a different pace of deployment. He also criticized – misleadingly – diplomatic understandings reached by Washington and Saigon on the nature and timing of potential American troop withdrawals.[65] But these were relatively minor quibbles. Much more concerning to him was what he called President Kennedy's "policies" and, later, President Johnson's "indecision," which Nixon claimed had "frittered away the advantage that massive pressure should have given us."[66] These alleged Democratic shortcomings were a serious problem, Nixon suggested in a 1963 speech to the American Society of Newspaper Editors, for "Communism is on the move. It is out to win. It is playing an offensive game." Any reluctance to "extend freedom," Nixon said, could lead the Soviets to "miscalculat[e] our will to resist." It was in this context that the United States had to "defend Vietnam."[67]

The problem, Nixon claimed in *Reader's Digest* the following year, was that Washington lacked the "will to win." The United States, he asserted, has "demonstrated that we have no real intention of winning this war. Instead, we are trying to achieve a precarious balance of not-quite-winning and not-quite-losing. Our allies in Asia are losing faith in us. Too often, they have seen us falter and renege on our decisions." Politicians' talk of accommodating communism – of withdrawing U.S. forces or of allowing Vietnam's neutralization ("surrender on the installment plan," Nixon called it) – was stoking fears that "the United States will weaken its resolve." The fact that Diem had recently been murdered in a coup "encouraged by the United States" represented "one of the blackest moments in the history of American diplomacy," he said. If Washington was willing to betray its longtime ally in Saigon, why should anyone trust the United States?[68]

American credibility was thus on the line. "What we *must* do," Nixon wrote, "is to instill in ourselves and our allies a determination to win this crucial war – and win it decisively. We must recognize that we are in a life-and-death struggle that has repercussions far beyond Vietnam, and that victory is essential to the survival of freedom." This was a war, in other words, with global implications. If the United States got out, communists would be encouraged by this display of American weakness and would pursue aggression elsewhere, he argued. Because the United States was the leader of the "free world," it would find it necessary to counter such hostility. But now it would be facing an emboldened communist enemy. The inevitable war would be even larger. "The present administration's policy" – he was referring to Johnson – only increased "the danger of major war." It was better to defeat the communists in Vietnam now.[69]

Nixon acknowledged that this hawkishness – what he called his "'win' policy" – opened him up to charges of "warmongering and endangering world peace." But, he insisted, "[t]he contrary is true. History shows that the appeasers, the compromisers who refuse to stand up against aggression, *have* to take a stand sooner or later – and always at a less favorable time and place." The current course of "compromise, vacillation, accommodation, and appeasement" thus had to be abandoned. Washington needed to decide on victory, which he defined as both the defeat of communism and "a free North Vietnam." Withdrawal, neutralization, or a military loss would only lead to a larger war, "probably with nuclear weapons." But "a victory for us in South Vietnam will shatter the myths of communist invincibility and of the inevitability of a Chinese takeover in Southeast Asia." This will halt the rising communist tide and may even cause its recession. The United States, he said, needed to overcome its crisis of confidence and marshal "the courage to use our power." It needed to develop the "will to win."[70]

Nixon continued to subscribe to the domino theory, telling the Executives Club of New York in January 1965 that "if Vietnam is lost" so will "Indonesia, Cambodia, Laos, Thailand, and all the rest" be lost. But the issue was not so much one pitting the United States against international communism. On the contrary, Nixon recognized the reality of the Sino–Soviet split, acknowledging that most of the Moscow leadership sought coexistence with the West. It was the "hardliners" in Beijing, he said, who remained hell-bent on global domination. "[W]hat we are dealing with in Vietnam is Chinese communist aggression." Yet while attentive to the nuances in the alleged communist threat, and aware of the nationalist desire for decolonization that swept through Asia after World War II, Nixon continued to dismiss the indigenous roots of the Vietnamese revolution. "If communist China were not instigating and supporting the Viet Cong," he insisted, "there would be no war in Vietnam today." The former vice president preferred to view the conflict through the prism of the Cold War. "The battle for Vietnam is the battle for Asia," he said. As for how to win it, Nixon counseled that the United States "'quarantine' the war and use American air and sea power to cut supply lines and destroy staging areas in North Vietnam and Laos which now make it possible for the guerrillas to continue their actions." The "South Vietnamese can handle the ground fighting," he suggested. "We should use American manpower only in the air and on the sea."[71]

Under no circumstances, he later wrote, should the United States seek a negotiated settlement. In the months between his January speech in New York and a missive he penned for the December 1965 issue of *Reader's Digest*, the war had begun to turn, he claimed. Where Nixon had been pessimistic before, he was optimistic now. "Today, after a recent visit to Southeast Asia, I am convinced that the communists are losing ground and that the South Vietnamese with our help have a good chance of victory." What had made the difference, he said, was not just "American air strikes in North Vietnam" but, ironically enough in light of his earlier advice, "our commitment of ground troops in South Vietnam." But "real victory" would not come quickly. It would take "two years or more of the hardest kind of fighting."[72]

Two years later, victory seemed as distant as ever. As 1968 approached, Nixon spotlighted the growing divisions in the United States between the left, liberals, and the Democratic Party, suggesting that this was doing harm to the American effort in Southeast Asia. Hanoi, he claimed, would persist with its "aggression" so long as the revolutionaries believed that millions of Americans opposed the war. During an April 1967 trip to Saigon, Nixon said it was "essential that the enemy be convinced that he cannot win the war militarily, that he cannot win it through a change in public opinion in the United States." What was needed, according to Nixon, was the mobilization of "free world opinion" and unity at home. Democratic criticisms of U.S. policy were giving "aid and comfort to the enemy" and needed to cease. "I recognize the right of dissent," he said, "but by golly, as I look around the world at the present time I am convinced that the divisions in the United States and the lack of understanding in Western Europe and the rest of the free world prolongs the war."[73]

Such criticisms allowed Nixon to blame the tactics – not the strategy, with which he essentially concurred – of the Johnson administration, together with the political disunity outside the Republican ranks, for the failure to achieve victory in Vietnam. The problem was thus one of "leadership," not policy. How to overcome the poor execution of an otherwise sound strategy? That would take a new president. And who better to take the presidential reins than the last Republican to nearly win the White House. On February 1, 1968, with the nation embroiled in furious debates about the war, Nixon formally announced his candidacy for that year's presidential election. Offering to bring peace with honor amid widespread frustration with Johnson and the Democratic Party, he exploited the American disgust with the war and, in August, captured the Republican nomination. By early September, with the November balloting just two months away, Nixon enjoyed a substantial lead in the polls over his Democratic counterpart, Hubert Humphrey. But then word leaked – especially through Henry Kissinger, who at the time was serving as a Republican consultant – that a negotiated settlement in Vietnam may be forthcoming.

By the spring of 1968, it had become clear that an American military victory, if possible at all, would take years to accomplish. At the same time, both Hanoi and the National Liberation Front had suffered extensive military setbacks during the Tet Offensive. The Johnson administration entered into quiet negotiations in Paris with the Vietnamese revolutionaries, which for several months they stalled. Then, that summer, the Soviet Union, which preferred to see Humphrey, not Nixon, in the White House, wrote to President Johnson that if the United States halted its bombing of North Vietnam, Moscow would press Hanoi. "I and my colleagues believe – and we have grounds for this – that a full cessation by the United States of bombardments...could promote a breakthrough." This was not a guarantee of peace, of course, but the Johnson administration believed that the Soviet offer represented Washington's best chance in years to bring to a close its contentious military involvement in Vietnam. The president announced a bombing halt five days before the election. This progress concerned the Republican candidate. With polls showing him beating his Democratic challenger, Nixon worried about what an agreement could mean for his ability to win. "Events could cut down a lead as big as ours," he justifiably feared.[74]

Nixon thus worked through unofficial channels, according to notes taken by his aide H. R. Haldeman, to "monkey wrench" the negotiations. He secretly encouraged the Saigon regime, which would have to agree to any terms, to resist a settlement, suggesting that it would do better in a Nixon administration. "Hold on. We are gonna win," Nixon emissary Anna Chennault assured RVN Ambassador Bui Diem. "Please tell your boss [RVN President Nguyen Van Thieu] to hold on."[75] There is evidence suggesting that the intervention was unnecessary and that the leadership in Saigon would have resisted the settlement regardless of what Washington thought.[76] Nevertheless, the fact that Nixon's campaign interfered in the negotiations was not insignificant. Indeed, Nixon's effort to scuttle an agreement was "potentially felonious," biographer John Farrell noted. Historian Ken Hughes was less reserved, unambiguously calling it a "crime committed to elect Nixon president."[77] President Johnson became aware of what he referred to as Nixon's "treason," but, given that it was just days before the election, he decided not to disclose it. Doing so would mean acknowledging U.S. surveillance not just of the South Vietnamese government – an ally – but also of the Republican candidate.[78] Nixon thus got away with attempting to undermine the possibility of an earlier end to the war – one which continued for another seven years, with hundreds of thousands of additional casualties.

Nixon narrowly won the election and, two months later, was inaugurated as the thirty-seventh president of the United States. It was now Nixon's war.

NOTES

1   John A. Farrell, *Richard Nixon: The Life* (New York: Doubleday, 2017), 12.
2   Woodrow Wilson, "Address at Des Moines, Iowa," September 6, 1919, *Addresses of President Wilson* (Washington: Government Printing Office, 1919), 60.
3   Farrell, *Richard Nixon*, 16, 29.
4   Farrell, *Richard Nixon*, 91.
5   Richard M. Nixon, "The 'Pink Sheet,'" September 1950, in Rick Perlstein, ed., *Richard Nixon: Speeches, Writings, Documents* (Princeton, NJ: Princeton University Press, 2008), 60–61.

6   Marilyn B. Young, John J. Fitzgerald, and A. Tom Grunfeld, eds., *The Vietnam War: A History in Documents* (Oxford: Oxford University Press, 2002), 12.

7   For more on the United States in the Vietnamese political imagination, see Mark Philip Bradley, *Imagining Vietnam and America: The Making of Postcolonial Vietnam, 1919–1950* (Chapel Hill: University of North Carolina Press, 2000), 10–44.

8   Young, et al., *The Vietnam War*, 19.

9   Nguyen Ai Quoc to Robert Lansing, June 18, 1919, in Young, et al., *The Vietnam War*, 21.

10 Vietnamese Declaration of Independence, in Young, et al., *The Vietnam War*, 27.

11 On the internal debates over U.S. support for the French recolonization and the reluctance to heavily commit, see Mark Atwood Lawrence, *Assuming the Burden: Europe and the American Commitment to War in Vietnam* (Berkeley: University of California Press, 2005).

12 H. Bruce Franklin, *Vietnam and Other American Fantasies* (Amherst: University of Massachusetts Press, 2000), 50.

13 State Department Review of Policy, September 1948, in Young, et al., *The Vietnam War*, 32.

14 Katherine Connor Martin, "George Orwell and the Origin of the Term 'Cold War,'" *OUPblog*, October 24, 2015, at https://blog.oup.com/2015/10/george-orwell-cold-war/ (accessed August 16, 2017).

15 Farrell, *Richard Nixon*, 218.

16 Young, et al., *The Vietnam War*, 34–36.

17 David F. Schmitz, *Thank God They're on Our Side: The United States and Right-Wing Dictatorships, 1921–1965* (Chapel Hill: University of North Carolina Press, 1999); and idem, *The United States and Right-Wing Dictatorships, 1965–1989* (Cambridge: Cambridge University Press, 2006).

18 Farrell, *Richard Nixon*, 218.

19 "Nixon Bids Vietnam Spur War Effort," *New York Times*, November 1, 1953.

20 "Nixon Bids Saigon Keep French Ties," *New York Times*, November 3, 1953.

21 "Nixon Disapproves Indo-China Truce," *New York Times*, November 5, 1953.

22 David F. Schmitz, *Richard Nixon and the Vietnam War: The End of the American Century* (Lanham, MD: Rowman & Littlefield, 2014), 3.

23 Richard Nixon, "Meeting the People of Asia," *Department of State Bulletin* 30:758 (January 4, 1954), 10.

24 Nixon, "Meeting the People of Asia," 12.

25 Dwight D. Eisenhower, "The President's News Conference of April 7, 1954," *Public Papers of the Presidents of the United States: Dwight D. Eisenhower, 1954* (Washington, DC: Government Printing Office, 1960), 383.

26 Nixon, "Meeting the People of Asia," 12.

27 Nixon, "Meeting the People of Asia," 13.

28 Richard M. Nixon, "The Chances for Peace Today: Dynamic Forces at Work on World Problems," *Vital Speeches of the Day*, October 15, 1955, 71. The United States was making a "huge expenditure of money and manpower," he said in an October 1955 speech, "[n]ot because we want territory. We have never asked for any, and we have acquired none. Not because we want the countries we aid to

be dependent, but because we want them to be independent. Not because we want war, but because we want peace. The United States is willing to accept any proposal leading towards peace except one that would mean surrender of our own freedom or the freedom of others, or one that would mean acquiescence in the enslavement of any peoples in the world." Nixon, "The Chances for Peace Today," 72.

29   Luther A. Huston, "Asian Peril Cited: High Aide Says Troops May Be Sent if the French Withdraw," New York Times, April 17, 1954. Nixon was identified as the source of the comments the next day; see "Digest of Nixon's Talk on Indo-China," New York Times, April 18, 1954.

30   "Digest of Nixon's Talk on Indo-China."

31   "Nixon Clarifies Position on Asia," New York Times, April 21, 1954.

32   "Nixon Clarifies Position on Asia"; Huston, "Asian Peril Cited."

33   Huston, "Asian Peril Cited."

34   Edward Miller, Misalliance: Ngo Dinh Diem, the United States, and the Fate of South Vietnam (Cambridge, MA: Harvard University Press, 2013), 51–53; Pierre Asselin, "Choosing Peace: Hanoi and the Geneva Agreement on Vietnam, 1954–1955," Journal of Cold War Studies 9:2 (Spring 2007): 97.

35   Joint Chiefs of Staff to the Secretary of Defense, March 12, 1954, in The Pentagon Papers: The Defense Department History of United States Decisionmaking on Vietnam, Senator Gravel Edition (Boston, MA: Beacon Press, 1971), I: 449.

36   Dwight D. Eisenhower, The White House Years: Mandate for Change, 1953–1956 (London: Heinemann, 1963), 372.

37   The Geneva Cease-Fire, July 20, 1954, in Marvin E. Gettleman, Jane Franklin, Marilyn B. Young, and H. Bruce Franklin, eds., Vietnam and America, second edition (New York: Grove Press, 1995), 67.

38   Final Declaration of the Geneva Conference, July 21, 1954, in Gettleman, et al., Vietnam and America, 75.

39   Walter Bedell Smith quoted in Gettleman, et al., Vietnam and America, 78.

40   Despatch from the Ambassador in Vietnam (Reinhardt) to the Department of State [Document 278], November 29, 1955, Foreign Relations of the United States, 1955–1957, Volume I: Vietnam (Washington, DC: Government Printing Office, 1985), 593.

41   Jessica M. Chapman, Cauldron of Resistance: Ngo Dinh Diem, the United States, and 1950s Southern Vietnam (Ithaca, NY: Cornell University Press, 2013).

42   Seth Jacobs, America's Miracle Man in Vietnam: Ngo Dinh Diem, Religion, Race, and U.S. Intervention in Southeast Asia (Durham, NC: Duke University Press, 2004).

43   "Nixon Hails Diem on Visit to Saigon," New York Times, July 7, 1956.

44   Richard M. Nixon, "'Peace without Surrender,'" U.S. News and World Report (April 15, 1955): 66.

45   Richard M. Nixon, "In the Cause of Peace and Freedom: Rule of Law Upheld," Vital Speeches of the Day 23:6 (January 1, 1957): 164.

46   Richard M. Nixon, "A Blunt Challenge to Our Free World: We Must Avoid Extremes of Panic and Complacency," Vital Speeches of the Day 24:5 (December 15, 1957): 131.

47   "Republicans: 'Now Is the Time…,'" *Time* (May 12, 1961): 14.

48   David Hunt, *Vietnam's Southern Revolution: From Peasant Insurrection to Total War* (Amherst, MA: University of Massachusetts Press, 2008), 6.

49   Robert K. Brigham, "Why the South Won the American War in Vietnam," in Marc Jason Gilbert, ed., *Why the North Won the Vietnam War* (New York: Palgrave, 2002), 97–116.

50   Program of the National Liberation Front of South Vietnam (1960), in Edward Miller, ed., *The Vietnam War: A Documentary Reader* (Malden, MA: Wiley Blackwell, 2016), 75–80.

51   Rusk quoted in Department of State, *A Threat to the Peace: North Viet-Nam's Effort to Conquer South Viet-Nam* (Washington, DC: Government Printing Office, 1961), Folder 11, Box 07, Douglas Pike Collection: Unit 11 – Monographs, Vietnam Archive, Texas Tech University, I: iii.

52   George McT. Kahin, *Intervention: How America Became Involved in Vietnam* (New York: Anchor Books/Doubleday, 1986), 471.

53   Department of State, *A Threat to the Peace*, i.

54   *The Pentagon Papers*, Senator Gravel Edition, I: 243.

55   Walt W. Rostow to Dean Rusk, July 13, 1961; Vietnam, General, 7/5/61-7/13/61; Box 193A; National Security Files; Countries; Papers of President Kennedy; John Fitzgerald Kennedy Library, Boston, MA.

56   William S. Turley, *The Second Indochina War: A Short Political and Military History* (Boulder, CO: Westview Press, 1986), 45.

57   Robert S. McNamara to Lyndon B. Johnson, December 21, 1963, in Young, et al., *The Vietnam War*, 67.

58   Robert Buzzanco, *Vietnam and the Transformation of American Life* (Oxford: Blackwell Publishers, 1999), 69; McNamara to Johnson, December 21, 1963, 67–68.

59   Eric Alterman, *When Presidents Lie: A History of Official Deception and Its Consequences* (New York: Penguin Books, 2004), 175.

60   M. A. Farber, "General Disputes Quote in CBS Trial," *New York Times*, November 30, 1984.

61   A. J. Langguth, *Our Vietnam: The War, 1954–1975* (New York: Simon & Schuster, 2000), 354.

62   *Who, What, When, Where, Why: Report from Vietnam by Walter Cronkite*, CBS Evening News, February 27, 1968, in Young, et al., *The Vietnam War*, 87.

63   Young, et al., *The Vietnam War*, 86.

64   Tom Engelhardt, *The End of Victory Culture: Cold War America and the Disillusioning of a Generation* (New York: Basic Books, 1995).

65   Richard Nixon, "Appraisal from Manila," November 4, 1966, in Perlstein, *Richard Nixon*, 117–120. For the full statement, see "An Appraisal of Manila," November 4, 1966, at https://cdn.nixonlibrary.org/01/wp-content/uploads/2017/07/24093905/An-Appraisal-of-Manila.pdf (accessed September 15, 2017).

66   Richard Nixon, "American Policy Abroad: Analysis and Recommendations," *Vital Speeches of the Day* 29:16 (June 1, 1963): 487; Jeffrey Kimball, *Nixon's Vietnam War* (Lawrence: University Press of Kansas, 1998), 29.

67   Nixon, "American Policy Abroad," 487–489.

68   Richard M. Nixon, "Needed in Vietnam: The Will to Win," *Reader's Digest* 85:508 (August 1964): 37–38, 40.

69   Nixon, "Needed in Vietnam," 38, 43.

70   Nixon, "Needed in Vietnam," 42–43.

71   Richard M. Nixon, "Facing the Facts in Vietnam: Get Out, Neutralize, or Win," *Vital Speeches of the Day* 31:11 (March 15, 1965): 337–339. On Nixon's recognition of postwar nationalism and the desire for decolonization, see Richard M. Nixon, "Asia After Viet Nam," *Foreign Affairs* 46:1 (October 1967): 112–113.

72   Richard M. Nixon, "Why Not Negotiate in Vietnam?" *Reader's Digest* 87:524 (December 1965): 49–50.

73   Kimball, *Nixon's Vietnam War*, 29–30; Tom Buckley, "Nixon Urges Halt to War Criticism," *New York Times*, April 15, 1967; "Nixon Says Asians Back U.S. on War," *New York Times*, April 8, 1967.

74   Farrell, *Richard Nixon*, 341. See also John A. Farrell, "Tricky Dick's Vietnam Treachery," *New York Times*, January 1, 2017; and John A. Farrell, "When a Candidate Conspired with a Foreign Power to Win an Election," *Politico*, August 6, 2017, at www.politico.com/magazine/story/2017/08/06/nixon-vietnam-candidate-conspired-with-foreign-power-win-election-215461 (accessed August 11, 2017).

75   Farrell, *Richard Nixon*, 343. See also Peter Baker, "Nixon Looked for 'Monkey Wrench' in Vietnam Talks to Help Win Race," *New York Times*, January 3, 2017.

76   Robert K. Brigham, *Reckless: Henry Kissinger and the Tragedy of Vietnam* (New York: PublicAffairs, 2018), 3–5.

77   Ken Hughes, *Chasing Shadows: The Nixon Tapes, the Chennault Affair, and the Origins of Watergate* (Charlottesville: University of Virginia Press, 2014), x.

78   Farrell, *Richard Nixon*, 342–343.

CHAPTER 2

Vietnamization and the Illusion of Peace

What to do? Having been sworn into office on January 20, 1969, Richard Nixon was presented with an immediate dilemma. He had just finished running on a purposely vague promise to bring about an "honorable end" to the war. What this meant was never clear. Nixon hoped to appeal to both proponents and opponents of U.S. policy, so while campaigning he spoke only in the most general of terms. It was important that he do so, he said, because wars are fluid and he did not wish to give away any "bargaining positions" months before potentially assuming office. He also, he suggested, did not wish to interfere with the Johnson administration's efforts to achieve peace in Southeast Asia.[1] Of course, his secretly conspiring to undermine a negotiated settlement in the final days of the 1968 campaign suggests just how mendacious and hypocritical Nixon could be. But publicly, unsure of what might work, he hoped to be all things to everybody. That offered a way into the White House.

His path was certainly made easier because of the implication that he had a "secret plan" – a term he did not disavow but never in fact used – to achieve a quick victory in Vietnam. And victory was indeed his goal, so long as victory was understood as "an honorable negotiated settlement."[2] This supposed plan, whose details were never disclosed, helped earn him favor with the millions of Americans tired of a war that the two most recent presidents, both of them Democrats, had vastly escalated. Yet Nixon had no magical formula, secret or otherwise. He spoke vaguely while campaigning about the importance of the Soviet Union in helping bring about a settlement, and he suggested that he would follow the lead of Dwight Eisenhower, who managed to end the bloody war in Korea when Nixon was vice president.[3]

Nixon did not want an endless war in Southeast Asia, yet, as an ardent cold warrior, he feared that a premature American withdrawal – essentially, quitting – would do serious damage to American "credibility" in the broader Cold War. What happened on the ground in Vietnam was less important to him than what a loss might mean for global geopolitics. "I certainly do not seek the Presidency for the purpose of presiding over the destruction of the credibility of the American power throughout the world," he told the press in August 1968.[4] The war was essentially a case of what he called "preventive diplomacy," a necessary battle to ensure that the United States faced no more "Viet Nam-type operations in Asia, Africa, Latin America, and other areas" in the future.[5] If the nation's enemies sensed American weakness, this would embolden them. That could not be allowed to happen. While suggesting a potential willingness to eventually negotiate with Beijing, Nixon continued to view China as an expansionist power and believed that the containment of communism was imperative.[6] So, again, what to do?

Nixon spent the initial months of his presidency trying to figure it out. On his first full day in office, he issued dozens of questions to top American officials in the United States and Vietnam in an effort to comprehend what he and his administration faced.[7] The responses from the national security establishment were disheartening. While there were "some divergencies on the facts," there was "general agreement" about the main issues, and the prognosis was almost entirely grim. Even with the recent strengthening in many respects of the U.S.-backed Saigon government, its armed forces "alone cannot now, or in the foreseeable future, stand up to both the VC and sizable North Vietnamese forces," an interagency summary concluded. Things looked little better for the United States. Following years of U.S. military escalation, it continued, "[w]e are not attritting enemy forces faster than they can recruit or infiltrate," and the revolutionaries retained "sufficient strength" to pursue their objectives. Indeed, the "enemy basically controls both sides' casualty rates."[8]

Politically, the Saigon government was "weakest" – "and the VC/NLF strongest" – in rural areas, which is where the overwhelming majority of Vietnamese lived, and it was "not clear" whether it "and other non-communist groups would be able to survive a peaceful competition with the NLF for political power in South Vietnam." The fact that the revolutionaries continued to negotiate with the United States in Paris was not a sign of "weakness" on their part but rather "a desire to pursue [their] objectives at lower costs," according to the summary. And then there was this: The Vietnamese were neither puppets of the Soviet Union and China nor did they do their bidding. "Hanoi is attempting to chart a course basically independent of Moscow and Peking," the American officials concluded.[9]

These were startling findings. They amounted to an admission – though a top secret one – that not only had years of U.S. intervention failed to improve the prospects for victory but that the revolutionaries painted as murderous thugs and aggressors by Washington and Saigon were in fact more popular than America's anticommunist clients. The verdict seemed clear: Nixon had inherited a stalemate, and there was little reason to suspect that things might improve. It would have taken a considerable suspension of one's critical faculties to draw an optimistic outlook from such a negative assessment. Yet that is precisely what the president did. In Nixon's mind, his Democratic predecessor may have failed, but Lyndon Johnson was no Richard Nixon. The new president could do better. And better would require further escalation.[10]

Yet Nixon knew that he was constrained by the political realities of 1969. America was a deeply divided nation, with a clear majority now expressing opposition to the war and a desire to see it end.[11] The depth of that opposition could be seen in the hundreds of thousands of people, from high school and university students to businessmen, educators, housewives, and even military personnel, taking to the streets or otherwise engaging in protest. Corporate executives decried the "sheer nonsense" of persisting with failed policies and condemned the war as unwinnable.[12] For refusing to be drafted while claiming conscientious objection, Muhammad Ali forfeited his heavyweight title and faced a five-year prison sentence.[13] The civil rights paragon Martin Luther King, Jr. explicitly denounced his own government as "the greatest purveyor of violence in the world today."[14] The collective message was unambiguous: The United States had to get out of Southeast Asia. The war had killed tens of thousands of Americans and many more Vietnamese, and it had left two nations deeply divided. And for what? The justifications of U.S. policymakers increasingly rang hollow.

Nixon wished to escalate the war, but he knew this would cause widespread outrage. He thus determined to say one thing and do another. His public statements would suggest and emphasize his quest for peace while his actions would deepen the violence. "I have not stepped up the war in Vietnam," he proclaimed at a March 14 news conference. While the United States would not hesitate to blunt a revolutionary offensive, "[w]e are trying to do everything that we can in the conduct of our war in Vietnam to see that we can go forward toward peace in Paris."[15] Then, on May 14, he took to the airwaves to outline what he saw as a reasonable proposal for "lasting peace." "I want to end this war," Nixon insisted in a nationally broadcast White House address.

> The American people want to end this war. The people of South
> Vietnam want to end this war. But we want to end it permanently
> so that the younger brothers of our soldiers in Vietnam will not
> have to fight in the future in another Vietnam someplace else in
> the world.

The United States could be flexible in its proposed solution, he said,
but any settlement had to "permit the South Vietnamese people to determine freely their own political future."[16]

Nixon then laid out the parameters as he envisioned them. There
would be a "withdrawal of all non-South Vietnamese forces, including
our own, from South Vietnam," and there would need to be "procedures
for political choice that give each significant group in South Vietnam a
real opportunity to participate in the political life of the nation." What
the United States was not seeking, he said, was military bases and military
ties. Washington was prepared to "agree to neutrality for South Vietnam
if that is what the South Vietnamese people freely choose," and it had
"no objection to reunification, if that turns out to be what the people of
South Vietnam and the people of North Vietnam want; we ask only that
the decision reflect the free choice of the people concerned."[17]

The Vietnamese revolutionaries should not view Nixon's offer as
evidence of timidity, he stressed. "[N]o greater mistake could be made
than to confuse flexibility with weakness or of being reasonable with
lack of resolution." His administration would continue, if necessary,
to wield a big stick. "If we are to move successfully from an era of
confrontation to an era of negotiation, then we have to demonstrate –
at the point at which confrontation is being tested – that confrontation with the United States is costly and unrewarding." Above all, the
president maintained, Washington could not accept a settlement that
"would amount to a disguised American defeat."[18]

This all sounded good to many of Nixon's compatriots, and that
was his goal. The president was able to present an image of himself as
a peace seeker, thus appealing to those tired of the seemingly endless
war, while maintaining the nation's military commitment – pleasing
the war's proponents – until the revolutionaries accepted Washington's
terms. But at the heart of Nixon's proposals was a fatal flaw. The proposals assumed that "North Vietnam," like the United States, was an
"outside force" in the country's south. Hanoi fundamentally disagreed.
Nixon's call to withdraw "all non-South Vietnamese forces, including
our own, from South Vietnam" was thus a nonstarter.[19] From the per-
spective of both the Saigon regime and the revolutionaries – and here
the latter pointed to the 1954 Geneva Accords as support – Vietnam

was a single nation. Years of American aggression had not altered this basic reality. To thus demand their withdrawal from the south as an "outsider force" was an insult that flew in the face of why the revolutionaries spent years fighting the Americans. It came down to this: Vietnamese were not foreigners in Vietnam.

As Nixon professed his desire for de-escalation and attempted to signal it to the American public by ordering the withdrawal of tens of thousands of the more than half a million American troops in the country – Henry Kissinger, his national security advisor, colorfully likened the danger of such withdrawals to "salted peanuts," as Americans would demand more and more – he covertly escalated the war.[20] On

Henry Kissinger

Henry Kissinger served as Richard Nixon's national security advisor as well as, beginning in 1973, his secretary of state. Given his mixed record and his involvement in some of the more sordid episodes in U.S. foreign policy – among them U.S. support for the 1973 overthrow of the elected Chilean president Salvador Allende and the green light he and President Gerald Ford gave to the 1975 Indonesian invasion of East Timor – Kissinger remains one of the most polarizing figures in the history of U.S. diplomacy.

Kissinger was born and raised in what is today Germany but fled, as a young Jew, from Nazi persecution in 1938. His family settled in New York. After a stint in the U.S. Army during World War II, Kissinger obtained his B.A., M.A., and Ph.D. degrees from Harvard before joining that university's faculty. Drawn to the practical world outside academia, he advised a number of government agencies, foreign policy organizations, and politicians in the 1950s and 1960s. When Nixon was elected in 1968, he named Kissinger his national security advisor.

With Nixon in the White House, Kissinger sought to centralize power in the National Security Council, working to exclude the State Department and Defense Department as much as possible from policymaking in Vietnam. He was an opponent of "Vietnamization" but lost the internal administration debate over whether to pursue the policy. Kissinger worried that Vietnamization's voluntary withdrawal of U.S. forces would undermine American leverage in negotiating a ceasefire with the Vietnamese revolutionaries. Those negotiations stood at the center of his agenda. He craved recognition as a great statesman and wanted to be known as the man who delivered an "honorable peace" in Vietnam.

Kissinger negotiated the agreement to end U.S. participation in the war largely in secret, keeping the details even from other members of the administration. For the most part, he also failed to consult the government in Saigon. This became a problem in 1972, when the RVN president Nguyen Van Thieu rejected the terms presented by Kissinger, seeing them as a betrayal of his government and of the Republic of Vietnam.

The negotiations culminated in the 1973 Paris Peace Accords, which resulted in the withdrawal of the last U.S. combat troops from Vietnam. For negotiating the accords, Kissinger and the Vietnamese revolutionary Le Duc Tho were awarded the 1973 Nobel Peace Prize. The designation of the prizes that year was deeply controversial, with two members of the Nobel committee resigning in protest.[1] For his part, Tho turned down the award, explaining that "peace has not yet really been established in South Vietnam."[2] Kissinger, who accepted the award, apparently felt otherwise.

1 Irwin Abrams, *The Nobel Peace Prize and the Laureates: An Illustrated Biographical History, 1901–2001*, Centennial Edition (Nantucket, MA: Science History Publications, 2001), 219.
2 Flora Lewis, "Tho Rejects Nobel Prize, Citing Vietnam Situation," *New York Times*, October 24, 1973.

one level, his plan involved the intentional projection of an irrational desire to defeat the Vietnamese at any cost. This, he hoped, would prompt them to succumb to American terms for a settlement. "I'm the one man in this country who can [achieve victory]," Nixon told his aide H. R. (Bob) Haldeman.

> They'll believe any threat of force that Nixon makes because it's Nixon. I call it the Madman Theory, Bob. I want the North Vietnamese to believe I've reached the point where I might do anything to stop the war. We'll just slip the word to them that, "for God's sake, you know Nixon is obsessed about Communism. We can't restrain him when he's angry and he has his hand on the nuclear button" and Ho Chi Minh himself will be in Paris in two days begging for peace.[21]

The Vietnamese revolutionaries needed to believe that the alternative to a negotiated settlement on terms favorable to the United States was their potential nuclear annihilation.

At the same time, the Soviet Union — and here Nixon evinced his mistaken assumption that the Soviets had far more influence over Hanoi and the NLF than they in fact did — needed to believe that their failure to compel the Vietnamese to make concessions and reach a favorable settlement with Washington could result in a nuclear holocaust. In certain respects, Nixon's madman theory followed a strategy that Dwight Eisenhower had pursued in ending the Korean War.

But as historian David Schmitz has noted, the context of 1969, when the Soviet Union was capable of a nuclear strike on the United States and that this would need to be considered in ensuring the Soviets' "own credibility with their allies," was quite different from that of 1953. Moscow had no such capability at that time.[22]

While projecting this image of Nixon as madman, the president also greatly escalated the violence by undertaking a "secret" – at least to the extent that it was not officially acknowledged – B-52 bombing campaign in Cambodia. He did so for a couple of reasons. Cambodia, which together with Laos neighbors Vietnam to the west, had remained officially neutral in the already years-long American campaign against Hanoi and the National Liberation Front. Yet the Vietnamese revolutionaries had allegedly used the country in several ways, including as a site of transit for personnel and materiel along two routes into South Vietnam. The first route, which the Americans called the Ho Chi Minh Trail (in Vietnam it was known as the Truong Son Road), extended through Laos and Cambodia. The second, known today as the Sihanouk Trail (Norodom Sihanouk was the Cambodian monarch and prime minister), began in the Cambodian port city of Sihanoukville and extended to the "sanctuaries" along the Vietnamese–Cambodian border. The United States began targeting these routes even before Nixon's arrival in the White House.

Yet Cambodia was significant to the United States for other reasons, too. According to U.S. officials in Saigon, it was used extensively as a sanctuary for Vietnamese revolutionary troops operating across the border.[23] Moreover, Nixon claimed, Cambodia fielded "the headquarters for the entire Communist military operation in South Vietnam."[24] The administration thus saw it as a perfectly appropriate target of American attacks. While the United States had in fact been engaged in air operations in Cambodia since at least 1965, it dramatically increased them under Nixon.[25] In early 1969, when the administration perceived an escalation in Vietnamese military activity as a revolutionary test of the new president's resolve, Nixon responded in a manner consistent with the madman theory. His initiation of a massive B-52 bombing campaign of neutral Cambodia was an attempt to demonstrate that his administration would not follow the usual rules.

This effort to send a political message to the Vietnamese proved devastating to the people of Cambodia. What became known as the Menu campaign – so named because American commanders called their different bombing operations Breakfast, Lunch, Supper, Dinner, Dessert, and Snack – and its successors killed, at minimum, tens of thousands of Cambodian civilians.[26] Just as significantly, the "U.S. economic and military destabilization of Cambodia" that "peaked in 1969–73 with the carpet bombing of Cambodia's countryside by American B-52s," concluded historian Ben Kiernan, was "probably the most important single factor in Pol Pot's rise."[27] Pol Pot was the general secretary of the Khmer Rouge, the Cambodian communist movement that would go on to institute one of the worst genocides of the twentieth century. The fledgling Khmer Rouge insurgency, which "had enjoyed relatively little support" before Nixon launched the B-52s, "profited greatly" from the Americans' assault from the sky, Kiernan wrote, using the "widespread devastation and massacre of civilians as propaganda for recruitment purposes and as an excuse for its brutal, radical policies and its purge of moderate Khmer communists."[28]

★★★★★

Public calls for peace alongside secret military escalation: This was the context when Richard Nixon sat before the cameras on November 3, 1969. The president saw his speech that night as an opportunity to present himself as a peacemaker before the American public. To do so, he would pursue what he called "Vietnamization." Vietnamization, whose most significant feature was the gradual withdrawal from Vietnam of American ground forces, sounded to many Americans like the United States was finally getting out of the war. This was not an accident. Nixon believed that two things above all else animated antiwar sentiment, and this sentiment, Nixon felt, constrained his ability to exercise American power. One of these was the draft, which the president changed by instituting a lottery system based on one's birthdate; "this way," wrote several historians, "everyone took their chances equally."[29] (In 1973, Nixon abolished conscription completely, ushering in what today remains an all-volunteer U.S. military.) The other was the deaths of American combat personnel. Since most of those deaths were of ground troops, their gradual withdrawal, Nixon believed, would reduce American fatalities and thus the antiwar mood.

But Vietnamization did not in fact mean diminishing the fight. On the contrary, persistence was necessary, the president said in his November speech, because the United States was "great," and a "nation cannot remain great if it betrays its allies and lets down its friends." The threat was real, according to Nixon. The "defeat and humiliation" of the United States in Vietnam "without question would promote recklessness in the councils of those great powers who have not yet abandoned their goals of world conquest." An American retreat, he continued, "would spark violence wherever our commitments help maintain the peace – in the Middle East, in Berlin, eventually even in the Western Hemisphere." Make no mistake, the president warned, a "precipitate withdrawal … would cost more lives. It would not bring peace; it would bring more war."[30]

Nixon understood that the American public was decreasingly in a fighting mood, however, so he had to convince it that continued war, though in modified form, was the only viable path to peace. Washington had made numerous legitimate efforts, both public and private, to settle the conflict, the president claimed. That "Hanoi has refused even to discuss our proposals" was clear evidence of the revolutionaries' unreasonable intransigence. "No progress whatever has been made except agreement on the shape of the bargaining table," he said, and this was not the Americans' fault. The "other side" had demonstrated an "absolute refusal to show the least willingness to join us in seeking a just peace," preferring instead to "wait for our next concession, and our next concession after that one, until it gets everything it wants."[31]

With the failure thus far of the "search for peace" through negotiations, the president described his other "plan to bring peace." This was the Nixon Doctrine, a policy "which not only will help end the war in Vietnam, but which is an essential element of our program to prevent future Vietnams." It went like this: If the Johnson administration had "Americanized the war in Vietnam" with its insertion of hundreds of thousands of American troops, the Nixon administration was now intent on "Vietnamizing the search for peace." This meant turning over much of the ground combat to allied Vietnamese forces, who would be strengthened by a "substantial increase" in the training and equipment supplied by the United States. American forces would begin coming home, with the "primary mission" of those remaining being "to enable the South Vietnamese forces to assume the full responsibility for the security of South Vietnam." At the same time, however, the American air war would continue. Vietnamization, in other words, meant "the complete withdrawal of all U.S. combat ground forces, and their replacement by South Vietnamese forces on an orderly scheduled timetable," together with ongoing U.S. aerial bombing. This was being done from a position of strength, not weakness, Nixon said. "As South Vietnamese forces become stronger, the rate of American withdrawal can become greater."[32]

Vietnamization may not have been the "easy way out" for the United States, Nixon admitted. It would have been much easier for him to "order an immediate, precipitate withdrawal of all Americans without regard to the effects of that action." But Vietnamization was "the right way," he said. His administration would not allow the "vocal minority" – the antiwar movement – to "impose" its views on the nation "by mounting demonstrations in the street." If these antiwar activists were to prevail "over reason and the will of the majority," then the United States had "no future as a free society." The president respected the "idealism" and the "concern for peace" of the "young people of this Nation," he claimed, but "any hope the world has for the survival of peace and freedom will be determined by whether the American people have the moral stamina and the courage to meet the challenge of free world leadership." The White House could thus not give in to their demands. "Let historians not record," Nixon said, "that when America was the most powerful nation in the world we passed on the other side of the road and allowed the last hopes for peace and freedom of millions of people to be suffocated by the forces of totalitarianism."[33]

The political divisions at home, Nixon suggested, were making it impossible for the administration to end the war. This was because the Vietnamese revolutionaries would not accept Washington's terms if they believed the United States was divided. And why should they? U.S. officials worried that Hanoi was content to wait things out until, given the growing pressure at home, Washington felt compelled to withdraw. A negotiated settlement – at least on terms acceptable to the administration – would thus require the American people to support U.S. policy, "for the more divided we are at home, the less likely the enemy is to negotiate at Paris. Let us be united for peace," he continued. "Let us also be united against defeat. Because let us understand: North Vietnam cannot defeat or humiliate the United States. Only Americans can do that."[34]

This was classic Nixon. In a stroke, the president identified continued war with peace and continued dissent with disloyalty. But it was even more than that. Those calling for the United States to get out of Vietnam were effectively calling for future American wars, he suggested, while those publicly demonstrating their opposition to U.S. policy were prolonging the war and thus American suffering. So who was killing American troops and upsetting the American public? The communists may have been firing the bullets, according to Nixon's logic, but the antiwar movement was keeping these young Americans in harm's way. Though the president couched his logic in lofty rhetoric about a "just and lasting peace," it essentially amounted to this: Americans who opposed the war bore responsibility for the deaths of their compatriots.[35] It was thus time for all Americans to support Vietnamization. Only a U.S. victory could bring the peace that Americans, and the world, desired.

The plan outlined in the November 3 address was not entirely new. Nixon had recommended pieces of it at various times in the past.

His call for South Vietnam to assume greater responsibility for its own preservation had been made early in the 1968 presidential contest, for example. "If they do not assume the majority of the burden in their own defense, they cannot be saved," he told an audience in Wisconsin that March.[36] By March 1969, two months into his presidency, Nixon had ordered the increased U.S. training of the South Vietnamese armed forces and, in the following months, the withdrawal of tens of thousands of American troops.[37] The growing emphasis on the self-reliance of U.S. client states would in fact form an essential part of what came to be called the Nixon Doctrine. Likewise, Nixon hinted at his conditional openness to NLF participation in a future Saigon government just days before the 1968 vote. A forced coalition government would amount to a "thinly disguised surrender," he said as the Republican nominee, but there could be a role for the NLF "provided they renounce the use of force and accept the verdict of elections."[38] These positions, like the ones Nixon articulated in his November 3 address, were intended to make Nixon look reasonable and committed to peace.

But things did not go entirely as the president had hoped. While a Gallup poll after the November 3 speech indicated that 77 percent of Americans supported the policies Nixon had just laid out – this is perhaps not surprising, given the extent to which it sounded like he was pulling the country out of the war – the honeymoon proved short-lived.[39] As would soon become clear, antiwar sentiment only increased.

Just two weeks before his address, on October 15, hundreds of thousands of Americans had participated in a "Moratorium to End the War" across the United States. This was an event that CIA operatives – both the CIA and the FBI illegally infiltrated and sought to neutralize the antiwar movement – warned was "shaping up to be the most widely supported public action in American history."[40] In Massachusetts, 100,000 people crowded onto the Boston Common. In New York City, 250,000 participated in protest activities. With the exception of the South, where the Moratorium was largely ignored, ordinary people from around the country showed up in huge numbers to listen to speakers, demonstrate their opposition, mourn those who had died, and discuss America's future in Southeast Asia.[41]

The president's supporters responded with a White House-orchestrated "Honor America" week from November 9 to 16. It featured parades, rallies, and countless "America, Love It or Leave It" signs.[42] As impressive as this show of support for Nixon appeared to be, however, it was dwarfed by a new "Mobilization Against the War" on November 15. That day, in Washington, DC, as many as 500,000 people congregated on the Mall to "rescue the nation from the warmakers." Another 250,000 gathered in San Francisco. It was the largest demonstration in American history.[43] Since the mid–1960s Americans had been protesting in significant numbers against the war. While these activists may have been despised by countless Americans – an animus successfully exploited by the Nixon administration – there was no doubt by the end of the decade that the hostility to the war that drove their actions was now broadly shared across the country.

Yet it was not just civilian protesters. By the late 1960s, a growing number of American veterans and active-duty troops were expressing their opposition to the conflict. This should not surprise us as much as it might. As early as 1945, when France decided to reclaim its former Vietnamese colony in the wake of World War II, the enlisted crewmen of several U.S. troopships whose job it was to transport French military personnel to Saigon let their views be known. Alarmed by U.S. support for what they called "the imperialist policies of foreign governments" and the French effort "to subjugate the native population," they organized a number of protest actions, from petitions and resolutions to calls for a congressional investigation.[44] And military dissent would persist. Less than a decade later, after Richard Nixon, then the vice president, floated a trial balloon about the United States potentially dispatching American troops to help support the struggling French campaign, an American Legion division with 78,000 members demanded that the Eisenhower administration refrain from doing so.[45]

This was only a prelude to the military protests that would follow. As antiwar sentiment grew in the mid–1960s, a relative handful of Americans in uniform began to publicly speak out. One of the first was U.S. Army Special Forces soldier Donald Duncan. Drafted in 1956 and deployed to Vietnam in 1964, Duncan was a heavily decorated former Green Beret when he authored a piece called "The Whole Thing Was a Lie" for the February 1966 issue of *Ramparts* magazine. "We weren't preserving freedom in South Vietnam," he wrote. "We are the Russian tanks blasting the hopes of an Asian Hungary," he said, comparing, in a particularly trenchant Cold War analogy, the United States to the Soviet Union during the Soviets' 1956 aggression against Hungarians seeking a more democratic future.[46] Duncan's opposition would be replicated exponentially as hundreds of thousands of Americans found themselves sent to Southeast Asia.

By the late 1960s and early 1970s, antiwar troops were distributing underground newspapers on military bases, veterans and active-duty servicepeople were leading marches and demonstrations, and thousands of GIs were being prosecuted for antiwar activities. Desertion, moreover, became a huge problem in the armed forces. During the 1971 fiscal year, 142 out of every 1,000 men on duty deserted. Indeed, between July 1, 1966, and December 31, 1973, the Department of Defense recorded 503,926 "incidents of desertion" within the military ranks.[47]

In Vietnam, combat personnel wore peace symbols, protested visiting officers, and gave antiwar salutes. Navy sailors rebelled and sabotaged their ships, air force pilots refused bombing missions, and ground troops defied direct orders.[48] This resistance was occasionally met with violence. In one of the most significant cases, U.S. soldiers were ordered to fire on a unit of their compatriots for having refused to participate in a search-and-destroy mission. The resistant troops fired back. Dozens of men were reportedly killed or wounded, and three helicopters were destroyed.[49]

Troops also engaged in "fragging." Fragging refers to the killing of officers through the use of fragmentation grenades. The Pentagon acknowledged 551 incidents of fragging with explosive devices by 1972, which left 86 people dead and more than 700 wounded. That figure does not include killing by rifle fire, however, which was a common method of dispensing with unpopular officers who crossed their units or recklessly put their troops' lives on the line.[50]

The problem of military dissent became so widespread that it raised concerns about the ability of the United States to continue waging war. By 1971, the *New York Times* was reporting on the concern that "the men in the [Army] ranks no longer have the esprit necessary to make first-class fighters." "Let's face it," one brigadier general told the paper. "We have units today that simply are not fit to go if the balloon goes up."[51] That same year, Colonel Robert Heinl took to the pages of the *Armed Forces Journal* to outline just how grave the situation had become. [See excerpts from Heinl's article in the documents at the end of this book.] "By every conceivable indicator," he wrote, "our army that now remains in Vietnam is in a state approaching collapse, with individual units avoiding or having refused combat, murdering their officers and noncommissioned officers, drug-ridden, and dispirited where not near mutinous."[52] There was, in other words, a practical logic to Nixon's desire to withdraw American combat forces. At the same time, the administration faced increasing political pressure to unwind the war with the growth in antiwar sentiment among American civilians. This frustrated the president, who felt it interfered with the time he needed for his policies to work. But the American public, which had been waiting for success in Vietnam for years, was not in a patient mood.

This growing dissent, both civilian and military, together with the public perception of an administration dialing down the American presence in Southeast Asia, was the backdrop for the widespread out-rage that greeted Nixon's April 1970 decision to expand the ground war to Cambodia. Already his administration had been engaged in a devastating, undisclosed B-52 bombing campaign in that country to weaken Hanoi and the NLF.[53] Nixon's various moves in attempt-ing to force a Vietnamese settlement on American terms had, in the months surrounding his November 3 address, all failed. It was time, the president believed, to try something new. The expansion of the ground war to Cambodia would be it. On April 30, just ten days after he announced the withdrawal of another 150,000 American troops by the following spring, Nixon took to the nation's airwaves and shocked the public by declaring that a U.S. and South Vietnamese invasion of Cambodia had commenced (Figure 2.1).[54]

Cambodia, according to Nixon, was "a small country of 7 million people" whose neutrality had been "blatant[ly]" violated by the Vietnamese revolutionaries – this, Nixon said, while the United States had "scrupulously respect[ed] the neutrality of the Cambodian people."

Figure 2.1 Like a teacher instructing his students, Richard Nixon used this prop to announce the U.S. invasion of Cambodia to a national television audience on April 30, 1970.
Getty Images: Bettmann/Contributor.

Despite the country hosting enemy sanctuaries along the Cambodia–Vietnam border, the United States had not "moved against" these sanctuaries because it "did not wish to violate the territory of a neutral nation."[55] This was only one of the lies in the speech. As we know, a year earlier Nixon had ordered the covert bombing of Cambodia by American B-52s, and just weeks before the April invasion the United States appeared to support the overthrow of the neutral head of state, Prince Norodom Sihanouk, who was replaced by the right-wing, U.S.-backed general Lon Nol. The coup regime almost immediately began receiving U.S. military, financial, and political support.[56]

By late April, when Nixon took to the public airwaves to announce what he denied was an invasion of Cambodia, he justified this "incursion," as he later called it, on the grounds of protecting the American troops remaining in Vietnam.[57] With thousands of Vietnamese revolutionaries "invading [Cambodia] from the sanctuaries" along the border and "encircling the capital of Phnom Penh," the Cambodian government had "sent out a call to the United States, to a number of other nations, for assistance." That assistance was essential, Nixon said, "[b]ecause if this enemy effort succeeds, Cambodia would become a vast enemy staging area and a springboard for attacks on South Vietnam along 600 miles of frontier – a refuge where enemy troops could return from combat without fear of retaliation." This threatened "not only the lives of our own men but the people of South Vietnam as well." He thus ordered the attack in Cambodia of what he called "the headquarters for the entire Communist military operation in South Vietnam."[58]

U.S. actions were not an expansion of the war into Cambodia, Nixon claimed. On the contrary, they were "indispensable" to the ongoing withdrawal of American forces from Vietnam and "winning the just peace we all desire." Nixon placed Hanoi on notice: The United States would be patient in working for peace and it would be conciliatory at the conference table, but it will not be "humiliated" or "defeated," he insisted. "We will not allow American men by the thousands to be killed by an enemy from privileged sanctuaries." Yet U.S. actions were also about something much bigger than the war in Southeast Asia. Drawing on the Cold War ideology that was central to Nixon's thinking, the invasion was essential to American global credibility. "If, when the chips are down, the world's most powerful nation, the United States of America, acts like a pitiful, helpless giant," he predicted, "the forces of totalitarianism and anarchy will threaten free nations and free institutions throughout the world."[59]

Already, Nixon said, "we live in an age of anarchy, both abroad and at home," with "mindless attacks" on civilized institutions, such as the nation's "great universities ... being systematically destroyed. Small nations all over the world," he continued, "find themselves under attack from within and from without." This threat, both global and domestic, required a firm response. Nixon acknowledged that the expansion into Cambodia might be unpopular. But, he claimed, he "rejected all political considerations in making this decision." How his party fared in the approaching midterm elections or in his own potential reelection in 1972 was immaterial, he said. "I would rather be a one-term President and do what I believe is right than to be a two-term President at the cost of seeing America become a second-rate power and to see this Nation accept the first defeat in its proud 190-year history."[60] Given the extent to which the invasion outraged so much of the American public, it did not seem unreasonable to suspect that Nixon might indeed not remain in office much longer.

Not only had he failed to consult Congress (which is of course vested under the Constitution with the power to declare war) on the momentous decision to invade Cambodia, but Nixon only notified Defense Secretary Melvin Laird and Secretary of State William Rogers – both of whom disagreed with the policy – at the last moment. Even Lon Nol, the new U.S.-supported head of the Cambodian military regime, was kept in the dark about the decision to invade his country; he had to learn about it from the U.S. chargé d'affaires, who himself learned about it from listening to Nixon's speech on the Voice of America radio network.[61]

For months the TV networks had deemphasized combat footage in their news programs, and most Americans, following television's lead, had come to believe that the war in Vietnam was winding down.[62] So when Nixon announced that he was expanding the ground war to Cambodia, the response was explosive. He had his supporters, of course. The right-wing organization Young Americans for Freedom circulated a "Support Our Fighting Men" petition and advertised how they "stand behind" Nixon.[63] But for millions of Americans, the invasion of Cambodia was an outrage. More than a third of the nation's colleges and universities shut down as faculty members and students joined demonstrations against U.S. policy. Two hundred and fifty State Department employees signed a letter of protest to the secretary of state. Members of Nixon's cabinet openly dissented.[64]

This broad opposition led to tragedy. At Kent State University on May 4, Ohio National Guard troops opened fire on unarmed students following days of fierce demonstrations and, on May 2, the burning of the campus ROTC (Reserve Officers' Training Corps) building. The guardsmen killed four and wounded another nine. Then, ten days later, the police shot and killed two students and injured twelve others at Jackson State College in Mississippi. Nixon, who had days earlier denounced student protesters as "bums" – "My child was not a bum," the father of Alison Krause, an honors student killed at Kent State, retorted – asked the president of Jackson State, "What are we going to do to get more respect for the police from our young people?"[65] Many Americans saw this as the wrong question. They wanted to know why student demonstrators had been shot and killed by their own government. An official report several months later concluded that the indiscriminate fire of the Ohio National Guard was "unnecessary, unwarranted, and inexcusable," while the police fusillade in Mississippi was "an unreasonable, unjustified overreaction."[66]

By that time Nixon had already pulled back from Cambodia. The invasion had been a disaster, inviting passage of the so-called Cooper–Church Amendment (named after Senators John Sherman Cooper, a Kentucky Republican, and Frank Church, a Democrat from Idaho), which cut off funding for U.S. operations in Cambodia. This was a big deal. The amendment represented Congress's first restriction on troop deployments during a war and, more specifically, the first vote to oppose presidential policy during the American campaign in Southeast Asia.[67] More broadly, the Cambodia invasion and its aftermath "marked the collapse of the madman policy and the end of Nixon's quest to secure a military victory in Vietnam," David Schmitz concluded. "The year 1970 was to Nixon's Vietnam policy what 1968 had been to Johnson's, and Cambodia was his Tet Offensive."[68]

Richard Nixon and Henry Kissinger on the Bombing of Cambodia, December 9, 1970

By December 1970, Nixon had grown frustrated with his inability to end the war on terms favorable to the United States. He complained to his national security advisor, Henry Kissinger, about what he considered the ineffectual bombing campaign in Cambodia, ordering him to ramp it up. "They have got to go in there and I mean really go in," Nixon instructed. "I want them to hit everything. I want them to use the big planes, the small planes, everything they can that will help out there, and let's start giving them a little shock." Nixon often demonstrated emotional instability, and this instability could easily translate into ill-considered policy directives. Kissinger's recognition of the president's shortcomings appeared in the sardonic order he then delivered to Alexander Haig, his military assistant:

> *Kissinger*: I just had a call from our friend. [...] [H]e wants a massive bombing campaign in Cambodia. He doesn't want to hear anything. It's an order, it's to be done. Anything that flies on anything that moves. You got that?

Kissinger's secretary, who transcribed the conversation, said it sounded like Haig was laughing.

Source: Elizabeth Becker, "Kissinger Tapes Describe Crises, War, and Stark Photos of Abuse," *New York Times*, May 27, 2004; Thomas Blanton and William Burr, eds., *The Kissinger Telcons*, National Security Archive Electronic Briefing Book No. 123, May 26, 2004, at https://nsarchive2.gwu.edu/NSAEBB/NSAEBB123/.

The president was not prepared to acknowledge the failure of the recent cross-border invasion – on the contrary, he publicly proclaimed it "the most successful operation of this long and very difficult war" – but after the Cambodia experience he would be forced to reframe U.S. efforts in Vietnam.[69] The basic policy dilemma faced by Washington was noted by Henry Kissinger: "Time is on [the revolutionaries'] side – the U.S. exodus from the South is irreversible and the [South Vietnamese government] can never stand on its own."[70] Uncertain about how to proceed, the administration chose stasis. Nixon would continue to gradually withdraw U.S. forces, which had come to be expected by the American public and which translated into additional congressional funding for the war. At the same time, he and his team recognized that each withdrawal weakened U.S. leverage with Hanoi, as the unilateral reduction of troops took away a bargaining chip that they might employ at the negotiating table. As these withdrawals proceeded, the United States would continue to try to strengthen the ARVN troops, even as the administration doubted their ability to successfully resist the revolutionaries.

Yet the administration had no good options going forward. Not knowing how best to proceed, the president redefined how success would be measured. Actual victory appeared unlikely, so the illusion of victory would have to suffice. Nixon knew that the American public wanted, more than anything, to see U.S. forces withdrawn. This,

combined with at least the short-term survival of the RVN government, would come to mean victory and thus "peace." If, in the longer
term, the absence of U.S. troops in Vietnam meant the inability of
the Saigon regime to survive, so be it. As long as Nixon could pull
Americans out of Vietnam without causing an immediate collapse of
the RVN government – a necessary interlude that came to be known as
the "decent interval" – he believed that U.S. global credibility would
remain intact. And if he could do this while pursuing détente with
China and the Soviet Union, and thus a considerable de-escalation of
Cold War tensions, he thought it might be sufficient to ensure his 1972
reelection.

The objective for the United States in the months following the
ill-fated Cambodia invasion was to minimize the fighting in southern
Vietnam and thus the vulnerability of the Saigon regime to collapse.
To accomplish this goal, Nixon ordered that whatever it took be done
to tie down PAVN forces in Laos and decrease the flow of supplies to
the revolutionaries in the south. And, he said, the Lon Nol regime in
Cambodia had to survive, whether through U.S. aid or through "covert operations, tactical air strikes, and support from other nations to
Phnom Penh."[71] While pursuing these goals, the administration would
continue to publicly profess its desire for a negotiated settlement, while
making itself look reasonable and the revolutionaries intransigent.
Such was the case with the president's national address on October 7,
1970, shortly after the NLF pledged to halt its attacks on American
forces in Vietnam in return for an American commitment to leave by
June 30, 1971.[72] Nixon worried about the public relations effect of the
NLF offer. He countered with a profession of his own peacemaking
desires, even if disingenuous. His five-part proposal on October 7 had
at its heart a "cease-fire-in-place" that, he said, may not "end the conflict" but would at least "end the killing." His proposals, if accepted by
the revolutionaries, would collectively "open the door to an enduring
peace in Indochina."[73]

With the cameras off, Nixon was more blunt. "As you know,
I don't think cease-fire is worth a damn, but now that we have done
it we are looking down their throats," he told Kissinger in a phone
call after the speech.[74] He was not especially interested in reaching a
negotiated settlement. His interest lay in the illusion of victory, which
meant a U.S. withdrawal without a pre-election collapse of the Saigon
regime. Winning the war "simply means … letting South Vietnam
survive," he confessed to Kissinger in April 1971. "That's all."[75] Along
those lines, he would undertake military strikes on the revolutionaries
not to send a signal to Hanoi but in an effort to "decrease the pressure"

on the RVN so that it would have time to build up its forces and preserve its government.[76]

Perhaps the principal effort to project RVN strength came in early 1971 with Operation Lam Son 719. This was an RVN incursion into southern Laos, accompanied by U.S. artillery and air support, which was intended to destroy revolutionary troops and disrupt revolutionary supply lines into southern Vietnam. It proved to be a fiasco. The American press, which had been barred from the initial assault, recorded desperate ARVN soldiers fleeing the combat by clinging onto the skids of American helicopters – causing some of them to crash – and pushing their wounded comrades out of the way in a frantic effort to escape. (The helicopter problem became so acute that American crews took to greasing the helicopters' skids.)[77] The ARVN campaign invited widespread criticism in Congress and the American press. U.S. policymakers were angry. "It would be hard to exaggerate the mystification and confusion caused here by the ARVN's latest scheme of maneuver which envisages a rapid pull-out from Laos," Henry Kissinger wrote to Ellsworth Bunker, the U.S. ambassador in Saigon.[78]

Publicly, the administration opted for deception. "[T]he South Vietnamese demonstrated that without American advisers they could fight effectively against the very best troops North Vietnam could put in the field," Nixon claimed in a televised April 7 address.

> Vietnamization has succeeded. [...] [T]he American involvement in Vietnam is coming to an end. The day the South Vietnamese can take over their own defense is in sight. Our goal is a total American withdrawal from Vietnam. We can and we will reach that goal through our program of Vietnamization if necessary. But we would infinitely prefer to reach it even sooner – through negotiations.[79]

The negotiations would have to wait. In the interim, Nixon announced in his April 7 speech that he was beginning the withdrawal of another 100,000 American troops, bringing the total withdrawn to 365,000, or "over two-thirds of the number who were there when I came into office."[80]

The government's leading minds were less sanguine than the president. Just three weeks after Nixon's assurance of RVN strength, a National Intelligence Estimate concluded that "the problems facing the GVN [Government of Vietnam], the uncertainties in South Vietnam about the magnitude, nature, and duration of future U.S. support, doubts concerning the South Vietnamese will to persist, the resiliency of the communist apparatus in South Vietnam, and North Vietnam's demonstrated ability and willingness to pay the price of perseverance are such that the longer term survival of the GVN is by no means yet assured."[81] This pessimistic prognosis, moreover, assumed that "a U.S. military support effort will be maintained beyond 1972 along with substantial amounts of U.S. economic assistance." This raised questions about the viability of the president's twin goals: the survival of the RVN regime together with "a total American withdrawal from Vietnam."[82]

Nixon, who was facing pressure from the general public, veterans, prisoner-of-war (POW) families, and Congress, took to saying publicly what Americans wanted to hear. Polls showed that 60 percent of respondents believed the war was a mistake, and over 70 percent favored a U.S. withdrawal.[83] This was reflected in ongoing protests. Vietnam Veterans Against the War (VVAW), which had first formed in 1967, sponsored an April 1971 demonstration in Washington during which combat veterans threw their Bronze Stars, Silver Stars, Purple Hearts, and campaign ribbons onto the steps of the U.S. Capitol. One of the organization's members, future senator and secretary of state John Kerry, powerfully spoke before the Senate Foreign Relations Committee, highlighting veterans' outrage over what Kerry called "this barbaric war." The whole military campaign had been a mistake, he said, and "[h]ow do you ask a man to be the last man to die for a mistake?"[84]

Public opinion became only more jaded when, in June 1971, the *New York Times* began publishing excerpts of what became known as the Pentagon Papers, a top secret study leaked to the press by one of its authors, Daniel Ellsberg. Commissioned by Defense Secretary Robert McNamara in 1967, the Pentagon Papers included thousands

The Pentagon Papers

The Pentagon Papers, which was officially titled "Report of the Office of the Secretary of Defense Vietnam Task Force," is the colloquial name given to a 3,000-page, top secret Defense Department study with 4,000 pages of accompanying documents that was commissioned by Robert McNamara in 1967. When they were leaked in 1971, the papers helped to further undermine confidence in U.S. foreign policy and the honesty and integrity of American officials. While a seemingly stale study of U.S.–Vietnam relations from 1945 to 1967, the

Pentagon Papers' revelations were in fact explosive, demonstrating that U.S. officials had lied to the American public for years. As McNamara reportedly told a friend when reading the report he had ordered, "You know they could hang people for what's in here."[1]

What was in there was indeed disturbing. The basic story of the war told by American leaders through the 1950s and 1960s was that Washington had been working assiduously to defend democracy and freedom in Southeast Asia against the imperial expansion of the Soviet Union and China. This meant supporting a free and independent South Vietnam, which was being besieged by communist aggressors. Suffice it to say that the Pentagon Papers complicated this simplistic tale.

Among other things, the papers acknowledged the widespread popular support that the Vietnamese revolutionaries enjoyed. They also detailed a much longer and deeper history of U.S. involvement in Vietnam than most Americans had been told, beginning with substantial U.S. aid to France as it was attempting to recolonize Vietnam in the decade following World War II. The papers deemed South Vietnam "essentially the creation of the United States," they outlined U.S. support for the 1963 coup to overthrow the RVN president Ngo Dinh Diem, they showed that the Tonkin Gulf incident was not the unprovoked aggression claimed by Lyndon Johnson, and they revealed a far more pessimistic outlook for the war than the rosy one publicly provided by U.S. officials.

Daniel Ellsberg, a former Marine and Pentagon staffer who worked on the study as an analyst for the RAND Corporation, by 1969 had grown increasingly disillusioned with the war, which he came to see as unwinnable and immoral. Together with his RAND colleague Anthony Russo, he surreptitiously photocopied the papers over a period of months with the goal of bringing them to the American public. He first leaked the documents to select members of Congress, but the senators and representatives with whom he shared them failed to act. Ellsberg then leaked the papers to the *New York Times*, which in June 1971 began excerpting them and publishing analyses of their significance.

The Nixon administration, which was not implicated in the perfidy the papers revealed (they covered only through 1967), nevertheless worried about what disclosure of the internal workings of U.S. foreign policy might suggest. It thus sought to enjoin the *Times* from further revelations. In response, Ellsberg provided copies of the documents to more than a dozen newspapers around the country, which proceeded to publish portions of them, and Senator Mike Gravel entered over 4,000 pages into the *Congressional Record*.

The Pentagon Papers, in an indirect way, also marked the beginning of the end for the Nixon presidency. The administration believed that it needed to neutralize Ellsberg, who Henry Kissinger called "the most dangerous man in America." The government charged him under the Espionage Act (its case was ultimately dismissed because of official misconduct), but the White House also wanted Ellsberg discredited publicly. It ordered a covert investigative unit that called itself the Plumbers – they fixed leaks – to burglarize Ellsberg's psychiatrist's office and find dirt that the administration could use against him. These were the same Plumbers who later broke into the Democratic National Committee headquarters in the Watergate complex in Washington, DC, setting in motion the Watergate scandal that undid Richard Nixon. Indeed, the Plumbers' illegal actions, including the break-in of Dr. Lewis Fielding's office, "helped form the basis for two of the three impeachment articles adopted against President Nixon by the House Judiciary Committee in July 1974."[2]

---

1 Marilyn B. Young, *The Vietnam Wars, 1945–1990* (New York: HarperPerennial, 1991), 211
2 David Rudenstine, *The Day the Presses Stopped: A History of the Pentagon Papers Case* (Berkeley: University of California Press, 1996), 348.

of pages of documents and analysis on the history of U.S. policymaking in Vietnam. The materials demonstrated – clearly and unequivocally – that American presidents and others had lied to the American public about the situation in Vietnam for years. The Nixon administration, whose policies were not addressed in the study (it ended with 1967), nevertheless worried about its revelations. The White House attempted through the judicial system to stop the materials' release on national security grounds. The Supreme Court refused to grant the administration's wish and allowed the papers publication to proceed. So the administration sought to discredit Ellsberg, including by having secret operatives illegally break into his psychiatrist's office to look for compromising material. This was the beginning of the Watergate scandal that ultimately brought down the president.

Antiwar sentiment continued to grow. Nixon worried about the disillusionment of the American public. He worried about protesting GIs. He worried about the war's effect on the worsening economy. And he worried about the calls by relatives of American POWs to end the war so that their loved ones could return home. Members of Congress contemplated a proposal that would require the withdrawal of all American troops by the end of 1971.[85] Nixon, recognizing the fragile environment in which he had to operate, ordered Henry Kissinger to soften the U.S. position in his sporadic secret talks with the revolutionaries in Paris. Perhaps the United States should no longer require mutual withdrawal (that is, both the United States and DRV) from South Vietnam, Nixon suggested to Kissinger. (Washington dropped the demand for mutual withdrawal in July 1972.)[86] But he was willing to go only so far. The administration hoped that its announced plans to meet with the Chinese leadership in Beijing – this was an enormous development, as the United States had recognized the government in Taipei since the 1949 end of the Chinese civil war – and the Soviet leadership in Moscow would convince the revolutionaries to accept the remaining U.S. terms. At the very least, Nixon hoped that his progress with the two major communist powers would distract the public from the war in Vietnam. It didn't.

Nixon remained stuck. The war continued to be a stalemate, and Hanoi refused to settle on terms favored by the United States. More than anything this meant Washington's insistence on preserving RVN President Nguyen Van Thieu – at least for a "decent interval." The president worried that American credibility would suffer a devastating blow if the United States was seen as having abandoned the RVN and caused its overthrow by the revolutionaries. The "decent-interval

A "Decent Interval"

On August 3, 1972, Richard Nixon and Henry Kissinger discussed whether and how the fate of South Vietnam might affect the United States and Nixon's presidency:

> *President Nixon*: Now let's look at that just a moment again, think about it some more, but let's be perfectly cold-blooded about it. If you look at it from the standpoint of our game with the Soviets and the Chinese, from the standpoint of running this country, I think we could take, in my view, almost anything, frankly, that we can force on Thieu. Almost anything. I just come down to that. You know what I mean? Because I have a feeling we would not be doing, like I feel about the Israeli, I feel that in the long run we're probably not doing them an in—uh, a disfavor due to the fact that I feel that the North Vietnamese are so badly hurt that the South Vietnamese are probably gonna do fairly well [*unclear*]. And also due to the fact—because I look at the tide of history out there, South Vietnam probably can never even survive anyway. I'm just being perfectly candid—I—
>
> *Kissinger*: In the pull-out area—
>
> *President Nixon*: [*Unclear—overlapping voices*] There's got to be—if we can get certain guarantees so that they aren't ... uh, as you

know, looking at the foreign policy process, though, I mean, you've got to be—we also have to realize, Henry, that winning an election is terribly important. It's terribly important this year, but can we have a viable foreign policy if a year from now or two years from now, North Vietnam gobbles up South Vietnam? That's the real question.

Kissinger: If a year or two years from now North Vietnam gobbles up South Vietnam, we can have a viable foreign policy if it looks as if it's the result of South Vietnamese incompetence. If we now sell out in such a way that, say, within a three- to four-month period, we have pushed President Thieu over the brink—we ourselves—I think, there is going to be—even the Chinese won't like that. I mean, they'll pay verbal—verbally, they'll like it—

President Nixon: But it'll worry them.

Kissinger: But it will worry everybody. And domestically in the long run it won't help us all that much because our opponents will say we should've done it three years ago.

President Nixon: I know.

Kissinger: So we've got to find some formula that holds the thing together a year or two, after which—after a year, Mr. President, Vietnam will be a backwater. If we settle it, say, this October, by January '74 no one will give a damn.

Source: Conversation 760-6, August 3, 1972, 8:28 a.m.–8:57 a.m., Oval Office, Nixon Public Library, reproduced in Ken Hughes, "Fatal Politics: Nixon's Timetable for Withdrawing from Vietnam," *Diplomatic History* 34:3 (June 2010): 500–501.

solution," as historian Jeffrey Kimball identified it, thus involved "withdrawing from the struggle without having achieved a clear-cut victory but having created conditions in South Vietnam that would avoid or postpone some future downfall of the Saigon regime – in essence, protecting America's credibility as a counterrevolutionary guarantor, an effective repeller of outside aggression, and trustworthy ally."[87] For Nixon and Kissinger, that downfall would have to occur long enough after the U.S. withdrawal that it appeared not to be caused by it. Rather, the RVN collapse would have to be perceived as "the result of South Vietnamese incompetence," Kissinger told Nixon in August 1972. If it was true that "South Vietnam probably can never even survive anyway," as Nixon confided to Kissinger in that same conversation, then, Kissinger responded, "we've got to find some formula that holds the thing together a year or two, after which ... Vietnam will be a backwater" and "no one will give a damn."[88]

The administration held out hope that Thieu's regime just might survive indefinitely, and, despite private doubts about its viability, the president never publicly suggested otherwise. For Nixon, "peace with honor" meant a negotiated settlement with the revolutionaries. The problem, however, was their ongoing refusal to accept American terms. In January 1972, shortly before his famous trip to Beijing, Nixon took to the nation's airwaves to charge the Vietnamese revolutionaries with duplicity and to publicly present what he called "a plan for peace that can end the war in Vietnam."[89] It included the withdrawal of all U.S. and allied forces, an exchange of prisoners of war, a ceasefire throughout Indochina, and a new presidential election in the south.[90] Nixon then left the United States for China. In the following months he was distracted by his journey to Beijing and strategic arms limitation talks with Moscow. When the Vietnamese revolutionaries launched a major offensive in March 1972, Nixon, worried that a blow to the RVN would undermine his claims of Vietnamization's success, escalated the U.S. air war and ordered the mining of the harbor in Haiphong, a large port city on the northern coast of Vietnam.[91] Of course, the fact that the United States found it necessary to intercede suggested just how unsuccessful Vietnamization had in reality been, with Saigon still dependent on American military support.

Yet Nixon eagerly wanted out of the war. When Kissinger met with the revolutionaries in Paris in July, he dropped the U.S. demand for mutual withdrawal. Hanoi reciprocated, no longer insisting on Nguyen Van Thieu's removal as president of the RVN. By late October, the terms of a settlement had been reached. This was the major breakthrough that the administration had sought. But Thieu rejected the agreement, believing its recognition of the NLF and its political arm, the Provisional Revolutionary Government, signaled the end of his RVN regime. And "Thieu is right, that our terms will eventually destroy him," Kissinger told Nixon on October 6. "Well, if they're that collapsible, maybe they just have to be collapsed," Nixon suggested. "That's another way to look at it, too. I mean, we have to – we've got to remember, we cannot keep this child sucking at the tit when the child is four years old. You know?"[92]

For domestic reasons, the White House was concerned. The 1972 presidential election was just days away, and any collapse of the settlement between the United States and the various Vietnamese parties could signal White House failure and ongoing war, undermining the president's reelection. Nixon and Kissinger thus presented the illusion of having achieved peace, claiming that an agreement had, at long last, been reached; all that remained was the resolution of some minor details.

It worked. Nixon was reelected in a landslide. His strategy of presenting himself as the president who delivered peace after years of war and decades of Cold War tensions proved successful. But in light of Thieu's rejection of the settlement, in late November negotiations with the revolutionaries resumed. Hanoi was agreeable to minor changes, but it refused to revisit the major provisions to which both it and Washington had consented weeks before. Kissinger threatened "savage" bombing if the DRV refused the new American demands. Nixon, who had earlier ordered his private pollster to predict the public response to bombing Hanoi (after researching the issue, he concluded that the reaction would be positive), broke off the talks in December.[93] He was concerned that the incoming Congress would cut off funding for the war, compelling him to bring the remaining American troops home. This would remove whatever leverage Washington still possessed. The time to reach a settlement was now. To force the issue, Nixon ordered a massive air campaign against the north coupled with the mining (again) of the Haiphong harbor.[94] In what became known as the "Christmas bombing" – a holiday season "gift" from the United States – American B-52s dropped tens of thousands of tons of bombs on Hanoi and Haiphong. More tonnage of bombs was dropped during the twelve-day campaign than the United States had used from 1969 to 1971.[95] Confounding the president's pollster, the domestic and global response was one of outrage, not support.

By early January 1973, the Democratic caucuses in Congress had voted to cut off all funding for the war following arrangements for U.S. troop withdrawals and the repatriation of prisoners of war. Less than three weeks later, the Paris Peace Accords that brought about an end to U.S. military intervention in Vietnam were finally signed. Nixon and Kissinger both claimed that the "Christmas bombing" forced Hanoi back to the bargaining table, where the revolutionaries finally accepted the revised American demands. But this is not true. The January terms were in fact virtually identical to those negotiated by Washington and Hanoi three months earlier. As an aide to Kissinger farcically put it, "We bombed the North Vietnamese into accepting our concessions."[96] The biggest difference now was that Thieu also accepted the settlement. Why? Because the RVN president was told by Nixon that his rejection of it would result in the "gravest consequences" for his government. His agreement, conversely, would guarantee the "full force" of the United States against Hanoi if the revolutionaries violated the accord, Nixon promised.[97] The "Christmas bombing" demonstrated what that full force might look like.

In a secret annex to the agreement, Nixon pledged to Hanoi that Washington would "contribute to the postwar reconstruction in North Vietnam without any political conditions." A figure of $3.25 billion was suggested, though this was contingent, Kissinger said, on Congress agreeing to appropriate such an amount.[98] Yet this all remained secret. Publicly, Nixon announced on January 23 that "we today have concluded an agreement to end the war and bring peace with honor in Vietnam and in Southeast Asia." The United States, he boasted, "did not settle for a peace that would have betrayed our allies, that would have abandoned our prisoners of war, or that would have ended the war for us but would have continued the war for the 50 million people of Indochina."[99]

But this was "yet one more deception," as David Schmitz put it.[100] Peace had not in fact come to Vietnam. The war would continue for another two years, though without direct American involvement. Nixon may have thought that he could again bomb Hanoi or otherwise assist the RVN after he pulled the United States out, but developments at home precluded this possibility. Some of these were congressional. In June 1973 Congress passed legislation that prohibited the White House from further military action in Vietnam, Cambodia, and Laos without congressional preapproval. Then, in July, Congress passed the War Powers Resolution, which constrained the president's warmaking abilities by requiring congressional notification within forty-eight hours of any military action and, within sixty days, congressional authorization to continue.[101] As Nixon found himself increasingly constrained by the legislature, his political fortunes sank. His administration ultimately imploded with the Watergate revelations. In August 1974, facing the near certainty of impeachment, he resigned the presidency in disgrace.

For Nixon, the war was over. It now belonged to Gerald Ford. For the Vietnamese, however, the suffering would continue.

NOTES

1   Robert B. Semple Jr., "Nixon Withholds His Peace Ideas," *New York Times,* March 11, 1968; David F. Schmitz, *Richard Nixon and the Vietnam War: The End of the American Century* (Lanham, MD: Rowman & Littlefield, 2014), 29–30.

2   Robert B. Semple Jr., "Nixon Says He Has Eased Views on Communist Bloc," *New York Times,* August 7, 1968.

3   On Nixon and the Soviet Union, see, for example, "Can the New Nixon Make
     It?" *Nation's Business* 56:1 (January 1968): 39. On "Eisenhower diplomacy," see
     "Nixon Urges Rise in Allied Soldiers," *New York Times*, March 15, 1968. Tech-
     nically, the war in Korea did not end; rather, a ceasefire was reached.
4   Semple Jr., "Nixon Says He Has Eased Views on Communist Bloc."
5   "Can the New Nixon Make It?" 39.
6   Semple Jr., "Nixon Says He Has Eased Views on Communist Bloc."
7   Henry Kissinger to the Secretary of State, Secretary of Defense, and Director of
     Central Intelligence, Situation in Vietnam: National Security Study Memoran-
     dum 1, January 21, 1969, at https://fas.org/irp/offdocs/nssm-nixon/nssm_001.
     pdf (accessed August 8, 2018).
8   Summary of Interagency Responses to NSSM 1 [Document 44], March 22,
     1969, in Edward C. Keefer and Carolyn Yee, eds., *Foreign Relations of the United
     States, 1969–1976*, Volume VI: Vietnam, January 1969–July 1970 (Washington,
     DC: Government Printing Office, 2006), 129–130.
9   Summary of Interagency Responses to NSSM 1, 130.
10   Schmitz, *Richard Nixon and the Vietnam War*, 44–45.
11   Hazel Erskine, "The Polls: Is War a Mistake?" *Public Opinion Quarterly* 34:1
     (Spring 1970): 134–135, 141–142, 150. Surprisingly in light of the widespread
     attention given to youth protests, those over 50 were more likely than those from
     21–29 years old to say that the war was a "mistake"; see Erskine, "The Polls?"
     144–145.
12   Melvin Small, *Antiwarriors: The Vietnam War and the Battle for America's Hearts
     and Minds* (Wilmington, DE: SR Books, 2002), 65; Nancy Zaroulis and Gerald
     Sullivan, *Who Spoke Up? American Protest Against the War in Vietnam, 1963–1975*
     (New York: Holt, Rinehart, and Winston, 1984), 153.
13   Charles DeBenedetti with Charles Chatfield, *An American Ordeal: The Antiwar Move-
     ment of the Vietnam Era* (Syracuse, NY: Syracuse University Press, 1990), 186. Ali
     also was fined $10,000. Both his prison sentence and fine were reversed on appeal.
     Marilyn B. Young, John J. Fitzgerald, and A. Tom Grunfeld, eds., *The Vietnam War:
     A History in Documents* (Oxford: Oxford University Press, 2002), 118–119.
14   Martin Luther King Jr., Riverside Church, New York City, April 4, 1967, in
     Young, et al., *The Vietnam War*, 122.
15   Richard Nixon, "The President's News Conference of March 14, 1969," in *Pub-
     lic Papers of the Presidents of the United States: Richard Nixon, 1969* (Washington,
     DC: Government Printing Office, 1971), 211.
16   Richard Nixon, "Address to the Nation on Vietnam," May 14, 1969, in *Public
     Papers of the Presidents of the United States: Richard Nixon, 1969*, 369, 372.
17   Nixon, "Address to the Nation on Vietnam," 371–372.
18   Nixon, "Address to the Nation on Vietnam," 370–371, 374.
19   Nixon, "Address to the Nation on Vietnam," 372.
20   Schmitz, *Richard Nixon and the Vietnam War*, 60. On the initial order to withdraw
     25,000 troops, see Richard Nixon, "Remarks Following Initial Meeting with
     President Thieu at Midway Island," June 8, 1969, in *Public Papers of the Presidents
     of the United States: Richard Nixon, 1969*, 443–444.

21   Young, et al., *The Vietnam War*, 131.

22   Schmitz, *Richard Nixon and the Vietnam War*, 46–47.

23   U.S. officials elsewhere tended to be skeptical of some of their colleagues' claims; see Kenton Clymer, *Troubled Relations: The United States and Cambodia since 1870* (DeKalb: Northern Illinois University Press, 2007), 94–95.

24   Richard Nixon, "Address to the Nation on the Situation in Southeast Asia," April 30, 1970, in *Public Papers of the Presidents of the United States: Richard Nixon, 1970* (Washington, DC: Government Printing Office, 1971), 407.

25   Taylor Owen and Ben Kiernan, "Bombs Over Cambodia," *The Walrus* (October 2006): 62–69.

26   Ben Kiernan, *The Pol Pot Regime: Race, Power, and Genocide in Cambodia Under the Khmer Rouge, 1975–79* (Chiang Mai, Thailand: Silkworm Books, 1997 [1996]), 24; Owen and Kiernan, "Bombs Over Cambodia," 67.

27   Kiernan, *The Pol Pot Regime*, 16.

28   Owen and Kiernan, "Bombs Over Cambodia," 63; Ben Kiernan, "The American Bombardment of Kampuchea, 1969–1973," *Vietnam Generation* 1:1 (1989): 4.

29   Young, et al., *The Vietnam War*, 129.

30   Richard Nixon, "Address to the Nation on the War in Vietnam," November 3, 1969, in *Public Papers of the Presidents of the United States: Richard Nixon, 1969*, 903.

31   Nixon, "Address to the Nation on the War in Vietnam," 903, 905.

32   Nixon, "Address to the Nation on the War in Vietnam," 905–906.

33   Nixon, "Address to the Nation on the War in Vietnam," 907–909.

34   Nixon, "Address to the Nation on the War in Vietnam," 909.

35   Nixon, "Address to the Nation on the War in Vietnam," 909.

36   UPI, "Nixon Urges Rise in Allied Soldiers," *New York Times*, March 15, 1968. Nixon later called for a "phasing-out" of American troops in Vietnam and a "fuller enlistment of our Vietnamese allies in their own defense." John W. Finney, "Nixon Asks Easing of U.S. War Role," *New York Times*, August 2, 1968; "Text of Nixon Statement to G.O.P. Platform Panel on the War," *New York Times*, August 2, 1968. Hints of Nixon's future position could be discerned in a major article he wrote for the establishment journal *Foreign Affairs* in 1967; see Richard M. Nixon, "Asia After Viet Nam," *Foreign Affairs* 46:1 (October 1967): 111–125, but especially 113–114.

37   Schmitz, *Richard Nixon and the Vietnam War*, 68; Nixon, "Remarks Following Initial Meeting with President Thieu at Midway Island," 443–444; Richard Nixon, "Statement on United States Troops in Vietnam," September 16, 1969, in *Public Papers of the Presidents of the United States: Richard Nixon, 1969*, 718.

38   R. W. Apple Jr., "Nixon Would Bar Forced Coalition in South Vietnam," *New York Times*, October 28, 1968.

39   Jeffrey Kimball, *Nixon's Vietnam War* (Lawrence: University Press of Kansas, 1998), 175.

40   DeBenedetti with Chatfield, *An American Ordeal*, 253. On the CIA and the antiwar movement, see, for example, Seymour M. Hersh, "Huge C.I.A. Operation Reported in U.S. Against Antiwar Forces, Other Dissidents in Nixon Years,"

New York Times, December 22, 1974. On the FBI and its COINTELPRO operations, see David Cunningham, *There's Something Happening Here: The New Left, the Klan, and FBI Counterintelligence* (Berkeley: University of California Press, 2004); and James Kirkpatrick Davis, *Assault on the Left: The FBI and the Sixties Antiwar Movement* (Westport, CT: Praeger, 1997). For a broader overview of American political repression, see Robert Justin Goldstein, *Political Repression in Modern America: From 1870 to 1976* (Urbana: University of Illinois Press, 2001).

41 DeBenedetti with Chatfield, *An American Ordeal*, 254.

42 Kimball, *Nixon's Vietnam War*, 174–175; DeBenedetti with Chatfield, *An American Ordeal*, 258–259.

43 DeBenedetti with Chatfield, *An American Ordeal*, 262–263; Kimball, *Nixon's Vietnam War*, 175; Young, et al., *The Vietnam War*, 137.

44 H. Bruce Franklin, *Vietnam and Other American Fantasies* (Amherst: University of Massachusetts Press, 2000), 50.

45 Franklin, *Vietnam and Other American Fantasies*, 51.

46 Richard Moser, *The New Winter Soldiers: GI and Veteran Dissent During the Vietnam Era* (New Brunswick, NJ: Rutgers University Press, 1996), 43–44.

47 Franklin, *Vietnam and Other American Fantasies*, 60–61.

48 Franklin, *Vietnam and Other American Fantasies*, 62–63, 65–68.

49 Franklin, *Vietnam and Other American Fantasies*, 63.

50 Franklin, *Vietnam and Other American Fantasies*, 64.

51 B. Drummond Ayres Jr., "Army Is Shaken by Crisis in Morale and Discipline," *New York Times*, September 5, 1971.

52 Col. Robert D. Heinl, Jr., "The Collapse of the Armed Forces," *Armed Forces Journal* 108:19 (June 7, 1971): 30.

53 The secret U.S. military actions in Cambodia were leaked but remained unknown to most Americans; see Clymer, *Troubled Relations*, 93.

54 Richard Nixon, "Address to the Nation on Progress Toward Peace in Vietnam," April 20, 1970, in *Public Papers of the Presidents of the United States: Richard Nixon, 1970*, 374.

55 Richard Nixon, "Address to the Nation on the Situation in Southeast Asia," April 30, 1970, in *Public Papers of the Presidents of the United States: Richard Nixon, 1970*, 406–407.

56 Kimball, *Nixon's Vietnam War*, 198–199. On the United States and the coup, see Clymer, *Troubled Relations*, 102–103; Ben Kiernan, *How Pol Pot Came to Power: Colonialism, Nationalism, and Communism in Cambodia, 1930–1975*, second edition (New Haven, CT: Yale University Press, 2004 [1985]), 300–302; and Kiernan, *The Pol Pot Regime*, 15.

57 Nixon, "Address to the Nation on the Situation in Southeast Asia," 407; Richard Nixon, "The President's News Conference of February 17, 1971," in *Public Papers of the Presidents of the United States: Richard Nixon, 1971* (Washington, DC: Government Printing Office, 1972), 162.

58 Nixon, "Address to the Nation on the Situation in Southeast Asia," 406–407.

59 Nixon, "Address to the Nation on the Situation in Southeast Asia," 408–409.

60   Nixon, "Address to the Nation on the Situation in Southeast Asia," 409–410.

61   Marilyn B. Young, *The Vietnam Wars, 1945–1990* (New York: HarperPerennial, 1991), 246, 248.

62   On decreasing network news coverage of the war, see Young, *The Vietnam Wars*, 245.

63   Sandra Scanlon, *The Pro-War Movement: Domestic Support for the Vietnam War and the Making of Modern American Conservatism* (Amherst: University of Massachusetts Press, 2013), 259.

64   Young, *The Vietnam Wars*, 248.

65   Hal W. Bochin, *Richard Nixon: Rhetorical Strategist* (New York: Greenwood Press, 1990), 66; Young, *The Vietnam Wars*, 248.

66   President's Commission on Campus Unrest, *The Report of the President's Commission on Campus Unrest* (Washington, DC: Government Printing Office, 1970), 289, 450.

67   Schmitz, *Richard Nixon and the Vietnam War*, 95.

68   Schmitz, *Richard Nixon and the Vietnam War*, 76, 104.

69   Richard Nixon, "Address to the Nation on the Cambodian Sanctuary Operation," June 30, 1970, in *Public Papers of the Presidents of the United States: Richard Nixon, 1970*, 476.

70   Memorandum from the President's Assistant for National Security Affairs (Kissinger) to President Nixon [Document 347], July 20, 1970, *Foreign Relations of the United States, 1969–1976*, Volume VI, Vietnam, January 1969–July 1970, 1137.

71   Schmitz, *Richard Nixon and the Vietnam War*, 111.

72   Schmitz, *Richard Nixon and the Vietnam War*, 112–113.

73   Richard Nixon, "Address to the Nation About a New Initiative for Peace in Southeast Asia," October 7, 1970, in *Public Papers of the Presidents of the United States: Richard Nixon, 1970*, 825, 827.

74   Editorial Note [Document 46], no date, *Foreign Relations of the United States, 1969–1976*, Volume VII, Vietnam, July 1970–January 1972 (Washington, DC: Government Printing Office, 2010), 123.

75   Conversation Between President Nixon and His Assistant for National Security Affairs (Kissinger) [Document 190], April 23, 1971, in *Foreign Relations of the United States, 1969–1976*, Volume VII, Vietnam, July 1970–January 1972, 575.

76   Schmitz, *Richard Nixon and the Vietnam War*, 116.

77   Young, *The Vietnam Wars*, 253.

78   Backchannel Message from the President's Assistant for National Security Affairs (Kissinger) to the Ambassador to Vietnam (Bunker) [Document 156], March 18, 1971, in *Foreign Relations of the United States, 1969–1976*, Volume VII, Vietnam, July 1970–January 1972, 467.

79   Richard Nixon, "Address to the Nation on the Situation in Southeast Asia," April 7, 1971, in *Public Papers of the Presidents of the United States: Richard Nixon, 1971*, 523–524.

80   Nixon, "Address to the Nation on the Situation in Southeast Asia," 524.

81 National Intelligence Estimate, NIE 53-71, South Vietnam: Problems and Prospects [Document 195], April 29, 1971, in *Foreign Relations of the United States, 1969–1976*, Volume VII, Vietnam, July 1970–January 1972, 598.

82 National Intelligence Estimate, 596.

83 Schmitz, *Richard Nixon and the Vietnam War*, 124.

84 "Vietnam Veterans Against the War: Testimony to the U.S. Senate Foreign Relations Committee (April 22, 1971)," in Marvin E. Gettleman, Jane Franklin, Marilyn B. Young, and H. Bruce Franklin, eds., *Vietnam and America: A Documented History*, second edition (New York: Grove Press, 1995), 456, 459, 462.

85 Schmitz, *Richard Nixon and the Vietnam War*, 127.

86 Schmitz, *Richard Nixon and the Vietnam War*, 129, 140.

87 Kimball, *Nixon's Vietnam War*, 90. For more on the "decent interval," see Larry Berman, *No Peace, No Honor: Nixon, Kissinger, and Betrayal in Vietnam* (New York: Free Press, 2001); Robert K. Brigham, *Reckless: Henry Kissinger and the Tragedy of Vietnam* (New York: PublicAffairs, 2018), 150–152; Gregory A. Daddis, *Withdrawal: Reassessing America's Final Years in Vietnam* (Oxford: Oxford University Press, 2017), 58, 180–181; Ken Hughes, "Fatal Politics: Nixon's Timetable for Withdrawing from Vietnam," *Diplomatic History* 34:3 (June 2010): 497–506; and Jeffrey Kimball, *The Vietnam War Files: Uncovering the Secret History of Nixon-Era Strategy* (Lawrence: University Press of Kansas, 2004), 121–198.

88 Transcript of a recorded conversation between Richard Nixon and Henry A. Kissinger, August 3, 1972, 8:28 a.m., at https://prde.upress.virginia.edu/conversations/4006748 (accessed November 8, 2018). See also Hughes, "Fatal Politics," 500–501.

89 Richard Nixon, "Address to the Nation Making Public a Plan for Peace in Vietnam," January 25, 1972, in *Public Papers of the Presidents of the United States: Richard Nixon, 1972* (Washington, DC: Government Printing Office, 1974), 100.

90 Nixon, "Address to the Nation Making Public a Plan for Peace in Vietnam," 103.

91 Schmitz, *Richard Nixon and the Vietnam War*, 139.

92 Transcript of a recorded conversation between Richard Nixon and Henry A. Kissinger, October 6, 1972, 9:30 a.m., at https://prde.upress.virginia.edu/conversations/4006749 (accessed November 8, 2018).

93 Young, *The Vietnam Wars*, 278.

94 Schmitz, *Richard Nixon and the Vietnam War*, 141.

95 Mark Philip Bradley, *Vietnam at War* (Oxford: Oxford University Press, 2009), 168.

96 Young, *The Vietnam Wars*, 279.

97 Backchannel Message from the President's Assistant for National Security Affairs (Kissinger) to the Ambassador to Vietnam (Bunker) [Document 248], January 5, 1973, *Foreign Relations of the United States, 1969–1976*, Volume IX, Vietnam, October 1972–January 1973 (Washington, DC: Government Printing Office, 2010), 906.

98 Young, *The Vietnam Wars*, 279.

99   Richard Nixon, "Address to the Nation Announcing Conclusion of an Agreement on Ending the War and Restoring Peace in Vietnam," January 23, 1973, in *Public Papers of the Presidents of the United States: Richard Nixon, 1973* (Washington, DC: Government Printing Office, 1975), 18, 20.

100 Schmitz, *Richard Nixon and the Vietnam War*, 143.

101 Schmitz, *Richard Nixon and the Vietnam War*, 143–144.

CHAPTER 3

Nixon and the Bloodbath Theory

Richard Nixon spent the first months of his presidency considering how to proceed in Vietnam, finding it difficult to settle on a firm course of action. Yet he knew what he did not want to do: pull the United States out in a manner that suggested retreat. This, he believed, would be devastating to American "credibility." How would the United States be viewed by the world – both its allies and its enemies – if it withdrew? Subscribing to Cold War ideology, Nixon worried that the nation's Communist enemies might feel emboldened, viewing withdrawal as evidence of weakness and an invitation to expand. U.S. allies, meanwhile, might question Washington's commitment to their security. How valuable are American pledges of support, foreign leaders could have wondered, if, in South Vietnam, the United States fled in the face of the Communist challenge?

While Nixon appreciated and worried about this dilemma, he faced a major problem at home: Most Americans had come to oppose the war.[1] That opposition, moreover, was increasingly moving abroad, with a growing number of U.S. troops expressing their dissent by demonstrating, deserting, refusing to obey orders, and even killing their officers. Nixon thus had his ideological work cut out for him. He had to convince both the public and the armed forces that the war was necessary but not endless. He had to demonstrate that he had a plan for bringing it to an end. This, the president said, would mean an outcome that reflected an "honorable" or "just" peace.[2] He consequently framed his course of action along two principal lines. One of these was strategic. A hasty withdrawal would lead to "a collapse of confidence in American leadership, not only in Asia but throughout the world," Nixon said in his November 3, 1969, address to the nation.[3] But American persistence in Vietnam was a moral imperative as well, he insisted. A staunch pragmatist, the president was not above appealing to an American sense of idealism. In doing so, he was simply echoing many of those who came before him.

When it came to the nineteenth-century conquest of North America, for example, some presidents, such as Andrew Jackson, implausibly claimed to be acting in Indian peoples' best interest. The "benevolent policy" of forcibly removing indigenous communities from their ancestral lands and opening them to white settlement, Jackson claimed, was not only "liberal but generous," "free[ing] [Indians] from the power of the states," "enabl[ing] them to pursue happiness in their own way," and "retard[ing] the progress of decay, which is lessening their numbers," with the government "kindly offer[ing the red man] a new home, and propos[ing] to pay the whole expense of his removal and settlement."[4] (Thomas Jefferson, writing decades earlier, was more blunt. "Nothing will reduce those wretches so soon as pushing the war into the heart of their country," he said in 1776. "But I would not stop there. I would never cease pursuing them while one of them remained on this side [of] the Mississippi."[5])

Similar discourses were applied overseas. When President William McKinley made the decision to colonize the Philippines in 1898, he described it as American munificence. "Wherever our flag floats, wherever we raise that standard of liberty," he told his fellow citizens, "it is always for the sake of humanity and the advancement of civilization."[6] And when President Harry S. Truman helped to usher in the Cold War in the late 1940s, it was not about American hegemony but the defense of freedom. It must be "the policy of the United States to support free peoples who are resisting attempted subjugation by armed minorities or by outside pressures," he told Congress in 1947. "The free peoples of the world look to us for support in maintaining their freedoms."[7]

Whether it was the gift of white Christianity in the eighteenth and nineteenth centuries or democracy promotion and humanitarian principles in the twentieth and twenty-first, American leaders have almost invariably characterized U.S. foreign policy as if it were driven by a charitable impulse. Unlike other world powers that pursued their own selfish interests, the United States, its dominant ideology suggests, is an "exceptional" nation whose objectives are selfless and fundamentally inconsistent with traditional imperial tendencies.

President Nixon, whose record of foreign policy has more often been described as "realist" than "idealist," recognized the rhetorical power of such exceptionalist thinking. Ordering an immediate American withdrawal would have been "a popular and easy course to follow," he claimed in his November 3 address, particularly as he could have "blame[d] the defeat" on his predecessor Lyndon Johnson. "This was the only way to avoid allowing Johnson's war to become Nixon's war," he said he had been counseled. But he "had a greater obligation than to think only of the years of my administration and of the next election," he continued. "I had to think of the effect of my decision on the next generation and on the future of peace and freedom in America and in the world."[8]

Among the various reasons the president identified for not ordering an immediate withdrawal of American troops, the first was rooted in what came to be known as the bloodbath theory. This was, in its essence, a fundamentally moral argument. "For the South Vietnamese," Nixon told his television audience, "our precipitate withdrawal would inevitably allow the Communists to repeat the massacres which followed their takeover in the North 15 years before. They then murdered more than 50,000 people and hundreds of thousands more died in slave labor camps." Yet this was not just a matter of the relatively distant past. "We saw a prelude of what would happen in South Vietnam," he predicted, "when the Communists entered the city of Hue last year. During their brief rule there, there was a bloody reign of terror in which 3,000 civilians were clubbed, shot to death, and buried in mass graves. With the sudden collapse of our support, these atrocities of Hue would become the nightmare of the entire nation – and particularly for the million and a half Catholic refugees who fled to South Vietnam when the Communists took over in the North."[9] With this, Nixon publicly entered – and sharply escalated – an ongoing debate about the nature and threat of the Vietnamese revolution.[10]

★★★★★

The debate that Nixon entered was one that played out at the level of both political and popular culture. In the months before his November speech, one of the country's most widely read newspaper columnists, Joseph Alsop, repeatedly predicted a massacre of "at least a million South Vietnamese … in the event of a nationwide Communist takeover."[11] Such a takeover, Alsop claimed, would make the Hue atrocities to which the president later referred "look like a Sunday school picnic."[12] (Just weeks before the president's November speech, Alsop increased the toll of the predicted "genocide in South Vietnam" to "a couple of million," basing this enumeration on what he said were official U.S. intelligence estimates of the consequences of an American "bug-out."[13])

John Wayne got in on the act, too. One of the country's best-known filmmakers and actors – and one whose politics skewed hard to the right – his 1968 picture *The Green Berets*, which fittingly enough opened on July 4 of that year, was widely panned by critics but still drew a large audience. The film dripped with right-wing talking points. Its opening sequence referred to the Vietnamese revolutionaries' "extermination of a civilian leadership, the intentional murder and torture of innocent women and children," and one of its most heart-wrenching scenes involved indigenous villagers slaughtered by "the Cong" because of their friendship with the United States. "We want to bring out that if we abandon these people, there will be a blood bath of over two million souls," Wayne told President Lyndon Johnson's press secretary while seeking White House assistance with the movie.[14] *The Green Berets* essentially served as a big-screen advertisement for the bloodbath theory.

President Nixon, like most other Americans of his generation, viewed the Vietnam War through the prism of the Cold War, and he understood the Cold War in uncomplicated binary terms. According to this thinking, the United States was an indispensable force in the defense of freedom, while the Soviet Union and its communist allies were totalitarian threats bent on global domination. This was thus a moral crusade. The world was, in fact, infinitely more complex than

Patrick Buchanan on Anti-Communism

The United States recognized that its military intervention was unpopular in South Vietnam. Nixon aide (and future politician and political commentator) Pat Buchanan thus proposed massively intervening in the South Vietnamese political system through a propaganda campaign, a proposal the president accepted. He, like others in the administration, worried that a Vietnamese antiwar candidate might jeopardize Nguyen Van Thieu's 1971 reelection – and, with it, U.S. policy in Vietnam.

> Elections, critical elections, come up in Vietnam next year. Anti-Communism, hopefully, will carry the day—but it would be utter folly to rest on our "hopes" after so many lives have been lost. A correspondent suggests that the Saigon Government begin now—with our help—a massive anti-Communist advertising campaign, portraying the atrocities of Hue, the horrors visited on Catholics and all religions by Communists, right now in preparation for those elections. Anti-Communism, like Cadillacs, is a good

commodity—but one does not see General Motors let Cadillac sell itself—it advertises all over America that Cadillac is the finest car in the country. Should we do less with "anti-Communism"? This seems to me the best way to set the stage for running into the ground any "peace" candidates.

Source: Patrick J. Buchanan to Richard M. Nixon, August 25, 1970, Folder: Buchanan, Patrick J., Box 809, Name Files, National Security Council Files, Nixon Presidential Materials Staff, National Archives II, College Park, MD.

Cold War ideology suggested, as many policymakers came to realize, but elected officials were not above exploiting these sorts of simplicities to sell U.S. policy to the public. In Cold War America, global politics played out like a Hollywood film. There were good guys and bad guys, and "we" were the good guys. Such a belief was widely shared in the 1940s and 1950s. The dilemma for Nixon, however, was that by the late 1960s millions of Americans had stopped subscribing to this fantasy. The Vietnam War saw to that.

When Nixon spoke to the nation on November 3, a substantial percentage of the American public had come to question whether their government was on the "wrong side" in its war in Vietnam. It was not that Americans had always supported earlier U.S. conflicts. The invasion of Mexico in 1846 engendered widespread opposition, for example, while the American conquest of the Philippines half a century later did the same.[15] World War I inspired a boisterous anti-war movement, and even World War II, which Americans have often simplistically come to remember as the "good war," saw an American military that was perhaps the least ideologically motivated in history.[16] But Cold War ideology, particularly when enforced by the punitive hand of the state, had made vocal dissent dangerous by the late 1940s. As numerous Americans had learned, political heterodoxy could lead to social ostracism, lost opportunities, or the collapse of one's livelihood. It could even invite Congressional investigation or surreptitious FBI "neutralization."[17] This had the unsurprising effect of encouraging docility.

Yet by the mid-1960s that docility would erode. The Vietnam War challenged Americans' moral sensibilities in ways that most other foreign policy campaigns would not. The "liberal consensus" – an ideological disposition characterized by hostility to communism and support for capitalism – began to collapse.[18] This was in considerable part because of growing political sympathy for the plight of the Vietnamese people. Whereas the U.S. government framed the Vietnamese conflict in aggressive terms – it was a case of a communist country called North Vietnam invading a freedom-loving country called South Vietnam – millions of Americans saw something quite different. To them, the Vietnamese enemy appeared to be engaged in an anti-imperialist revolution, with a hostile Washington attempting to impose its will on a resistant Southeast Asian people. The outcome was there for all the world to see: hundreds of thousands of Vietnamese lives lost and young Americans returning home in coffins.

With even some U.S. policymakers doubting the propriety of the American campaign, the Nixon White House desperately sought to recapture the moral high ground. The bloodbath theory was instrumental in its effort to do so. Its logic was quite simple. If the United States were to withdraw from Vietnam, the theory went, there would be a massive campaign of bloody retaliation by the communists against those millions of Vietnamese who either worked with the United States or supported the American intervention. To prevent such genocidal violence, Washington had an obligation to remain in Vietnam.

The theory's political brilliance was its reversal of the war's moral calculus. Those pushing continued warfare – the sort of people who, in a conflagration that had already destroyed millions of lives, might otherwise be denounced as warmongers – could ostensibly claim the moral high ground, arguing that what was an admittedly brutal war was in fact the only thing preventing even more brutal communist atrocities. Conversely, the war's opponents, under the logic of the theory, became morally reprehensible: their opposition to the war implied tacit support for genocide. "Now that America is [in Vietnam]," Nixon said just days after invading neighboring Cambodia, "if we do what many of our very sincere critics think we should do, if we withdraw from Vietnam and allow the enemy to come into Vietnam and massacre the civilians there by the millions, as they would – if we do that, let me say that America is finished insofar as the peacekeeper in the Asian world is concerned."[19]

In other words, an American withdrawal would not only be a strategic defeat for the United States but a moral one as well. As the Republican governor of Oregon, Tom McCall, said in an official statement to the press less than an hour after Nixon's November 3 address, "our immediate capitulation" would not only end U.S. preeminence as a world power and destroy the nation's self-confidence but would "scar our souls with the remorse of a people who, wearily after 200 years, first stamped their approval on genocide."[20] This was not acceptable. The United States could not allow such a slaughter to unfold. It had to persist in Vietnam. Or so the argument went.

The problem – or at least one of them – was its inconsistency. Contrary to Nixon's claim about Washington's self-declared role as "the peacekeeper in the Asian world," the United States was anything but. In fact, the foreign policy establishment had just endorsed an episode of mass killing – this one in Indonesia – only a few years before. When, in 1965, the Indonesian armed forces and their allies began to slaughter hundreds of thousands of alleged communists following a supposed coup attempt, Washington did "everything in its power," wrote historian Brad Simpson, "to encourage and facilitate the army-led massacre."[21] In the end, perhaps half a million Indonesians lay dead following what the CIA called "one of the worst mass murders of the 20th century."[22] American support for the butchery was "enthusiastic," Simpson found.[23] *Time* magazine, reflecting U.S. policymakers' belief that Indonesian leftists were essentially "unworthy victims," celebrated the outcome of the "boiling bloodbath" as the "West's best news for years in Asia."[24]

At the very least, this raised questions about the sincerity of American principled concern. But there were even more fundamental questions at issue in the case of Vietnam. Among these was a philosophical one. Was it appropriate to perpetrate a bloodbath – as the American war had by most accounts become – in order to ostensibly prevent one? Such reasoning sounded to critics a lot like what an unnamed U.S. officer once infamously told AP correspondent Peter Arnett about the Vietnamese provincial capital of Ben Tre: "It became necessary to destroy the town to save it."[25] The point was starkly made by dozens of American soldiers stationed at Fort Bliss. "No one wants to witness a 'blood bath' in Viet Nam," they wrote to the president shortly after his November 3 speech. "The slaughter which you predict will occur upon our withdrawal is certainly an ugly possibility. But the slaughter in which we are now participating has already cost 40,000 American lives and hundreds of thousands of Vietnamese lives. [...] We urge you to end our part in this massacre."[26]

A second question was more speculative. Would the Vietnamese revolutionaries in fact have slaughtered hundreds of thousands of their compatriots if the United States precipitately withdrew? While this may be ultimately unanswerable in the context of 1969, it prompts a third, related question. Were there credible grounds to believe that a postwar slaughter would unfold?

This was the debate into which Nixon waded in his November television address. The first question is fundamentally moral and ethical, with no easy answer. It could generate an infinite number of responses by an infinite number of people. Some might make a "lives lost" versus "lives saved" calculation, while others might point to a dictum often, but erroneously, attributed to the Hippocratic Oath: "First, do no harm." The second question – the one about whether a bloodbath would have ensued – is impossible to answer. It is what historians call a "counterfactual," as the United States did not withdraw in 1969 (or in 1970, 1971, or 1972). We thus have no way of knowing what *might* have happened. This brings us to the third question, which might be rephrased this way: Were Nixon and other proponents of the bloodbath theory drawing on solid evidence in predicting a genocidal future?

Of the three questions, this one offers the most straightforward answer. The historian Edwin Moise put it bluntly. "The documentary evidence for the bloodbath theory seems to have been spurious almost in its entirety," he concluded.[27] Still, this third question merits further examination. In poring over the details of this history, we discover an object lesson in its manipulation for political ends. We can, in other words, learn a great deal about how political leaders use – or, as is often the case, misuse – evidence in their efforts to win over the public.

While we cannot know what might have happened to America's Vietnamese allies in 1969, we do know what happened – or, rather, did not happen – when the combat ended in 1975. There was no mass slaughter of the vanquished. This is not to suggest that all was harmonious, however. The victorious revolutionary leadership in Hanoi had hundreds of thousands of its defeated adversaries placed in "re-education camps," where many were brutalized, where due process did not exist, where the conditions were typically appalling, and where, for some, the confinement persisted for years. But the genocidal retaliation confidently predicted by Nixon and his political sympathizers never occurred. Two right-wing scholars (one of whom became a Pentagon official in the Reagan administration) did later assert that there had been tens of thousands of executions, thus purporting to confirm a milder version of the bloodbath theory. But their methodology was deeply flawed and convincingly refuted.[28] There is a scholarly consensus today that no mass executions were carried out by the victors.

Curiously, some defenders of U.S. policy in Vietnam have pointed to neighboring Cambodia to suggest the legitimacy of the administration's bloodbath argument.[29] This is because while there was no postwar bloodbath in Vietnam, there was a genocide in Cambodia. Yet these partisans tend to overlook a few important points. For one, Cambodia is not Vietnam. Its history has often been intertwined with that of Vietnam, but its history is nevertheless a separate history. For another, U.S. policy arguably precipitated the Cambodian genocide, with the Khmer Rouge – the communist insurgents who seized power in 1975 – owing its growing strength in the early 1970s in considerable part to the Nixon administration. Historian Ben Kiernan, who is perhaps the world's foremost scholar of the Cambodian atrocities, wrote that the "U.S. eco-nomic and military destabilization of Cambodia" under Richard Nixon was "probably the most important single factor in [Khmer Rouge leader] Pol Pot's rise."[30] It is also telling that, when the genocidal nightmare in Cambodia finally ended, it was thanks to the same Vietnamese revolu-tionaries that the Nixon administration had painted as savage tyrants. To be sure, the Vietnamese invasion that drove the Khmer Rouge out of Phnom Penh in the late 1970s was not driven by altruistic concerns, but its humanitarian effect – immediate and substantial – was undeniable.

Moreover, it is difficult to square the Nixon's administration's alleged concern for human rights in Vietnam with its behavior elsewhere in Asia. Here, the case of Cambodia may be instructive. When the Khmer Rouge overthrew the U.S.-backed Lon Nol dic-tatorship in 1975 and accelerated their genocidal policies, Secretary of State Henry Kissinger, Nixon's closest foreign-policy advisor – he and the president were so close that observers often took to jointly calling them Nixinger – appeared utterly unfazed (Figure 3.1).

Figure 3.1 Richard Nixon worked closely with his Harvard-trained national security
     advisor, Henry Kissinger, in crafting U.S. foreign policy. Here, the two men
     speak on the White House grounds on September 16, 1972.
     dpa Picture-Alliance /Alamy Stock Photo.

"You should ... tell the Cambodians that we will be friends with them," Kissinger instructed Thailand's foreign minister on November 26, 1975. "They are murderous thugs, but we won't let that stand in our way."[31]

Nixon was out of office by then – he resigned during the Watergate scandal in 1974 – but it was not just Kissinger who expressed such sentiments. Perhaps most tellingly, he and Nixon averted their eyes from East Pakistan – which eventually became Bangladesh – as the Pakistani military slaughtered hundreds of thousands of Bengalis in 1971. The White House decision to enable the atrocities, which included openly sympathizing with and quietly rearming the perpetrators, invited one of the most forceful official dissents in the history of U.S. diplomacy. In what became known as the "Blood Telegram," the American Consul General in Dhaka, together with twenty other members of the diplomatic corps, berated Nixon and Kissinger's indifference to human suffering. "Our government has failed to denounce atrocities," they wrote to Washington.

> Our government has failed to take forceful measures to protect its citizens while at the same time bending over backwards to placate the West Pak[istan] dominated government and to lessen [the] likely and deservedly negative international public relations impact against them. Our government has evidenced what many will consider moral bankruptcy, ironically at a time when the USSR sent [Pakistan] President Yahya a message defending democracy, condemning [the] arrest of [the] leader of [the] democratically elected majority party (incidentally pro-West)[,] and calling for [an] end to repressive measures and bloodshed. In our most recent policy paper for Pakistan, our interests in Pakistan were defined as primarily humanitarian, rather than strategic. But we have chosen not to intervene, even morally, on the grounds that the Awami [i.e., East Pakistan] conflict, in which unfortunately the overworked term genocide is applicable, is purely [an] internal matter of a soverign [sic] state. Private Americans have expressed disgust. We, as professional public servants[,] express our dissent with current policy and fervently hope that our true and lasting interests here can be defined and our policies redirected in order to salvage our nation's position as a moral leader of the free world.[32]

The Blood Telegram suggests a Nixon administration utterly unconcerned with human rights.

While this disregard for humanitarian principles in Asia calls into question the veracity of the administration's stated concern for the prospect of Vietnamese genocide, the evidence it cited for the likely Vietnamese bloodbath suggests the political utility of moral arguments made by American officials. An analysis of the bloodbath theory's evidentiary foundation not only opens an important window into the recent Vietnamese past but also offers an opportunity to explore the empirical underpinnings of U.S. political discourse. To what extent, we might ask, was the bloodbath theory a mere rhetorical ploy to justify a devastating American war? And does this suggest something larger about U.S. foreign policy? While the answers to these questions may ultimately be unknowable, the administration's manipulation of the historical record is certainly suggestive.

At the outset, I should note that the question of whether the evidence upon which Nixon relied for the bloodbath theory was credible is a complicated one. Its answer requires considerable nuance. When Nixon posited the bloodbath theory in his November 3 address, he cited two episodes as evidentiary support. The first of these was what has been called the "land reform executions" of the mid-1950s. The second was the Hue Massacre. In both cases, the president pointed to these atrocities as clear-cut examples of the sort of postwar political retribution that the bloodbath theory suggested. Yet both were anything but clear-cut.

Nixon provided no context and no source when he spoke assuredly in his November 3 address about "the massacres which followed [the communists'] takeover in the North 15 years before," citing the "murder" of "more than 50,000 people" while "hundreds of thousands more died in slave labor camps." For those unfamiliar with recent Vietnamese history, which was the case with most Americans in the 1960s, the land reform atrocities would have seemed a striking example of the sort of communist barbarity which Nixon claimed to be fighting. The president's language suggested a simple story in which the Vietnamese revolutionaries "took over" – as opposed to "liberated" – "the North" in 1954 and proceeded to slaughter tens of thousands of innocents.

The takeover to which Nixon was referring was the Viet Minh victory over France after nearly a decade of French attempts to recolonize this piece of its pre–World War II empire. The Viet Minh, which was a front organization led by communists, was the most popular political force in Vietnam, having formed during the Second World War in opposition to the Japanese occupation and then, following the Japanese surrender, worked to secure an independent Vietnamese state in the face of postwar French aggression.

As the Viet Minh had battled the French, they pursued social revolution in the northern countryside. They did so for reasons of both principle and politics. "It was an opportunity for the Communists both to win the gratitude of the poor and to develop a political structure in the villages, recruiting cadres from among the peasants," wrote Edwin Moise, probably the leading scholar of the land reform campaign.[33] Recognizing the importance of land in this overwhelmingly agricultural nation but also the inequities in its possession, the revolutionaries instituted land reform policies that sought to provide Vietnamese peasants with workable plots of their own. As part of the campaign, a number of landlords were to be killed. These policies, which were enacted in 1953, quickly escalated, with thousands of villagers executed following trumped-up charges and sham legal proceedings. It is not known how many people were killed, but the most widely cited estimate is that of Moise, who concluded in 1983 that it was "probably on the rough order of 5,000 and almost certainly between 3,000 and 15,000."[34] The executions ended in 1956, when the government in Hanoi acknowledged that serious excesses had occurred and launched a campaign to rectify the "errors."[35] The land reform atrocities were, by all accounts, horrifically brutal.

But nuance still matters. According to numerous historians, the atrocities represented a radical departure from the planners' original goals. "Until 1956," Gabriel Kolko wrote, "the land reform organizational structure was functioning not only independently of the Party but often against it, basing its power on the poor peasantry."[36] Marilyn B. Young argued that the program spiraled out of control when handled by local officials, as "[a]ncient village grievances, religious differences, petty spite, and a growing paranoia frequently left villages not transformed, but deeply embittered."[37] Lien-Hang T. Nguyen echoed the sentiment, pointing to how "an atmosphere of fear, distrust, paranoia, and greed" resulted in "neighbors turn[ing] against one another."[38] Other scholars, such as Alex-Thai D. Vo, have conversely written that "Ho Chi Minh and the DRV's leaders were deeply involved in the development and implementation of the program; as such they were fully aware of, and arguably responsible for, its many 'errors' and injustices."[39]

Whatever the case, there is little doubt that in 1969, when Richard Nixon first publicly pointed to the land reform atrocities in support of the bloodbath theory, he did so as a propagandist drawing from a sketchy empirical foundation. The source most favored at that time by proponents of the theory was former schoolteacher Hoang Van Chi. Two days before Nixon's November 3 speech, as its final language was still being drafted, National Security Council staffer Sven Kraemer pointed to Chi as an "objective scholar" whose U.S. government-funded book, *From Colonialism to Communism*, contained "the most detailed account" of the atrocities.[40] In the speech's immediate aftermath, when questions were raised about its factual accuracy, Chi was the first person identified among the "best scholars" whose work supported the president's claims.[41]

The Vietnamese author, by that time working for the U.S. government broadcaster Voice of America, derived his supposed credibility from allegedly having close, firsthand knowledge of the land reform campaign through 1955, when he left his home in Thanh Hoa province, which is in northern Vietnam, for the south, where he took a position in the new Ngo Dinh Diem government's Ministry of Information. But, as later revealed, Chi did not have the firsthand knowledge of land reform policy that he suggested; he was in fact only a schoolteacher before leaving Thanh Hoa.[42] His published writings, moreover, relied on what political scientist D. Gareth Porter characterized as "a series of falsehoods, non-existent documents, and slanted translations."[43] Chi was a notorious anticommunist at the time of his book's 1964 publication, but even so, Edwin Moise concluded, his "work is in general so unreliable that it cannot be trusted even when what he says is favorable to the Communists."[44]

Make no mistake: The land reform executions about which he wrote were cruel, vicious, and criminal. But they were not the carefully planned, politically inspired mass murder alleged by Hoang Van Chi, and they were not the communist retribution suggested by the president. Their predictive power for postwar Vietnam was, at best, negligible. None of this seemed to concern the White House, however. That Nixon continued to cite the land reform atrocities after his 1969 speech, especially as the bloodbath theory faced a growing number of challenges, suggests the extent to which the president prioritized rhetorical power over factual accuracy.

We can see this in both his private and public remarks. Nixon was all over the place in identifying the likely number of victims if the United States were to withdraw, for example. Would it have been hundreds of thousands, as he indicated in a meeting with British counterinsurgency specialist Sir Robert Thompson just days before his November 3 speech?[45] Or would it have been millions, as he insisted in a news conference several months later?[46] Sometimes he himself wasn't sure. In a quiet April 1970 conversation with Henry Kissinger about his coming speech on the invasion of Cambodia, the two men went back and forth for roughly four minutes about how to characterize the bloodbath's victims. Would it be "better to say hundreds of thousands" or "millions" would be killed? Nixon wondered. And should these victims be "South Vietnamese" or "noncommunist Vietnamese," which broadly suggested indiscrimination, or should they more specifically be those who "oppose" or "stand up" to the "communists"? The president appeared to settle on "hundreds of thousands" who "have dared to oppose" or "dared to fight" the "communist invasion."[47] But in fact, when he delivered his address four days later, he punted. "[T]o take the easy political path" and "bring all of our men home immediately," Nixon insisted in his televised April 30 announcement, would be "to desert 18 million South Vietnamese people, who have put their trust in us and to expose them to the same slaughter and savagery which the leaders of North Vietnam inflicted on hundreds of thousands of North Vietnamese who chose freedom when the Communists took over North Vietnam in 1954."[48]

The point is not which was the "better" argument, as Nixon put it. Rather, the point is the evident lack of empirical rigor that Nixon brought to his bloodbath allegations. And these allegations, with their foundation in a mischaracterization of the land reform executions, were aired repeatedly. Just over two months later, in a July 1, 1970, news conference, the president hyped the "blood bath ... when the North Vietnamese took over in North Vietnam" in responding to a question about the survivability of a communist bloc-leaning South Vietnam.[49] The following year, when stressing the importance of saving Asian lives, Nixon cited the "half million, by conservative estimates, in North Vietnam who were murdered or otherwise exterminated by the North Vietnamese after they took over from the South."[50] Another time – this one in 1972 – he claimed that "a minimum of 50,000 were murdered, assassinated" from 1954 to 1956 and that "at least half a million" others perished in "slave labor camps," attributing the latter statistic to "the Catholic Bishop of Danang, whom I talked to when I was there in 1956 in South Vietnam."[51]

The attribution to the bishop was notable because it was a rare moment in which the president publicly cited a source for his bloodbath claims. But it also points to the reason why he may have avoided doing so. How? In short, Nixon could not have spoken to the Catholic bishop of Danang in 1956, when he was serving as vice president, because there was no Catholic bishop of Danang in 1956. The city did not have a bishop until 1963, according to the Hierarchy of the Catholic Church database.[52] This is significant, as there was virtually no support in contemporaneous scholarship for Nixon's claim that half a million Vietnamese had been killed by communists in such "slave labor camps," and the only source he identified did not exist. It is possible that another Catholic bishop may have told him about this, but even if that were true, it was a weak foundation on which to ground policy and render presidential pronouncements. Moreover, it raises questions about why, if the president had learned this in 1956, he failed to mention it for thirteen years. Given his undeniable hostility to communism and his vocal support for the Vietnam campaign as vice president, one would think that he might have disclosed the alleged deaths of half a million people at the hands of America's enemies at that time. This would have only strengthened the American claim of communist inhumanity. But Nixon never said a word.

The effort to portray revolutionary atrocities as "ideologically-inspired mass murder," as Gareth Porter called it, was apparent in the Hue Massacre, too.[53] During the Tet Offensive in 1968, the Vietnamese revolutionaries captured portions of Hue, a former imperial capital, for several weeks. In one of the most brutal battles of the war, U.S. and RVN military forces gradually drove the revolutionaries out of the city. When the fighting finally stopped, Hue lay in ruins. Robert Shaplen of the *New Yorker* wrote that "[n]othing I saw during the Second World War in the Pacific, during the Korean war, or in the Vietnam war so far has been as terrible, in terms of destruction and despair, as what I saw in Hue."[54] Approximately three out of every four houses had been completely destroyed or seriously damaged, and bomb craters forty feet wide and twenty feet deep "staggered" the streets near the walls of the ancient Citadel. Most of the city's population had been rendered homeless, and thousands of civilians and military personnel lay dead, with "bodies stacked into graves by fives – one on top of another," wrote Scripps-Howard correspondent Don Tate.[55]

This overall destruction was not the "nightmare" to which Nixon was referring in his November 3 address, however – perhaps because the United States bore some responsibility for it. Rather, the president had in mind what he called the "bloody reign of terror in which 3,000 civilians were clubbed, shot to death, and buried in mass graves" by the revolutionaries. "With the sudden collapse of our support," he warned the American public, "these atrocities of Hue would become the nightmare of the entire nation."

As with the land reform executions, the president was not entirely making things up. There were indeed executions by the revolutionaries in Hue. While precise figures are contested, at the very least hundreds of civilians were killed.[56] Tran Thi Thu Van, who published her work under the pen name Nha Ca, movingly described the "gigantic death of the entire city," including the summary executions by young people she knew, in her celebrated memoir *Mourning Headband for Hue*. "It is precisely here among our own generation," she said in just one example, "that there was Doan, who at some point studied in the same school with me, attended a university in Saigon, then suddenly returned to Hue wearing a red band on her arm and carrying a gun at her side, enthusiastic about tracking down this person and shooting that person, becoming an evil spirit on the deathbed of Hue."[57] But Nixon's portrayal of the atrocities as a frenzied purge that served as a harbinger of a defeated RVN was a serious mischaracterization of what transpired.

In an article published in the flagship magazine of mainline American Protestantism at the time of Nixon's November 3 address, two graduate students, D. Gareth Porter and Len Ackland, provided a very different portrait of the events in Hue. They detailed how the killing happened in various stages. While acknowledging that a relatively small number of those dubbed "enemies of the people" were killed immediately – in Gia Hoi, a district containing about a quarter of the city's population, these "enemies" consisted of four members of Hue's special police – with others in the following days, the bulk of the executions, they found, "were not the result of a policy on the part of a victorious government but rather the revenge of an army in retreat."[58] This was principally due to the fact that residents who had initially been slated for re-education – especially soldiers, policemen, and those who worked for the RVN and the United States – found themselves facing execution when it became clear that the revolutionaries would not be able to hold Hue indefinitely.

Of course, these circumstances do not excuse the murder of civilians. Political killing – on all sides – has a long history in Vietnam, just as it does elsewhere. But the circumstances do provide a quite different context than the one suggested by most pro-war partisans. If the Nixon administration's argument was that the atrocities in Hue portended the fate of hundreds of thousands, or even millions, of Vietnamese following an American withdrawal, his critics, including a number of distinguished scholars and journalists, offered a vigorous rebuttal, arguing that what had transpired under wartime conditions had little predictive value for a postwar Vietnam. George McT. Kahin, for example, a political scientist and director of the Southeast Asia Program at Cornell University, took to the pages of the New York Times just weeks after Nixon's speech to dispute the president's bloodbath claims. Kahin, who by that time was widely known as the coauthor of an influential 1967 book, The United States in Vietnam, wrote in the Times that Nixon was factually wrong about both the Hue atrocities and the land-reform executions.[59] But he was not only wrong on the facts, Kahin charged. The president's suggestion that such atrocities were what awaited Vietnamese civilians made it "much more difficult for Americans to trust in a negotiated peace settlement," according to Kahin.[60] Under Nixon's logic, the only moral course of action for the United States would be continued war.

New York Times columnist Tom Wicker followed this up with a blistering critique of what the paper's headline writers called "Mr. Nixon's scary dreams." To the extent that Americans were led to believe in the bloodbath specter, Wicker wrote, "the President makes it harder to justify any end to the war that would appear to give North Vietnam opportunity for such a massacre; that is, almost *any* compromise settlement." This was especially troubling, he continued, because the evidentiary basis on which the president was making his claims was deeply flawed. "[S]ince Mr. Nixon's staff is perfectly capable of pointing out an untruth no President should wish to assert, his insistence on the bloodbath seems to stem from something stronger than evidence. It is as though he wills it to be true, even though it isn't, both to justify the war and his policy, and to confirm the anti-Communism on which rests so much of his public life. Believing, perhaps, has made it so."[61]

★★★★★

As Wicker suggested, the bloodbath theory seemed to be necessary for Nixon and his supporters. Their entire geopolitical worldview was predicated on a vision of communist totalitarianism and brutality – of which there was certainly plenty. Yet the empirical bar when it came to communism was set low. Charges against communists required little or no evidence. It was one thing to claim, as did Nixon adviser Pat Buchanan, that a "policy of atrocity is the policy of the enemy we confront in Vietnam." Such assertions were unlikely to meet with resistance in respectable Washington

The My Lai Massacre

The My Lai Massacre was the most infamous American atrocity of the Vietnam War. On the morning of March 16, 1968, a unit of U.S. Army soldiers entered Son My village in Quang Ngai Province in central Vietnam and, expecting to find NLF insurgents but encountering only civilians, proceeded to slaughter – in some cases after sexually assaulting – nearly everyone they could. By the official Vietnamese count, the Americans killed 504 villagers, most of them women, children, and elderly men. As far as the U.S. Army was initially concerned, however, "128 Communists" had been killed in "a bloody day-long battle."[1]

The massacre was covered up for well over a year. Nine days after Nixon's November 3 address, an intrepid journalist named Seymour Hersh broke the My Lai story. Hersh's report caused a major stir. Countless antiwar activists viewed the slaughter as the logical outcome of an immoral and even criminal U.S. war. Both supporters of U.S. policy and critics of the antiwar movement – many of them at the core of Nixon's "silent majority" – felt otherwise. A poll in Minnesota, for example, found that nearly half (49 percent) of respondents did not believe "the charges of mass murder are true."[2] Among Americans who did, many were dismissive. Of the 79 percent of Americans who disapproved of Lieutenant William Calley's conviction for overseeing the atrocities, according to a *Newsweek* poll, 20 percent did not think the massacre amounted to a crime.[3] "It was good," a 55-year-old elevator starter in Boston approvingly said of the killing. "What do they give soldiers bullets for – to put in their pockets?"[4] When *Time* magazine surveyed 1,608 American households about what happened, 65 percent of respondents "shrug[ged] off My Lai, reasoning that 'incidents such as this are bound to happen in a war.'"[5]

The Nixon administration, for its part, sought to stoke what it called the "backlash" to the My Lai reports – though while being careful to ensure that its contribution, as Henry Kissinger put it, "could not be attributable to the White House."[6] Nixon recognized that the backlash fueled support for his policies and for a growing number of Americans associating with the "silent majority."

Despite the wartime denial of many Americans, there is no doubt that the atrocities occurred. Months before Hersh broke the story, Ron Ridenhour, a GI serving in Vietnam, had gotten word of what transpired from fellow soldiers and wrote to a number of political and military officials in Washington. This prompted an investigation that led to charges against several individuals. The highest ranking among them was Lt. Calley, who was convicted by a military jury in 1971 and sentenced to life imprisonment and hard labor. Calley's conviction met with widespread opposition. Some Americans felt the massacre was not criminal. Millions of others believed that people more senior to Calley shared responsibility for the atrocities but had escaped justice. The day after his sentencing, President Nixon had Calley transferred from the military prison at Fort Leavenworth, Kansas, to house arrest at Fort Benning, Georgia. He was confined to house arrest for three-and-a-half years before his conviction was overturned on several technicalities.

Historical scholarship and investigative reporting in the decades since the war has revealed just how commonplace U.S.-perpetrated massacres were. The one at My Lai may have been unusual for the hundreds of victims it produced, but the killing of Vietnamese civilians – whether by ground troops or through more seemingly impersonal means such as bombing – essentially became an everyday affair.

1 "My Lai: An American Tragedy," *Time,* December 5, 1969.
2 "Many Disbelieve My Lai Reports," *Minneapolis Tribune*, December 21, 1969; see also "Poll Finds Doubters on My Lai," *Washington Post*, December 22, 1969.
3 *"Newsweek* Poll on My Lai," in Marilyn B. Young, John J. Fitzgerald, and A. Tom Grunfeld, eds., *The Vietnam War: A History in Documents* (Oxford: Oxford University Press, 2002), 134.
4 "Doves Recoil but Hawks Tend to See 'Massacre' as Just Part of War," *Wall Street Journal*, December 1, 1969.
5 "The War: New Support for Nixon," *Time* (January 12, 1970): 12.
6 Henry A. Kissinger to Richard M. Nixon, December 4, 1969, Folder: My Lai Incident (2 of 2), Box 1004, Alexander M. Haig Special File, National Security Council Files, Nixon Presidential Materials Staff, National Archives II, College Park, MD.

society. It was quite another, however, to claim that the My Lai massacre – the March 1968 killing of 504 Vietnamese civilians by American forces in Quang Ngai province – suggested something deeper about the United States. That was verboten. The killing at My Lai is "against everything we stand for and are fighting for," Buchanan suggested as a Nixon talking point. "Any individual who cannot see the difference between the isolated acts of members of the American army ... and the premeditated and systematic atrocities of its Communist enemy in the field does not know what this war is about – or what his society is about."[62]

Unfortunately for Nixon, fewer and fewer Americans appeared able to see this difference.

NOTES

1 George C. Herring, *America's Longest War: The United States and Vietnam, 1950–1975*, fourth edition (Boston: McGraw-Hill, 2002), 210–213.

2 On a "just peace," see Richard Nixon, "Remarks at the Siemens Factory, West Berlin," February 27, 1969, *Public Papers of the Presidents of the United States: Richard Nixon, 1969* (Washington, DC: Government Printing Office, 1971), 158. On an "honorable peace," see Richard Nixon, "Annual Budget Message to the Congress, Fiscal Year 1971," February 2, 1970, *Public Papers of the Presidents of the United States: Richard Nixon, 1970* (Washington, DC: Government Printing Office, 1971), 47. Nixon was certainly not alone in using these terms. See, for example, Lyndon B. Johnson, "The President's News Conference," February 26, 1966, *The American Presidency Project*, at www.presidency.ucsb.edu/ws/?pid=28103 (accessed April 13, 2018).

3 Richard Nixon, "Address to the Nation on the War in Vietnam," November 3, 1969, *Public Papers of the Presidents of the United States: Richard Nixon, 1969*, 902.

4 Andrew Jackson, "Message of the President of the United States, to Both Houses of Congress, at the Commencement of the Second Session of the Twenty-first Congress," December 7, 1830, *Register of Debates*, 21st Congress, 2nd Session, ix–x, at https://memory.loc.gov/cgi-bin/ampage?collId=llrd&fileName=010/llrd010.db&recNum=430 (accessed January 24, 2018).

5 Thomas Jefferson to John Page, August 5, 1776, Founders Online, at https://founders.archives.gov/documents/Jefferson/01-01-02-0202 (accessed January 31, 2018).

6 Susan A. Brewer, *Why America Fights: Patriotism and Propaganda from the Philippines to Iraq* (Oxford: Oxford University Press, 2009), 26.

7 Harry S. Truman, "Special Message to the Congress on Greece and Turkey: The Truman Doctrine," March 12, 1947, *The American Presidency Project*, at www.presidency.ucsb.edu/ws/?pid=12846 (accessed January 24, 2018).

8 Nixon, "Address to the Nation on the War in Vietnam," 901–902.

9   Nixon, "Address to the Nation on the War in Vietnam," 902.

10 In fact, Nixon had nodded to the bloodbath theory months earlier, when, in his May 14 nationwide address, he said that to "abandon [millions of South Vietnamese men, women, and children who placed their trust in us] now would risk a massacre that would shock and dismay everyone in the world who values human life." His caution received relatively little attention, however. Richard Nixon, "Address to the Nation on Vietnam," May 14, 1969, *Public Papers of the Presidents of the United States: Richard Nixon, 1969*, 370.

11 Joseph Alsop, "Reds' Hue Murder Spree Could Be a Prediction," *Los Angeles Times*, May 16, 1969.

12 Joseph Alsop, "More Blood on Our Hands?" *Los Angeles Times*, September 16, 1969.

13 Joseph Alsop, "Hue Massacre Foreshadowed Results of 'Bug-out' by U.S.," *Washington Post*, October 15, 1969.

14 Wayne quoted in Lawrence H. Suid, *Guts and Glory: The Making of the American Military Image in Film*, revised edition (Lexington: University Press of Kentucky, 2002), 248.

15 See, for example, Amy S. Greenberg, *A Wicked War: Polk, Clay, Lincoln, and the 1846 U.S. Invasion of Mexico* (New York: Alfred A. Knopf, 2012); and Stephen Kinzer, *The True Flag: Theodore Roosevelt, Mark Twain, and the Birth of the American Empire* (New York: Henry Holt and Company, 2017).

16 Michael C. C. Adams, *The Best War Ever: America and World War II* (Baltimore, MD: Johns Hopkins University Press, 1994), 88.

17 On the FBI's secret effort to neutralize dissent, see Nelson Blackstock, *COINTELPRO: The FBI's Secret War on Political Freedom* (New York: Vintage Books, 1976); Ward Churchill and Jim Vander Wall, *Agents of Repression: The FBI's Secret Wars against the Black Panther Party and the American Indian Movement* (Boston: South End Press, 1988); David Cunningham, *There's Something Happening Here: The New Left, the Klan, and FBI Counterintelligence* (Berkeley: University of California Press, 2004); James Kirkpatrick Davis, *Assault on the Left: The FBI and the Sixties Antiwar Movement* (Westport, CT: Praeger, 1997); and James Kirkpatrick Davis, *Spying on America: The FBI's Domestic Counterintelligence Program* (New York: Praeger, 1992).

18 On the "liberal consensus," see Godfrey Hodgson, *America in Our Time* (Garden City, NY: Doubleday, 1976), 67–98.

19 Richard Nixon, "The President's News Conference of May 8, 1970," May 8, 1970, *Public Papers of the Presidents of the United States: Richard Nixon, 1970*, 419.

20 Governor McCall's Statement on President Nixon's Vietnam Message, November 3, 1969, Folder: SP 3-56/PRO, [11/4/69]-11/13/69, Box 107, Subject Files: Speeches (Ex), White House Central Files [hereafter WHCF], Nixon Presidential Materials Staff [hereafter NPMS], National Archives II, College Park, MD [hereafter NA II].

21 Bradley R. Simpson, *Economists with Guns: Authoritarian Development and U.S.-Indonesian Relations, 1960–1968* (Stanford, CA: Stanford University Press, 2008), 193.

22 Central Intelligence Agency, *Indonesia – 1965: The Coup that Backfired*, Research Study, December 1968, 71, at www.foia.cia.gov/CPE/ESAU/esau-40.pdf (accessed January 26, 2010). Amnesty International concluded that the atrocities "rank among the most massive violations of human rights since the Second World War." Amnesty International, *Political Killings by Governments* (London: Amnesty International Publications, 1983), 34.

23 Simpson, *Economists with Guns*, 193.

24 "Indonesia: Vengeance with a Smile," *Time* 88:3 (July 15, 1966): 22, 26. On "worthy and unworthy victims," see Edward S. Herman and Noam Chomsky, *Manufacturing Consent: The Political Economy of the Mass Media* (New York: Pantheon Books, 1988), 37–86.

25 Associated Press, "Major Describes Move," *New York Times*, February 8, 1968; William M. Hammond, *Reporting Vietnam: Media and Military at War* (Lawrence: University Press of Kansas, 1998), 115.

26 Robert T. Park, et al., to Richard M. Nixon, November 17, 1969, Folder: SP 3-56/Con, 11/6/69 – 2/16/70, Box 113, Subject Files: Speeches (Gen), WHCF, NPMS, NA II.

27 Edwin E. Moise, *Land Reform in China and North Vietnam: Consolidating the Revolution at the Village Level* (Chapel Hill: University of North Carolina Press, 1983), 217.

28 Beginning in 1985, Jacqueline Desbarats and Karl D. Jackson attempted to prove that, by a conservative estimate, at least 65,000 persons had been executed in Vietnam from 1975 to 1982. Jacqueline Desbarats and Karl D. Jackson, "Vietnam 1975–1982: The Cruel Peace," *Washington Quarterly* 8:4 (Fall 1985): 169–182; and Jacqueline Desbarats and Karl D. Jackson, "Political Violence in Vietnam: The Dark Side of Liberation," *Indochina Report* [Singapore] 6 (April–June 1986): 1–29. Their scholarship was persuasively refuted, however. Gareth Porter and James Roberts, "Creating a Bloodbath by Statistical Manipulation," *Pacific Affairs* 61:2 (Summer 1988): 303–310. Still, in an essay published in 1990, Desbarats revised her estimate of executions upward to "possibly more than 100,000 Vietnamese people" without engaging, let alone even acknowledging, Porter and Roberts's critique of her and Jackson's methodology. Jacqueline Desbarats, "Repression in the Socialist Republic of Vietnam: Executions and Population Relocation," in John Norton Moore, ed., *The Vietnam Debate: A Fresh Look at the Arguments* (Lanham, MD: University Press of America, 1990), 196–197.

29 Donald W. Beachler, "Arguing About Cambodia: Genocide and Political Interest," *Holocaust and Genocide Studies* 23:2 (Fall 2009): 214–238.

30 Ben Kiernan, *The Pol Pot Regime: Race, Power, and Genocide in Cambodia Under the Khmer Rouge, 1975–79* (Chiang Mai, Thailand: Silkworm Books, 1997 [1996]), 16. See also Michael Haas, *Cambodia, Pol Pot, and the United States: The Faustian Pact* (New York: Praeger, 1991).

31 Taylor Owen and Ben Kiernan, "Bombs Over Cambodia: New Light on U.S. Air War," *Asia-Pacific Journal: Japan Focus* 5:5 (May 2, 2007): 3.

32 U.S. Consulate (Dacca) to Secretary of State, Dissent from U.S. Policy Toward East Pakistan, April 6, 1971, at https://nsarchive2.gwu.edu//NSAEBB/

NSAEBB79/BEBB8.pdf (accessed January 17, 2018). For more on this issue, see Gary J. Bass, *The Blood Telegram: Nixon, Kissinger, and a Forgotten Genocide* (New York: Alfred A. Knopf, 2013).

33   Moise, *Land Reform in China and North Vietnam*, 5.

34   Moise, *Land Reform in China and North Vietnam*, 217, 222. Moise later wrote that "probably fewer than 8,000 landlords and would-be opponents of the regime were put to death," although many others, he continued, "were sent to reeducation camps." Edwin E. Moise, "Land Reform," in Spencer C. Tucker, ed., *Encyclopedia of the Vietnam War: A Political, Social, and Military History* (Oxford: Oxford University Press, 2000), 219.

35   Moise, *Land Reform in China and North Vietnam*, 146.

36   Gabriel Kolko, *Anatomy of a War: Vietnam, the United States, and the Modern Historical Experience* (New York: Pantheon Books, 1985), 66.

37   Marilyn B. Young, *The Vietnam Wars, 1945–1990* (New York: HarperPerennial, 1991), 50.

38   Lien-Hang T. Nguyen, *Hanoi's War: An International History of the War for Peace in Vietnam* (Chapel Hill: University of North Carolina Press, 2012), 34.

39   Alex-Thai D. Vo, "Nguyen Thi Nam and the Land Reform in North Vietnam, 1953," *Journal of Vietnamese Studies* 10:1 (Winter 2015): 2.

40   Sven Kraemer to Alexander M. Haig, November 1, 1969, Folder: Haig's Vietnam File – Vol. 3, November–December 1969 (2 of 2), Box 1008, Alexander M. Haig Special File, National Security Council Files [hereafter NSCF], NPMS, NA II; Hoang Van Chi, *From Colonialism to Communism: A Case History of North Vietnam* (New York: Praeger, 1964). To write about the land reform campaign, Hoang Van Chi received a grant from the CIA-backed Congress for Cultural Freedom, and his 1964 book's publication was later subsidized by the U.S. Information Agency. Hoang Van Chi, *From Colonialism to Communism*, xii; D. Gareth Porter, "The Myth of the Bloodbath: North Vietnam's Land Reform Reconsidered," *Bulletin of Concerned Asian Scholars* 5:2 (September 1973): 3.

41   Lt. Colonel Sweitzer [Robert Schweitzer] to Alexander M. Haig, November 6, 1969, Folder: Haig's Vietnam File – Vol. 3, November–December 1969 (1 of 2), Box 1008, Alexander M. Haig Special File, NSCF, NPMS, NA II.

42   "Hoang Van Chi," Wikipedia, n.d., https://en.wikipedia.org/wiki/Hoang_Van_Chi (accessed March 6, 2018); Porter, "The Myth of the Bloodbath," 2.

43   Porter, "The Myth of the Bloodbath," 3.

44   Moise, *Land Reform in China and North Vietnam*, 222.

45   Memorandum of Conversation [Attachment to John H. Holdridge to Henry Kissinger, October 24, 1969], October 17, 1969, Folder: MemCon – The President, Sir Robert Thompson, et al., October 17, 1969, Presidential/HAK MemCons, NSCF, NPMS, NA II.

46   Nixon, "The President's News Conference of May 8, 1970," 419.

47   Conversation No. 333-21, Executive Office Building, April 26, 1972, Nixon White House Tapes, NPMS, NA II.

48   Richard Nixon, "Address to the Nation on the Situation in Southeast Asia," April 30, 1970, *Public Papers of the Presidents of the United States: Richard Nixon, 1970*, 409–410.

49 Richard Nixon, "A Conversation with the President about Foreign Policy," July 1, 1970, *Public Papers of the Presidents of the United States: Richard Nixon, 1970*, 548.

50 Richard Nixon, "Panel Interview at the Annual Convention of the American Society of Newspaper Editors," April 16, 1971, *Public Papers of the Presidents of the United States: Richard Nixon, 1971* (Washington, DC: Government Printing Office, 1972), 542.

51 Richard Nixon, "The President's News Conference of July 27, 1972," July 27, 1972, *Public Papers of the Presidents of the United States: Richard Nixon, 1972* (Washington, DC: Government Printing Office, 1974), 745–746.

52 "Diocese of Da Nang," *The Hierarchy of the Catholic Church*, n.d., at www.catholic-hierarchy.org/diocese/ddana.html (accessed January 19, 2018).

53 Porter, "The Myth of the Bloodbath," 11–12.

54 Robert Shaplen, "Letter from Saigon," *New Yorker* (March 23, 1968): 122.

55 D. Gareth Porter, "The 1968 'Hue Massacre,'" *Indochina Chronicle* 33 (June 24, 1974): 8.

56 Two days before Nixon's speech claiming a toll of three thousand, an NSC staffer notified the White House that "approximately a thousand civilian men, women, and children" had been executed. Sven Kraemer to Alexander M. Haig, November 1, 1969. Douglas Pike, a wartime USIA analyst widely cited by proponents of the bloodbath theory as a dispassionate expert despite engaging in what he called "my effort to discredit the Viet Cong," wrote in 1988 that he thought "about 1,200 [were executed] but it could be less, for there are many who simply vanished." Douglas Pike to Patricia Way, November 11, 1988. (I am grateful to Grover Furr of Montclair State University for furnishing me with a copy of this document.) This is considerably fewer than Pike's wartime estimate of approximately 2,800 victims; see Douglas Pike, *The Viet-Cong Strategy of Terror* (Saigon: United States Mission, Viet-Nam, 1970), 30–31. The later uncertainty acknowledged by Pike rings true. As Mark Bowden noted in his 2017 book on the 1968 battle in Hue, there is no doubt that "the Front engaged in a systematic effort to find and punish those allied with the Saigon regime, just as that regime undertook its own reprisals when the battle ended." But with respect to the bodies found in mass graves that were attributed by pro-war elements to the NLF's executions, "without careful examination it would be impossible to say with certainty how they perished. The sheer number of dead [during the fighting in Hue] necessitated hasty mass burials." Mark Bowden, *Hue 1968: A Turning Point of the American War in Vietnam* (New York: Atlantic Monthly Press, 2017), 495–496.

57 Nha Ca, *Mourning Headband for Hue: An Account of the Battle for Hue, Vietnam 1968*, trans. Olga Dror (Bloomington: Indiana University Press, 2014), 7–9.

58 D. Gareth Porter and Len Ackland, "Vietnam: The Bloodbath Argument," *The Christian Century* (November 5, 1969): 1415–1416.

59 George McTurnan Kahin and John W. Lewis, *The United States in Vietnam* (New York: Dial Press, 1967).

60 George McT. Kahin, "Topics: History and the Bloodbath Theory in Vietnam," *New York Times*, December 6, 1969.

61   Tom Wicker, "Mr. Nixon's Scary Dreams," *New York Times*, May 12, 1970.

62   Pat Buchanan to Henry Kissinger, Q's and A's for the President's Briefing Book, December 5, 1969, Folder: My Lai Incident (1 of 2), Box 1004, Alexander M. Haig Special File, NSCF, NPMS, NA II. Nixon echoed this sentiment in his news conference a few days later; see Richard Nixon, "The President's News Conference of December 8, 1969," *Public Papers of the Presidents of the United States: Richard Nixon, 1969*, 1003–1004.

CHAPTER 4

The "Great Silent Majority" and Right-Wing Revanchism

Richard Nixon was masterful at exploiting white resentment. While his November 3 speech was fundamentally an address on U.S. policy in Vietnam, we remember it today mostly for a clever coinage he employed as he was winding down. "And so tonight – to you, the great silent majority of my fellow Americans – I ask for your support," he pleaded near the tail end of his thirty-two-minute address. It proved a brilliant stroke.

Silent majority: It sounds so simple and so innocuous. But in invoking the term, Nixon was both acknowledging and exacerbating the deep polarization in American society. As he certainly knew, by 1969 a clear majority of Americans opposed the war in Vietnam.[1] But – and this is where Nixon saw an opening – a substantial majority also opposed the antiwar protesters.[2] This is not as incongruous as it may seem. Americans, wrote political scientists Benjamin Page and Robert Shapiro, "have a long history of distaste for demonstrators and protesters, even peaceful ones, a distaste accentuated by official efforts to discredit and red-bait [them]."[3] And if there were two political skills that Nixon could count among his most finely honed, they were discrediting and red-baiting his opponents. His people were "the non-shouters" and "the non-demonstrators," he proudly declared. As president he would stand with those he called the "forgotten Americans."[4]

Nixon's appeal to this supposed majority of supporters drew on larger, extant discourses that were already circulating in American political culture. At the center of these were issues of patriotism, race, and class. But his invocation of a "silent majority" also carried with it a powerful implication: that the radicalism that seemed to be everywhere by late 1969 was not actually representative and that those Americans who were "silent" had in fact been silenced. And who was responsible for this silencing? Nixon hardly needed to say. The culprits would have been well known to the self-described freedom-loving Americans who made up the president's base.

That base was comprised of the people country-and-western star Merle Haggard spotlighted just weeks before Nixon's address in his hit song "Okie from Muskogee." The "silent majority," to borrow from Haggard's 1969 anthem, meant those Americans who, in a time of growing youth experimentation and student revolt, "don't smoke marijuana," "don't take our trips on LSD," "still wave Old Glory down at the courthouse," and "still respect the college dean."

Their silencers included the "Eastern Liberal Press," as conservative champion and 1964 Republican presidential candidate Barry Goldwater characterized the mainstream media.[5] The media was joined – at least in the minds of this supposed majority – by Hollywood and other smut peddlers whose immoral filth was polluting the minds and degrading the morals of the nation's children. The East Coast political establishment, against whom Nixon claimed to be leading the charge, as well as antiwar intellectuals, who two weeks before the president's address were memorably denounced by his vice president, Spiro Agnew, as "an effete corps of impudent snobs," were also among the silencers.[6] And we of course must not forget the campus radicals, that vocal cadre of young leftists that the president would come to condemn as "bums."[7]

If these folks did not in fact silence anyone, no matter. It was the right's perception of being silenced that was important. The conservative general public of what some politicians call "middle America" was alarmed by the activism and unrest they saw on the nation's streets and the challenge they perceived to America's natural order. The United States was a white, Christian nation, they believed. It always had been. Coming to terms with the black freedom struggles, with their upending of racial segregation and insistence on black equality, was proving difficult enough. Now young people were denouncing U.S. foreign policy and questioning whether the United States was the greatest nation on earth.

It was too much. When the president invoked the "great silent majority," he struck a chord that proved political gold. Countless Americans enthusiastically responded. "I have just listened to your speech about the war in Viet Nam," Mrs. Dennis W. Harrison of the conservative hotbed of Orange County, California, wrote to the president. "I decided that I have remained silent long enough."[8]

★★★★★

The 1960s witnessed tremendous change. Not all Americans embraced it. This was particularly true when it came to the thorny issue of race. For decades – and especially since World War II – black Americans had fought to throw off the shackles of white oppression. Since the late nineteenth century they had lived under a system of legal, or de jure, segregation in the South and actual, or de facto, segregation elsewhere. Where segregation was legal, as it had been in education until the U.S. Supreme Court said otherwise in its 1954 *Brown v. Board of Education* decision, blacks were forced into separate and typically unequal facilities. But all across the United States they lived in segregated neighborhoods, attended segregated schools, and suffered worse health outcomes and fewer economic opportunities than their white counterparts. Blacks were not alone in enduring racial oppression – all sorts of people of color faced either outright bigotry or more subtle forms of discrimination – but racism against blacks seemed especially pronounced.

The freedom struggles of the mid-twentieth century sought to change that. Countless black Americans, at times joined by white and other allies, waged an organized, nonviolent campaign against racial oppression. They engaged in consciousness raising, they marched and demonstrated, they wrote letters and signed petitions, and they undertook innumerable acts of civil disobedience. For doing so they were often denounced by reactionaries as communists and subversives (and, in the case of white activists, as "race traitors" and "nigger lovers"), and they endured the violence and terror of white Americans who sought to preserve the racial status quo. By the mid-1960s, the years of agitation began to show results. To the horror of many whites, especially in the South, in 1964 Congress passed the Civil Rights Act, which, among other things, outlawed discrimination based on race, color, religion, sex, or national origin, and it followed up a year later with the 1965 Voting Rights Act. The latter piece of legislation prohibited racial discrimination at the polls – a serious concern in Southern states, where whites had employed a variety of creative means to prevent blacks from exercising the franchise and attaining political power. Both acts were signed by the Democratic president Lyndon B. Johnson, who championed a number of progressive reforms at home while, paradoxically, deepening America's brutal war in Vietnam abroad.

The War in Music

Music reflected the deep divisions in American society in the 1960s and 1970s. Country-and-western, which grew in popularity during this period, generally resonated with those who supported the war or were hostile to those opposing it. For the antiwar movement, both folk and rock spoke to its opposition to U.S. foreign policy and to millions of Americans' hope for a more peaceful and decent future. Two songs released in the months surrounding Richard Nixon's November 3 address help illustrate this division.

Just a few weeks before Nixon's speech, Merle Haggard, a rising country star whose family relocated from Oklahoma to Bakersfield, California, during the Great Depression, released his 1969 hit "Okie from Muskogee," which he wrote with Roy Edward Burris. The song spoke to millions of Americans' disgust with the antiwar movement and the counterculture more broadly. With the lyrics' reproach of burning draft cards, smoking marijuana, or questioning authority, Haggard aligned himself with those supposedly strait-laced and law-abiding Americans who Nixon would soon dub the "silent majority." It was a huge hit, rising to the top of the Billboard country music charts and landing Haggard four awards from the Country Music Association: single of the year, album of the year, male vocalist of the year, and entertainer of the year.

If Merle Haggard spoke to Nixon's political base, Crosby, Stills, Nash, and Young identified with the antiwar movement that so outraged the president. A multinational group of singer-songwriters (David Crosby and Stephen Stills were American, Graham Nash was British, and Neil Young was Canadian), the band made a splash at the Woodstock music festival in August 1969, just months before Nixon's November 3 address. Following the May 4, 1970, killing of four unarmed students by the Ohio National Guard at Kent State University, Neil Young wrote and composed "Ohio," which, with lyrics that warned of "tin soldiers ... gunning us down," appeared to blame Richard Nixon ("Nixon's comin'") for the carnage that day. There were questions at the time about the extent to which rock stars should be identified with the serious political activists who opposed the war and whether the musicians were capitalizing on popular sentiment. Still, the song proved an enormous critical and commercial success, remaining in the top forty for seven weeks.[1]

---

1 H. Bruce Franklin, ed., *The Vietnam War in American Stories, Songs, and Poems* (Boston: Bedford Books of St. Martin's Press, 1996), 213.

For many Americans, the civil rights victories represented a long overdue step toward the nation's promise of universal freedom. But not all white Americans embraced the change. For them, the specter of blacks living in their formerly all-white neighborhoods, attending their

children's once all-white schools, and otherwise disrupting their racially homogenous social existence was unacceptable. They responded
in various ways. For the most extreme, violence and terror offered one
possible solution. Others, such as perhaps most infamously the residents of Boston, protested (sometimes violently) school busing, which
was the practice by districts of achieving court-ordered integration by
transporting children to schools outside their racially segregated neighborhoods.[9] By far the most common response, however, was "white
flight," or the abandonment by whites of their once-segregated city
neighborhoods for suburban communities that they attempted to in-
oculate from black penetration. Yet white flight represented more than
just "a physical relocation," historian Kevin Kruse noted. "It was a
political revolution," with "white southern conservatives ... forced to
abandon their traditional, populist, and often starkly racist demagoguery and instead craft a new conservatism predicated on a language of
rights, freedoms, and individualism."[10]

.   Many of these whites − especially middle-class suburbanites −
denied that they were racist and rejected the crude white supremacy
of earlier decades. They did not wear sheets, burn crosses, or carry
torches. They appreciated Nixon's assurance that they − a crucial part
of the "silent majority," or what in 1968 he was calling the "forgotten Americans" − were "not racists or sick."[11] Still, they proved quite
susceptible to what historian Edward H. Miller called "sophisticated
encoded appeals to unacknowledged bigotry."[12] These often upwardly
mobile, middle-class professionals and housewives resisted, through
their identities as homeowners, taxpayers, and school parents, the
changes overseen by the Johnson administration. Their concerns were
reflected in the language of declining property values, "big government," high taxes, and unsafe classrooms. They embraced a form of
spatial segregation that effectively maintained their largely homogenous neighborhoods and mostly white schools, and they increasingly
worried that the Democratic Party, with its growing support for civil
rights and the African American community, no longer represented
them.[13]

These were people that, by the late 1960s, Nixon hoped to reach.
But he also played to poor whites and the white working class, getting
them to craft political identities rooted in race rather than class. During
the nineteenth century the Democrats, who dominated Southern politics, had been the avowed party of white supremacy. But beginning
especially with the Great Depression of the 1930s, the party built itself
into a broad, national coalition that included blue-collar whites, farm-
ers, intellectuals, racial and religious minorities, and, oddly enough,

Southern white supremacists. What they shared was a sense of class consciousness and a commitment to many of the progressive reforms of Franklin D. Roosevelt's New Deal. By the time of the 1968 presidential campaign, Nixon, in what came to be known as the "Southern strategy," believed that working- and middle-class whites – and not just Southerners – could be persuaded to vote Republican (Figure 4.1). He believed that race could be used as a wedge with which to peel them away from the Democratic Party. Nixon was not the first political figure to make this calculation – nor would he be the last – but he proved extremely effective at a critical moment in American history. Like Barry Goldwater and others before him, Nixon recognized that countless white Americans in the country's blossoming suburbs objected to the forced integration of their neighborhoods and schools, and he was confident he could bring them into the Republican fold.

Figure 4.1 Employing race as a wedge with which to divide white Americans from the Democratic Party, Richard Nixon proved masterful in pursuing what Republicans came to call their "Southern strategy." Here, Nixon appears in Georgia while campaigning for the White House on May 31, 1968.
Everett Collection Historical/Alamy Stock Photo.

They would become his "silent majority." And he succeeded. By the end of the twentieth century, the white South and much of white suburban America was solidly in the GOP camp.

Richard Nixon's great contribution to the growth of the political right was his mastery of the politics of resentment. He recognized that the social changes of the 1960s had left millions of white Americans feeling unsettled, aggrieved, and afraid. Rather than appeal to their better angels and assure them that such changes to the racial status quo were an essential development in the nation's democratic progress, Nixon saw political advantage in stoking anger and fear over black bodies in previously white spaces. He generally avoided doing so explicitly, however. Rather, he used code words and insinuation. Political analysts refer to this as "dog-whistle politics," a phrase suggesting that, just like a high-frequency call that only dogs can hear, politicians will employ coded language that only certain people will detect. What might sound innocuous to most members of the electorate might be heard differently by others. This is especially the case with seemingly color-blind but racially loaded terms such as *states' rights* or *law and order*.

Nixon's chief of staff, H. R. Haldeman, acknowledged the president's wholehearted embrace of dog-whistle politics. As Haldeman recorded in his diary following a "deep discussion" with his boss, Nixon "emphasized that you have to face the fact that the *whole* problem is really the blacks. The key is to devise a system that recognizes this while not appearing to."[14] Or, as Nixon's former chief domestic adviser, John Ehrlichman, wrote in a 1982 confessional, the "subliminal appeal to the antiblack voter was always in Nixon's statements and speeches." The 1968 campaign, he said, came down to this: "we'll go after the racists."

As morally despicable as such a strategy may seem to many Americans, Nixon's tactical brilliance resided in his ability, as Ehrlichman put it, to "always couch[] his views in such a way that a citizen could avoid admitting to himself that he was attracted by a racist appeal." Under such logic, Republican voters could justify their support for the party by claiming that "[t]here were plausible reasons to be against open housing that had nothing to do with the fact that most public-housing-dwellers are black," for example. Or, "[b]using is bad because it wastes education money, not because it mixes the races."[15]

Lee Atwater, a Southern political strategist who served as chairman of the Republican National Committee, infamously explained the GOP's thinking in a 1981 interview with political scientist Alexander Lamis. "You start out in 1954 by saying, 'Nigger, nigger, nigger,'" Atwater began.

> By 1968 you can't say "nigger" – that hurts you, backfires. So
> you say stuff like, uh, forced busing, states' rights, and all that
> stuff, and you're getting so abstract. Now, you're talking about
> cutting taxes, and all these things you're talking about are
> totally economic things and a byproduct of them is, blacks get
> hurt worse than whites.... "We want to cut this" is much more
> abstract than even the busing thing, uh, and a hell of a lot more
> abstract than "Nigger, nigger."[16]

While Atwater's career and admission followed the Nixon presidency,
its logic was virtually identical to that embraced and advanced by the
California Republican.

To be sure, Nixon trafficked in more than just coded racial appeals.
He was capable of the crudest sorts of racist expression, though he
worked to confine his explicit bigotry to private conversations. "Henry,
let's leave the niggers to [Secretary of State William Rogers] and we'll
take care of the rest of the world," he once told his national security
advisor, Henry Kissinger, in a discussion about U.S. policy in Africa.
Indeed, Nixon "frequently" used the terms "niggers," "jigaboos," and
"jigs," wrote historian David Schmitz.[17] Another time he complained
about the "little Negro bastards on the welfare rolls" who "live like
a bunch of dogs."[18] This is consistent with the view ascribed to him
by Ehrlichman, his former aide: the president believed that "blacks
were *genetically inferior* to whites."[19] Africans were "child-like," Nixon
told Kissinger in 1971; Kissinger then followed up with a racist char-
acterization ("savages") of his own.[20] Africans might progress in the
very long term, Nixon confided to his personal secretary, Rose Mary
Woods, in 1973, but it would take time. Disputing his secretary of
state's more positive assessment of them – that, as Nixon paraphrased it,
"they are strong and some of them are smart" – the Republican president's "own view" of "the black thing" was more pessimistic. "I think
[William Rogers is] right if you're talking in terms of 500 years. I think
it's wrong if you're talking in terms of 50 years. What has to happen
is they have to be, frankly, inbred. And, you just, that's the only thing
that's going to do it, Rose."[21]

Nixon also revealed a deep wellspring of anti-Semitism. He denounced Robert Vesco (who happened to be Roman Catholic) as a
"cheap kike," and he consistently railed against American Jews, who
Nixon was convinced were out to get him.[22] "I won't mind one goddamn but to have a little anti-Semitism if it's on that issue [poten-
tially torpedoing a 1973 U.S.-Soviet summit]," the president said to
Kissinger, who was Jewish, in 1973. "They put the Jewish interest

above America's interest and it's about goddamn time that the Jew in America realizes he's an American first and a Jew second."[23] Whatever perceived shortcomings Jews may have had might not have been their fault, however – at least according to Nixon. "The Jews are just a very aggressive and abrasive and obnoxious personality," he explained.[24] And then there was this from a conversation on presidential appointments: "No Jews. We are adamant when I say no Jews."[25]

Yet these were all private remarks. Publicly, Nixon preferred dog whistles. Along these lines, perhaps no president in history more effectively exploited the term *law and order*. This was a notion that grew out of opposition to the civil rights movement of the 1950s and 1960s, and it operated on several levels. Whereas activists believed that sometimes unjust laws needed to be broken to demonstrate their opposition to them – an example would be black "freedom riders" in 1961 using what were legally "whites-only" restrooms or segregated lunch counters in Southern bus terminals – white reactionaries denounced such "civil disobedience" as disrespect for the sanctity of law. For these white conservatives, the actions of the civil rights activists were criminal, not political, and they refused to accept them as morally driven statements of principled opposition. More broadly, whites pointed to the rising crime rate in the 1960s and blamed it on desegregation. As noted by legal scholar Michelle Alexander, however, the crime wave, while complex, "can be explained" not by the civil rights reforms of that decade but "in large part by the rise of the 'baby boom' generation – the spike in the number of young men in the fifteen-to-twenty-four age group, which historically has been responsible for most crimes." This spike coincided with a sharp rise in the unemployment rate for black men, she notes, "but the economic and demographic factors contributing to rising crime were not explored in the media. Instead, crime reports were sensationalized and offered as further evidence of the breakdown in lawfulness, morality, and social stability in the wake of the Civil Rights Movement."[26]

Perhaps nothing scared white Americans in the 1960s more than the specter of black violence. The urban riots that scarred a number of American cities – Los Angeles, Newark, Detroit, and elsewhere – as well as the uprisings that followed the 1968 assassination of Martin Luther King Jr., underscored the danger. So, too, did media coverage of radical black activists, such as members of the Black Panther Party, openly carrying guns to defend themselves, they said, against police brutality. For many white Americans, such scenes offered a clear demonstration of what the decade's civil rights reforms had unwelcomely wrought. "Choose the way of [the Johnson] administration and you have the way of mobs in the street," Republican presidential candidate Barry Goldwater famously declared in a 1964 speech.[27] So whites were increasingly presented with a choice. They could go with a Democrat who embraced the changes to the social order that allegedly ushered in this violence, or they could go with a Republican who promised to restore law and order. The United States wasn't ready for Goldwater in 1964 – while taking several states in the South, he was otherwise trounced at the polls by Lyndon Johnson – but by 1968 they appeared ready for Nixon.

The White House would not come easily to the California Republican, however. He had to overcome not just one opponent but two. In addition to Hubert Humphrey, the Minnesota Democrat who had served as Johnson's vice president, Nixon faced a challenge from third-party candidate George Wallace. Wallace was a notorious segregationist

The Inaugural Address of Governor George C. Wallace, January 14, 1963

George Wallace was perhaps the nation's most infamous segregationist. He proudly announced his opposition to integration and hostility to federal interference in his inaugural address as Alabama's newly elected governor in 1963. Below is an excerpt:

> Today I have stood, where once Jefferson Davis stood, and took an oath to my people. It is very appropriate then that from this Cradle of the Confederacy, this very Heart of the Great Anglo-Saxon Southland, that today we sound the drum for freedom as have our generations of forebears before us done, time and time again down through history. Let us rise to the call of freedom-loving blood that is in us and send our answer to the tyranny that clanks its chains upon the South. In the name of the greatest people that have ever trod this earth, I draw the line in the dust and toss the gauntlet before the feet of tyranny ... and I say ... segregation today ... segregation tomorrow ... segregation forever.
>
> The Washington, D.C. school riot report is disgusting and revealing. We will not sacrifice our children to any such type school system – and you can write that down. The federal troops in Mississippi could better be used guarding the safety of the citizens of Washington, D.C., where it is even unsafe to walk or go to a ballgame – and that is the nation's capital. I was safer in a B-29 bomber over Japan during the war in an air raid, than the people of

Washington are walking in the White House neighborhood. A closer example is Atlanta. The city officials fawn for political reasons over school integration and THEN build barricades to stop residential integration – what hypocrisy!

Let us send this message back to Washington by our representatives who are with us today ... that from this day we are standing up, and the heel of tyranny does not fit the neck of an upright man ... that we intend to take the offensive and carry our fight for freedom across the nation, wielding the balance of power we know we possess in the Southland. ... that WE, not the insipid bloc of voters of some sections ... will determine in the next election who shall sit in the White House of these United States ... that from this day ... from this hour ... from this minute ... we give the word of a race of honor that we will tolerate their boot in our face no longer ... and let those certain judges put *that* in their opium pipes of power and smoke it for what it is worth.

Source: The Inaugural Address of Governor George C. Wallace, January 14, 1963, Montgomery, AL, Alabama Department of Archives and History, at http://digital.archives.alabama.gov/cdm/ref/collection/voices/id/2952.

who, following his 1962 election as governor of Alabama, infamously proclaimed in his inaugural address, "Segregation now! Segregation tomorrow! Segregation forever!"[28] His ambitions transcended the governor's mansion, however. Wallace unsuccessfully sought the Democratic nomination for the presidency in 1964 – again, this was a time when Southern whites overwhelmingly identified with the Democratic Party, which had unabashedly embraced white supremacy since the nineteenth century – and then appeared on the American Independent Party ticket in 1968.

The dynamics of that presidential race, in which Wallace ran to Nixon's right as a third-party candidate with a coded appeal to white voters, "quickly push[ed] Nixon toward race-baiting," wrote legal scholar Ian Haney López.[29] Without such subtle race-based appeals, Nixon worried that Wallace might split the white vote, allowing Humphrey to emerge victorious. Nixon thus sought to neutralize the Alabamian. This meant two things. He would need to earn the endorsement of the nation's most high-profile elected segregationist (that is, other than Wallace) and those who looked to him for guidance, and he had to appeal to the political pragmatism of whites who feared four more years of a Democrat in the White House.

Through the figure of Strom Thurmond, Nixon did both. Thurmond was a U.S. senator from South Carolina who once ran for president as the Dixiecrat, or States' Rights Democratic Party, candidate on a segregationist platform. That was in 1948. By 1964 the national Democratic Party's increasing alliance with the civil rights movement had become intolerable to him. Thurmond left the party that year, pronouncing himself a Republican. He was, other than Wallace, the most nationally renowned elected official openly pining for the racist status quo. Winning his support – and thus ultimately defusing the attraction to white Americans of Wallace – was, as Nixon biographer John Farrell put it, "the key to the [Republican] nomination."[30] Nixon did so by appealing to both Thurmond's pragmatism – the South Carolinian wanted a Republican to win – and his racial prejudices. The former vice president told Thurmond that *Brown v. Board of Education*, the 1954 Supreme Court decision that overturned the "separate but equal" doctrine that had been used to justify legal segregation since the *Plessy v. Ferguson* case in 1896, was now settled law. But, Nixon said, a "strict construction" of the Constitution limited the federal government's ability to enforce it, and he would appoint only "strict constructionists" to the courts. This, together with the promise that he would consult the senator on a vice-presidential candidate, was sufficient to earn Thurmond's endorsement.[31] With Thurmond and many of his segregationist backers behind him, Nixon prevailed in the 1968 election – but just barely. Wallace still managed to claim 13.5 percent of the national vote and carry five Southern states, with Nixon topping the Democratic candidate Humphrey by only 0.7 percent.[32]

Nixon employed a lexicon as both candidate and president that, while not as fierce as it would become by the early 1970s, nevertheless oozed dog-whistle politics. "Law and order" was his bread and butter. The Republican recognized that calling for "order" was a racially coded way of calling for a crackdown on African Americans. And so did the white Americans he was hoping to win over. As one Wallace supporter bluntly put it in 1968, "I like his stand on 'law and order.' You know – the niggers."[33] A 1968 Gallup poll found that 81 percent of respondents agreed that "law and order has broken down in this country," with the majority blaming "Negroes who start riots" and "Communists."[34]

For Nixon, this provided an opening. He could appeal to white racism without employing the sort of explicitly racist language that, by the late 1960s, might discredit a candidate seeking national acceptance and respect. *Law and order* was perfect for this sort of thing. As the political scientists Amy Lerman and Vesla Weaver wrote, the term "allowed politicians to implicitly appeal to racial concerns without directly calling up discredited norms of racial dominance."[35] It was, after all, whites frustrated with the civil rights gains of the mid-1960s who made it a concern. This was, in other words, no coincidence. "The most ardent opponents of civil rights legislation and desegregation were the most active on the emerging crime issue," Michelle Alexander wrote.[36] Or, as noted by Weaver, "[t]he same actors who had fought vociferously against civil rights legislation shifted the 'locus of attack' by injecting crime onto the agenda. Fusing crime to anxiety about ghetto revolts, racial disorder – initially defined as a problem of minority disenfranchisement – was redefined as a crime problem, which helped shift debate from social reform to punishment."[37]

This played to Nixon and the Republicans' strengths. After all, no one favored crime. But what was meant by "crime"? And who was responsible for it? What was meant by "order"? More often than not, elected officials advocating "law and order" did not explicitly refer to African Americans. The connection was instead implied, with the issue serving as what Haney López called "a proxy language for race."[38] But not always. Sometimes politicians illustrated precisely who they had in mind. Gerald Ford, the Republican House leader and future vice president who became president following Nixon's 1974 resignation, in 1966 bemoaned how the "war against crime" was being lost and chastised Lyndon Johnson's Democratic administration for failing "to protect our people in their homes, on the streets, at their jobs." For Ford, the nature of the criminal threat was not ambiguous: it was young black men. "When a Rap Brown and a Stokely Carmichael are allowed to run loose, to threaten law-abiding Americans with injury and death, it's time to slam the door on them and any like them – and slam it hard!" Ford declared of two of the nation's best-known black-power activists.[39]

Yet for Nixon, who as president took over stewardship of America's war in Vietnam, it was not strictly – or only just – about race. Without a doubt, Nixon made innumerable race-based appeals to white voters that drew on their fear of black bodies and black violence. But he also conflated the law-and-order issue with the antiwar activism that he worried would cripple his administration's foreign policy. "[T]he distinction between antiwar and civil rights demonstrators, between heckling protesters and street muggers, seemed almost nonexistent" to Nixon's base, historian Dan Carter wrote.[40] This was reflected in that earlier-cited 1968 poll that found that respondents blamed not only "Negroes who start riots" but also "Communists" for the breakdown in social order. "Communists" was a reference to the hundreds of thousands of young people taking to the streets by the late 1960s. Whose interests were they serving? Nixon, a master red-baiter, would have felt no need to tar the activists explicitly. Their waving of National Liberation Front flags at antiwar demonstrations was damning enough. Countless Americans came to view the antiwar movement as at best communist dupes and at worst anti-American subversives. It is little wonder that most of the country approved of Chicago police officers' wanton violence against protesters – an official commission called it a "police riot" – outside the 1968 Democratic convention.[41] The same appeared to be true when dozens of construction workers attacked antiwar activists in New York City in May 1970.[42] The rise of revolutionary groups in the years that followed, including violent offshoots of the antiwar movement, only heightened the sense that Americans now lived amidst unceasing social turbulence.

Nixon's twinned appeal to anti-black and pro-war Americans in a law-and-order sense was illustrated in a notorious television ad his campaign ran in 1968. With an ominous musical background and a spitfire montage of photographs showing angry protesters, bloodied bodies, white law enforcement personnel, and urban destruction, Nixon offered a calm and reassuring message: "It is time for an honest look at the problem of order in the United States," he said. (He, for one, refused to be silenced.) "Dissent is a necessary ingredient of change," Nixon continued. "But in a system of government that provides for peaceful change, there is no cause that justifies resort to violence. Let us recognize that the first civil right of every American is to be free from domestic violence. So I pledge to you: We shall have order in the United States." This was followed by a white-lettered plea set against a black background: "THIS TIME VOTE LIKE YOUR WHOLE WORLD DEPENDED ON IT." And then the solution: "NIXON."[43]

Upon seeing the ad, Nixon was ecstatic, reportedly remarking that it "hits it right on the nose. It's all about those damn Negro-Puerto Rican groups out there."[44] And it was indeed a politically brilliant appeal. The commercial featured images that would not have been unusual in the media landscape of 1968, and it cleverly appropriated the term "civil rights" to insist that the first of all such rights was freedom from criminal violence. In other words, the ad subtly suggested that the greatest civil rights victims in the late 1960s were not African Americans or other people of color who continued to face both personal and structural impediments to equal citizenship. Rather, the greatest victims were the millions of law-abiding whites forced to endure unrest on the nation's streets. In this way, Nixon neatly conflated the politics of resentment with the feeling of victimhood at the heart of many conservatives' sense of identity.[45]

By the early 1970s, Nixon appeared to have found a strategy to jointly attack what he perceived as two of the nation's biggest threats while concurrently appealing to his "silent majority." This was the "war on drugs." As readers of this book will likely know, the toll of this "war" by the twenty-first century was vast. It included millions of Americans – a grossly disproportionate share of them African American – subject to the criminal justice system (and its often attendant disenfranchisement), with millions of others quietly suffering addiction. It included numerous countries contending with a history of U.S. military intervention. And it included the expenditure of billions of seemingly wasted dollars, with billions more in health care spending, as drugs continued to remain plentiful and easily attainable throughout the United States. This "war on drugs" was of course not just a Republican war. Democratic president Bill Clinton enthusiastically got on board in the 1990s, for example. But it was Richard Nixon who first declared it.

Nixon, like nearly all elected officials who undertake major policy initiatives, framed what he was doing in benevolent terms. Drug abuse was "public enemy number one," he said in launching the campaign, "a national emergency" afflicting "both the body and the soul of America."[46] But John Ehrlichman, the Watergate co-conspirator who served faithfully as Nixon's chief domestic aide, offered a very different explanation for the "war" in a 1994 interview with journalist Dan Baum. "You want to know what this was really all about?" Ehrlichman asked Baum. He then told him.

> The Nixon campaign in 1968, and the Nixon White House after that, had two enemies: the antiwar left and black people. You understand what I'm saying? We knew we couldn't make it illegal to be either against the war or black, but by getting the public to associate the hippies with marijuana and blacks with heroin, and then criminalizing both heavily, we could disrupt those communities. We could arrest their leaders, raid their homes, break up their meetings, and vilify them night after night on the evening news. Did we know we were lying about the drugs? Of course we did.[47]

The quote was published years after Ehrlichman's death and, given its explosive nature, several Nixon aides disputed their former colleague's sincerity. They suggested that Ehrlichman was being sarcastic, and they claimed that "John never uttered a word or sentiment that suggested he or the President were 'anti-black.'"[48] In fairness, it should be noted that Ehrlichman probably also felt betrayed by Nixon, who had declined to pardon him for his Watergate crimes. Yet given what we know of Nixon's racial views, his attack on dissent, and the cold pragmatism that drove his politics, Ehrlichman's more cynical explanation for the administration's "war on drugs" hardly seems implausible.

Regardless of intent, there is no doubt that the drug war disproportionately harmed African Americans, and "law and order," including opposition to drug-related crime, became a central plank of right-wing political agitation in the decades following Nixon's presidency.

So, too, did the issue of "states' rights." The term *states' rights* is a loaded one, carrying with it a heavy connotation of anti-black racism. When the Southern states seceded in the 1860s to form the Confederacy – secessions that of course prompted the Civil War – they did so in the name of maintaining the right of the states to preserve slavery. In the decades since, and consistent with what is called the Lost Cause myth, conservatives have claimed that the war was not in fact about slavery; rather, they say, the secessions represented a principled stand against the encroachment or consolidation of federal power and the threatened destruction of the Southern way of life. Historians almost universally find this claim nonsensical. Not only was secession unambiguously about slavery, as revealed, for example, in South Carolina's Declaration of the Immediate Causes of Secession – South Carolina's population had the highest percentage of slaves and it was the first state to leave the Union – but the southern states in fact opposed states' rights, such as the right of states outside the South to refuse to enforce the 1850 federal Fugitive Slave Act.[49]

So while the origins of the Civil War are, for many Americans, grounded in what is in scholarly accounts a myth of "states' rights," that term came to denote something similarly race-based in the mid-twentieth century. In particular, white Southerners increasingly resisted the passage of civil rights laws and the end of legal segregation not by making avowedly white-supremacist arguments but by claiming to uphold the right of states to maintain their local systems in the face of heavy-handed federal intervention. Such a framework made it sound like *states' rights* was an argument over deeply held principles, not the preservation of racist institutions. Much like *law and order*, however, the position served as a code for "anti-black." While Nixon, always a political opportunist, frequently employed subtle appeals to race as a political strategy while paying lip service to support for civil rights, as the 1960s progressed he did not push the language of states' rights as forcefully as he would that of law and order. This is not to say, however, that he avoided the states' rights issue altogether. Rather, he just did so more quietly. This was something of a departure from his earlier run for the presidency.

When Nixon first sought the White House in 1960 – an election he lost to the Democratic candidate, John F. Kennedy – he hired I. Lee Potter as his southern campaign director. Potter, a Virginian, "supported state segregation laws," wrote historian Joshua Farrington, and Nixon more and more took to "emphasizing states' rights in southern speeches" despite knowing that this was a "mainstay of rhetoric against desegregation." The GOP candidate would declare, for example, that Republicans "stand for strengthening the states and our opponents stand for weakening them." He also highlighted, as Farrington put it, "his belief in not only states' rights, but local control of education, a phrase directly associated in southern politics with federally imposed school desegregation." Nixon told Dwight Eisenhower, in whose administration he then served as vice president, that "in the south the thing that appeals most is a statement to the effect that we are not going to weaken states' rights but we are going to strengthen them." Along these lines, Nixon, in a speech in Nashville, favorably quoted the slave-owning nineteenth-century president Andrew Jackson to the effect that "[m]y countrymen will [ever] find me arresting measures which encroach on the rights of the states." The *Louisville Courier-Journal* charged him with "playing footsie with the segregationists."[50]

The coming years would reveal just how much Nixon enjoyed playing footsie. As he attempted to revive his political career and prepare for a run at the presidency, Nixon laid the groundwork for an electoral victory in the South. As this required winning the allegiance of the arch-segregationist Strom Thurmond, the Californian and supposed civil rights champion offered the longtime South Carolina senator what one historian called "absolution."[51] When asked by a reporter in 1966 whether he found it "embarrassing" to share a party affiliation with "ol' States' Rights Strom," Nixon responded that "Strom is no racist. Strom is a man of courage and integrity."[52] Two years later, in attempting to capture the Republican nomination, Nixon, as noted earlier, pledged to appoint only "strict constructionists" to the Supreme Court, and he vowed that he would choose a running mate "acceptable to all sections of the party" – an unambiguous reference to Southern racists such as Thurmond.[53]

Nixon of course was elected. At his inauguration, he appeared to champion civil rights and racial justice, publicly promising "to give life to what is in the law," to make freedom's promise "real for black as well as for white." Behind closed doors, however, he said that "nothing should happen in the South without checking with [Harry] Dent," the former top Thurmond aide who served as Nixon's special White House counsel.[54] Dent immediately got to work on delaying the withdrawal of federal funds from five Southern school districts that had failed to file court-ordered desegregation plans. The president instructed his Department of Health, Education, and Welfare to ensure that any desegregation plan be "developed in method and content in such a manner as to be inoffensive to the people of South Carolina" and every other Southern state.[55]

This was Nixon whistling white solidarity, though he backed off the more explicit states' rights language that marked his 1960 run for the White House. Ronald Reagan, over a decade later, showed little such hesitation. The former California governor turned presidential

Ronald Reagan and the Noble Cause

Ronald Reagan, a one-time "New Dealer to the core" who made a name for himself in Hollywood before moving right politically and serving two terms as California governor, did not occupy the White House during the Vietnam War.[1] But his eight-year presidency, from 1981 to 1989, did coincide with a concerted postwar effort to reimage the conflict in American memory. Much of this reimaging was cultural. Having largely avoided films about the war during its peak years, Hollywood took to Vietnam with gusto in the decades that followed, producing everything from serious-minded dramas, such as *The Deer Hunter* (1978), *Platoon* (1986), and *Full Metal Jacket* (1987), to cartoonish, right-wing schlock – think Chuck Norris in *Missing in Action* (1984) or the finely-chiseled (and nearly always bare-chested) Sylvester Stallone in *Rambo: First Blood Part II* (1985).

But the reimaging was not just cultural. Indeed, Hollywood found itself following Washington's lead. Democrat Jimmy Carter, the first president elected after the war ended, claimed in 1977 that the war's destruction had been "mutual" – a bizarre statement that drew on a curious accounting – while explaining that "we went to Vietnam without any desire to capture territory or to impose American will on other people. We went there to defend the freedom of the South Vietnamese."[2] Of course, the United States was in Vietnam precisely in order to impose its will on the Vietnamese people. Unable to destroy the Vietnamese revolutionaries politically – they were simply too popular – the Americans sought to destroy them militarily.

But Ronald Reagan took the transformation of American memory to unprecedented heights. When campaigning for the White House in 1980, the charismatic Republican called on Americans to cast aside the "Vietnam syndrome," which Reagan attributed to "the North Vietnamese aggressors," and re-envision the war as an admirable pursuit. "It is time we recognized that ours was, in truth, a noble cause," he told a gathering of Veterans of Foreign Wars (VFW) members that August. "A small country newly free from colonial rule sought our help in establishing self-rule and the means of self-defense against a totalitarian neighbor bent on conquest."[3] Reagan, who would trounce Carter at the polls two-and-a-half months later, repeatedly drew on a fallacious recollection of the war's history. In a 1982 news conference, for example, he erroneously claimed that North Vietnam and South Vietnam had been separate countries prior to French colonization, that Ho Chi Minh had refused to honor the call for elections demanded by the Geneva accords, and that Ho had "closed the border" between the northern and southern regroupment zones.[4]

Reagan's rewriting of the war's history was in many ways prescriptive. "There is a lesson for all of us in Vietnam," he told the VFW in that 1980 address. "If we are forced to fight, we must have the means and the determination to prevail or we will not have what it takes to secure the peace. And while we are at it, let us tell those who fought in that war that we will never again ask young men to fight and possibly die in a war our government is afraid to let them win."

Reagan was propagating an unfounded myth that civilian bureaucrats, together with the "liberal media" and the antiwar movement, had essentially conspired to undermine what should have been an American military victory in Vietnam. Is it any wonder that John Rambo (Stallone), the Reagan era's favorite fictional veteran, had only one question for Colonel Sam Trautman (Richard Crenna), his trusted commanding officer, after accepting one last mission in Vietnam? "Do we get to win this time?" Rambo asked. That "get to" was essential. And Trautman's answer was revealing: "This time it's up to you."

The spare but penetrating exchange encapsulated the right-wing mythmaking that characterized the postwar era. Reagan had to have been pleased.

---

1 David Farber, *The Rise and Fall of Modern American Conservatism: A Short History* (Princeton, New Jersey: Princeton University Press, 2010), 165.

2 "The President's News Conference of March 24, 1977," *Public Papers of the Presidents of the United States: Jimmy Carter, 1977* (Washington, DC: Government Printing Office, 1977), I: 501.

3 Ronald Reagan, "Address to the Veterans of Foreign Wars Convention in Chicago," August 18, 1980, *The American Presidency Project*, at www.presidency.ucsb.edu/documents/address-the-veterans-foreign-wars-convention-chicago.

4 "The President's News Conference, February 18, 1982," *Public Papers of the Presidents of the United States: Ronald Reagan, 1982* (Washington, DC: Government Printing Office, 1983), I: 184–185.

aspirant clearly recognized the value of race-baiting in opening his 1980 general election campaign. He did so at Mississippi's Neshoba County Fair, where he solicited what the GOP official who invited him called "George Wallace–inclined voters."[56] The fair was just outside the town of Philadelphia (not to be mistaken with the Pennsylvania city of the same name), which was probably best known for the gruesome 1964 murders of James Chaney, Andrew Goodman, and Michael Schwerner, three civil rights activists working on a black voter registration campaign who were killed by Ku Klux Klansmen with the support of local law enforcement. (Their case was later made into the popular 1988 film *Mississippi Burning*.) "I believe in states' rights," Reagan declared at the fair that day.[57] As he uttered this statement, which since the 1950s had become code for hostility to integration, Reagan was well aware that he was addressing racist whites in a place notorious for its violent opposition to the black freedom struggle. But he saw political utility in the act.

Besides, Reagan, like other political opportunists, knew that coded language offered plausible deniability. The absence of explicitly racist appeals meant that the utterer could deny that he (or in some cases she) was being racist. White (and black) Americans may have known exactly who Reagan meant when he railed against Cadillac-driving "welfare queens" or "strapping young bucks" using food stamps to buy T-bone steaks, but the fact that the California Republican never explicitly said they were black allowed him to deny the charges of racism lobbed his way.[58]

George H. W. Bush, Reagan's vice president and Republican successor in the White House, followed closely in his GOP predecessors' footsteps. Though not at first. Through the spring and summer of 1988 – still relatively early in the presidential contest – Bush had avoided the sort of race-baiting employed by Reagan, Nixon, and other Republicans before him. Perhaps as a result, he found himself trailing in the polls. But his campaign manager, Lee Atwater – the same Lee Atwater quoted earlier about the need to move rhetorically from "nigger, nigger, nigger" to "forced busing" and ultimately "cutting taxes" – had a solution. His name was William Horton – or "Willie," as the Republicans preferred to call him, feeling that it sounded more sinister.[59] Horton was a convicted murderer in Massachusetts who escaped while on a weekend furlough and then stabbed a man and raped his fiancée. Significantly, Horton was black and the woman was white, and Bush's Democratic challenger, the Massachusetts governor Michael Dukakis, had earlier vetoed a measure rendering Horton and other convicted murderers ineligible for furlough. For an opportunist peddling in racist demagoguery, this was like manna from heaven. "It's a wonderful mix of liberalism and a big black rapist," one Bush aide said. It provided an extraordinary, though racially explosive, opening through which to attack the Massachusetts liberal. An ad was produced featuring Horton's mug shot and a photograph of his arrest, and it ended with the tag line "Weekend Prison Passes: Dukakis on Crime." Following the Horton blitz, more than 10 percent of Dukakis voters switched their allegiance to Bush, and the Republican took the lead in the polls.[60] He ultimately won.

As we would soon see, however, dog-whistle politics has not been the exclusive presidential purview of the Republican Party. Four years after Bush's 1988 victory, the Democratic candidate in 1992, Bill Clinton, positioned himself as a "New Democrat" – that is, as Ian Haney López noted, one "resistant to black concerns, tough on crime, and hostile to welfare." To prove it, and seeking to prevent a potential "Willie" Horton moment of his own, Clinton broke from his campaign during the New Hampshire primary to return to Arkansas, where he was governor, to oversee the execution of Ricky Ray Rector, a black man convicted of two murders who had survived a self-inflicted gun-shot wound to the head (the surgeon who saved his life called it "a classic prefrontal lobotomy" that rendered him "totally incompetent") and lived in an impaired mental state. Such was Rector's intellectually debilitated condition that he elected not to eat the dessert accompanying his final meal so that he could save it "for later." Of course, for those facing the needle, there was no "later." Rector seemed not to comprehend that, however. His scheduled death by lethal injection raised moral questions about the state killing someone unable to comprehend what was happening or why. But Clinton was unfazed. He allowed the execution to proceed. "I can be nicked a lot," he reportedly said, "but no one can say I'm soft on crime."[61]

Clinton also made it a point during the campaign to play golf at a segregated Little Rock country club, and he admonished the hip hop artist Sister Souljah and tussled with the civil rights icon Jesse Jackson.[62] Both were black. This was no coincidence. "The day he told off that fucking Jackson is the day he got my vote," a white electrician in Philadelphia disclosed.[63] Once elected, Clinton continued to pander to whites, escalating the "war on crime," pushing for "three strikes" sentencing requirements, and ending Aid to Families with Dependent Children, the welfare program for impoverished kids that, as Haney López notes, "had been a staple of the New Deal approach since 1936, but which the right had trashed in racist terms for encouraging poor black women to have children out of wedlock."[64] What we saw with Bill Clinton, in other words, was a Democratic president signaling to white voters that he understood and would address their racial fears and concerns.

★★★★★

Richard Nixon neither introduced nor monopolized race-based pol-iticking. But seeking and then entering the White House at a critical moment in twentieth-century history, he heightened and popularized it, demonstrating how elections could be won through the exploitation of voters' fears, resentments, and anxieties. Nixon of course differed in important respects from Reagan, Bush, and other Republican presi-dents, just as he did from the Democrat Clinton. But he did share with all of them a propensity to capitalize on society's deep polarization for political gain – this during a decade when society was perhaps more polarized than at any time since the Civil War. The civil rights battles, the conflict in Southeast Asia, the American Indian movement, and the struggle for women's equality: all of these divided America. Nixon only furthered this division.

The irony is that Nixon himself was widely distrusted by many of the conservatives that populated his base. They saw in the Californian someone with, yes, a long record as a staunch anticommunist, but one who proved only too willing to seek normalization with Beijing and détente with the Soviet Union. They saw a Republican open to a guar-anteed annual income – a notion that reeked of socialism to the political right – and a champion of big government responsible for the creation of the Environmental Protection Agency. The leftist intellectual Noam Chomsky called Nixon "in many respects the last liberal president."[65] And – at least in looking at the late twentieth century – Chomsky was, I think, right. Whatever his policy initiatives – and Nixon was indeed a complicated figure – he blazed the trail as a major-party candidate in exploiting the nation's differences, in the process laying the foundation for the decades of right-wing agitation to come.

NOTES

1   See, for example, Hazel Erskine, "The Polls: Is War a Mistake?" *Public Opinion Quarterly* 34:1 (Spring 1970): 134–135, 141–142.

2   Joel Lefkowitz, "Movement Outcomes and Movement Decline: The Vietnam War and the Antiwar Movement," *New Political Science* 27:1 (March 2005): 14–15.

3   Benjamin I. Page and Robert Y. Shapiro, *The Rational Public: Fifty Years of Trends in Americans' Policy Preferences* (Chicago: University of Chicago Press, 1992), 350.

4   Richard Nixon, "Address Accepting the Presidential Nomination at the Repub-lican National Convention in Miami Beach, Florida," August 8, 1968, *American Presidency Project*, at www.presidency.ucsb.edu/ws/?pid=25968 (accessed June 16, 2018).

5   "Goldwater Bestows Pins on Reporters Who Ride His Plane," *New York Times*, September 20, 1964. And how Nixon hated the press. At one point in 1972, his

"hatchet man" Charles Colson ordered future White House "Plumber" E. Howard Hunt to "stop [journalist Jack] Anderson at all costs." Hunt, together with fellow "Plumber" G. Gordon Liddy, began hatching plans to assassinate Anderson. Their plans came to a halt with the unfolding Watergate scandal. Gil Troy, "When Nixon's Henchmen Plotted to Assassinate a Journalist with LSD," *The Daily Beast*, January 20, 2017, at www.thedailybeast.com/when-nixons-henchmen-plotted-to-assassinate-a-journalist-with-lsd (accessed January 28, 2017).

6   Marjorie Hunter, "Agnew Says 'Effete Snobs' Incited War Moratorium," *New York Times*, October 20, 1969.

7   Juan de Onis, "Nixon Puts 'Bums' Label on Some College Radicals," *New York Times*, May 2, 1970; Richard Nixon, "The President's News Conference," May 8, 1970, *Public Papers of the Presidents of the United States: Richard Nixon, 1970* (Washington, DC: Government Printing Office, 1971), 417.

8   Mrs. Dennis W. Harrison to Richard Nixon, November 4, 1969, Folder: SP 3-56/PRO, 11/21/69 (1 of 2), Box 107, Subject Files: Speeches (Ex), White House Central Files [hereafter WHCF], Nixon Presidential Materials Staff [hereafter NPMS], National Archives II, College Park, MD [hereafter NA II].

9   On the violent response to busing in Boston, see Ronald P. Formisano, *Boston Against Busing: Race, Class, and Ethnicity in the 1960s and 1970s* (Chapel Hill: University of North Carolina Press, 2004 [1991]).

10   Kevin M. Kruse, *White Flight: Atlanta and the Making of Modern Conservatism* (Princeton, NJ: Princeton University Press, 2005), 6.

11   Nixon, "Address Accepting the Presidential Nomination at the Republican National Convention in Miami Beach, Florida," August 8, 1968.

12   Edward H. Miller, *Nut Country: Right-Wing Dallas and the Birth of the Southern Strategy* (Chicago: University of Chicago Press, 2015), 6.

13   For several recent scholarly works that address these issues, see Kruse, *White Flight*; Matthew D. Lassiter, *The Silent Majority: Suburban Politics in the Sunbelt South* (Princeton, NJ: Princeton University Press, 2006); Lisa McGirr, *Suburban Warriors: The Origins of the New American Right* (Princeton, NJ: Princeton University Press, 2001); and Miller, *Nut Country*.

14   H. R. Haldeman, *The Haldeman Diaries: Inside the Nixon White House* (New York: G. P. Putnam's Sons, 1994), 53. Emphasis in the original.

15   John Ehrlichman, *Witness to Power: The Nixon Years* (New York: Simon & Schuster, 1982), 222–223.

16   Rick Perlstein, "Exclusive: Lee Atwater's Infamous 1981 Interview on the Southern Strategy," *Nation*, November 13, 2012, at www.thenation.com/article/exclusive-lee-atwaters-infamous-1981-interview-southern-strategy/ (accessed June 7, 2018).

17   David F. Schmitz, *The United States and Right-Wing Dictatorships* (New York: Cambridge University Press, 2006), 82.

18   James Warren, "Nixon on Tape Expounds on Welfare and Homosexuality," *Chicago Tribune*, November 7, 1999, at http://articles.chicagotribune.com/1999-11-07/news/9911070165_1_oval-office-tapes-nixon-john-d-ehrlichman (accessed July 26, 2018).

19   Ehrlichman, *Witness to Power*, 223. Emphasis in the original.

20   "Conversation Between President Nixon and the President's Assistant for National Security Affairs (Kissinger)" [Document 57], September 28, 1971, *Foreign Relations of the United States, 1969–1976, Volume XXVIII: Southern Africa* (Washington, DC: Government Printing Office, 2011), 144–145.

21   Adam Nagourney, "In Tapes, Nixon Rails About Jews and Blacks," *New York Times*, December 11, 2010.

22   Stanley I. Kutler, ed., *Abuse of Power: The New Nixon Tapes* (New York: Free Press, 1997), 451. On Nixon and American Jews, see Nagourney, "In Tapes, Nixon Rails About Jews and Blacks."

23   Elspeth Reeve, "Some Newly Uncovered Nixon Comments on the Subjects of Jews and Black People," *Atlantic*, August 21, 2013, at www.theatlantic.com/politics/archive/2013/08/some-new-comments-richard-nixon-subject-jews-and-blacks/311870/ (accessed January 17, 2018).

24   Nagourney, "In Tapes, Nixon Rails About Jews and Blacks."

25   Reeve, "Some Newly Uncovered Nixon Comments on the Subjects of Jews and Black People."

26   Michelle Alexander, *The New Jim Crow: Mass Incarceration in the Age of Colorblindness*, revised edition (New York: New Press, 2012), 41. I am indebted to Alexander's book for its identification of a number of important sources.

27   Barry Goldwater, "Peace Through Strength: Private Property, Free Competition, Hard Work," September 3, 1964, *Vital Speeches of the Day* 30:24 (October 1, 1964): 744.

28   Dan T. Carter, *From George Wallace to Newt Gingrich: Race in the Conservative Counterrevolution, 1963–1994* (Baton Rouge: Louisiana State University Press, 1996), 1.

29   Ian Haney López, *Dog Whistle Politics: How Coded Racial Appeals Have Reinvented Racism and Wrecked the Middle Class* (New York: Oxford University Press, 2014), 22–23.

30   John A. Farrell, *Richard Nixon: The Life* (New York: Doubleday, 2017), 328. Nixon faced challenges for the Republican nomination from several figures, including Ronald Reagan, then the governor of California, and Nelson Rockefeller, the wealthy governor of New York.

31   Rick Perlstein, *Nixonland: The Rise of a President and the Fracturing of America* (New York: Scribner, 2008), 284.

32   Robert Cook, *Sweet Land of Liberty? The African-American Struggle for Civil Rights in the Twentieth Century* (London: Routledge, 2013 [1998]), 253.

33   Michael W. Flamm, *Law and Order: Street Crime, Civil Unrest, and the Crisis of Liberalism in the 1960s* (New York: Columbia University Press, 2005), 165.

34   Alexander, *The New Jim Crow*, 46.

35   Amy E. Lerman and Vesla M. Weaver, "Race and Crime in American Politics: From Law and Order to Willie Horton and Beyond," in Sandra M. Bucerius and Michael Tonry, eds., *The Oxford Handbook of Ethnicity, Crime, and Immigration* (Oxford: Oxford University Press, 2014), 43–44.

36   Alexander, *The New Jim Crow*, 42.

37   Vesla M. Weaver, "Frontlash: Race and the Development of Punitive Crime Policy," *Studies in American Political Development* 21:2 (Fall 2007): 230.
38   Haney López, *Dog Whistle Politics*, 51.
39   Ford quoted in Weaver, "Frontlash," 249.
40   Carter, *From George Wallace to Newt Gingrich*, 29.
41   "The Whole World Was Watching: Public Opinion in 1968," Roper Center for Public Opinion Research, Cornell University, n.d., at https://ropercenter. cornell.edu/the-whole-world-was-watching/ (accessed August 1, 2018).
42   Emanuel Perlmutter, "Head of Building Trades Unions Here Says Response Favors Friday's Action," *New York Times*, May 12, 1970. For an important corrective to the myth of working-class hostility to the antiwar movement, see Penny Lewis, *Hardhats, Hippies, and Hawks: The Vietnam Antiwar Movement as Myth and Memory* (Ithaca, NY: Cornell University Press, 2013).
43   Nixon-Agnew Victory Committee campaign advertisement, 1968, at www. youtube.com/watch?v=swyFqRB3dxY (accessed July 24, 2018).
44   Alexander, *The New Jim Crow*, 47.
45   "Far from being an invention of the politically correct," political scientist Corey Robin wrote, "victimhood has been a talking point of the right ever since Burke decried the mob's treatment of Marie Antoinette." Corey Robin, *The Reactionary Mind: Conservatism from Edmund Burke to Sarah Palin* (Oxford: Oxford University Press, 2011), 58.
46   Richard Nixon, "Remarks About an Intensified Program for Drug Abuse Prevention and Control," June 17, 1971, *Public Papers of the Presidents of the United States: Richard Nixon, 1971* (Washington, DC: Government Printing Office, 1972), 738; Richard Nixon, "Special Message to the Congress on Drug Abuse Prevention and Control," June 17, 1971, *Public Papers of the Presidents of the United States: Richard Nixon, 1971*, 739, 748.
47   Dan Baum, "Legalize It All," *Harper's Magazine* (April 2016): 22.
48   Hilary Hanson, "Nixon Aides Suggest Colleague Was Kidding About Drug War Being Designed to Target Black People," *HuffPost*, March 25, 2016, at www.huffingtonpost.com/entry/richard-nixon-drug-war-john-ehrlichman_ us_56f58be6e4b0a3721819ec61 (accessed July 24, 2018). Ehrlichman's children also questioned the account; see Tom LoBianco, "Report: Aide Says Nixon's War on Drugs Targeted Blacks, Hippies," *CNN*, March 24, 2016, at www.cnn. com/2016/03/23/politics/john-ehrlichman-richard-nixon-drug-war-blacks-hippie/index.html (accessed July 26, 2018). Ehrlichman died in 1999.
49   Eric Foner, *Give Me Liberty! An American History*, Seagull fifth edition, vol. 1 (New York: W. W. Norton & Company, 2017), 515. A good, focused analysis of the Southern states' rejection of states' rights can be found in James W. Loewen, "Using Confederate Documents to Teach about Secession, Slavery, and the Origins of the Civil War," *OAH Magazine of History* 25:2 (April 2011): 36–38.
50   Joshua D. Farrington, *Black Republicans and the Transformation of the GOP* (Philadelphia: University of Pennsylvania Press, 2016), 101–102. Jackson's full statement was slightly different: "Solemnly impressed with these considerations, my countrymen will ever find me ready to exercise my constitutional powers in

arresting measures which may directly or indirectly encroach upon the rights of the States or tend to consolidate all political power in the General Government." Second Inaugural Address of Andrew Jackson, March 4, 1833, at http://avalon. law.yale.edu/19th_century/jackson2.asp (accessed July 30, 2018).

51   Dan T. Carter, *The Politics of Rage: George Wallace, the Origins of the New Conservatism, and the Transformation of American Politics*, second edition (Baton Rouge: Louisiana State University Press, 2000), 329.

52   Perlstein, *Nixonland*, 89.

53   Perlstein, *Nixonland*, 284.

54   Richard Nixon, "Inaugural Address," January 20, 1969, *Public Papers of the Presidents of the United States: Richard Nixon, 1969* (Washington, DC: Government Printing Office, 1971), 1, 3; Perlstein, *Nixonland*, 362. "When I look back, my biggest regret now is anything I did that stood in the way of the rights of black people," Dent ruefully told the *Washington Post* in 1981 as he made the transition into full-time ministry. Patricia Sullivan, "Harry Dent; Advised Key Republicans," *Washington Post*, October 3, 2007, at www.washingtonpost.com/wp-dyn/content/article/2007/10/02/AR2007100202225.html (accessed July 31, 2018).

55   Richard Reeves, *President Nixon: Alone in the White House* (New York: Simon & Schuster, 2001), 117.

56   David Farber, *The Rise and Fall of Modern American Conservatism: A Short History* (Princeton, NJ: Princeton University Press, 2010), 190.

57   Farber, *The Rise and Fall of Modern American Conservatism*, 191.

58   Haney López, *Dog Whistle Politics*, 4.

59   Kathleen Hall Jamieson, *Dirty Politics: Deception, Distraction, and Democracy* (New York: Oxford University Press, 1992), 128–130.

60   Haney López, *Dog Whistle Politics*, 105–106; National Security PAC, "Bush & Dukakis on Crime," 1988, at www.youtube.com/watch?v=Io9KMSSEZ0Y (accessed July 31, 2018).

61   Haney López, *Dog Whistle Politics*, 108–109. See also Kenneth O'Reilly, *Nixon's Piano: Presidents and Racial Politics from Washington to Clinton* (New York: Free Press, 1995), 411–412.

62   O'Reilly, *Nixon's Piano*, 410.

63   Carter, *From George Wallace to Newt Gingrich*, 100.

64   Haney López, *Dog Whistle Politics*, 109–110.

65   Noam Chomsky, *Rogue States: The Rule of Force in World Affairs* (Chicago: Haymarket Books, 2015 [2000]), 102.

Conjuring Nixon in the Twenty-First Century

On July 10, 2015, just weeks after announcing his run for president of the United States, Donald Trump declared to several thousand Republicans from the stage of a Phoenix rally that "[t]he silent majority is back, and we're going to take the country back."[1] The response from the crowd was electric. When he followed up seconds later with a promise to "make America great again," the audience went wild. Finally, here was a candidate speaking for them, not the "special interest groups" or the "liberal elites" scheming to perpetuate "globalism."

Trump was, of course, invoking a term made famous by Richard Nixon, with politicians and activists long claiming to represent a silent majority when seeking or securing power. In 1932, for example, Democratic contender Franklin D. Roosevelt cited his support for the "forgotten man at the bottom of the economic pyramid" in campaigning against Republican incumbent Herbert Hoover.[2] A decade-and-a-half later, Nixon picked up on the theme when running for Congress.[3] By 1968, when the former vice president became the Republican-endorsed candidate for president, he had turned the idea into a right-wing populist call. Speaking that year before the assembled crowd at the Republican National Convention, Nixon professed to be listening to "the voice of the great majority of Americans, the forgotten Americans – the non-shouters, the non-demonstrators."[4] While subsequent presidents, such as "New Democrat" Bill Clinton, harkened the "quiet, troubled voice of the forgotten middle class," the idea of a silent majority resonated especially on the political right, with Tea Party activists during the Barack Obama administration insisting they would be "silent no more."[5]

It is not clear whether Donald Trump was familiar with this history when hearkening the silent majority from that Arizona stage. Trump was not generally known for his historical or intellectual acuity. Among other things, he confused the Baltics and the Balkans in lambasting leaders of the former for the wars in the latter; appeared to believe that the nineteenth-century abolitionist Frederick Douglass was alive; mused that Andrew Jackson, who died sixteen years before the Civil War, was "really angry" about it; and blamed Canada, which did not exist in the early nineteenth century, for burning down the White House during the War of 1812.[6] It is thus entirely possible that Trump was too ignorant to understand the origins or significance of the term. But given the consistent race-baiting – if not outright racism – he demonstrated as both a candidate and as president, this cannot be assumed.

Either way, it was clear by 2015 that the silent majority was indeed back, and Richard Nixon would increasingly become Donald Trump's lodestar (Figure 5.1). Trump, like Nixon, made "law and

Figure 5.1 When campaigning for the presidency in 2015, Donald Trump announced that "the silent majority is back." The message clearly resonated with many Americans. Here, audience members listen to the Republican candidate during a rally at the University of Northern Iowa on January 12, 2016. Getty Images: Joe Raedle/Staff.

order" a rallying cry of his presidency, railing against undocumented immigrants for the extraordinary number of crimes he falsely accused them of committing.[7] "You wouldn't believe how bad these people are. These aren't people, these are animals, and we're taking them out of the country at a level and at a rate that's never happened before," Trump said.[8] At other times he denounced the "horrendous" immigrants who arrived because of the diversity visa lottery or questioned why "all these people from shithole countries" had been allowed into the United States.[9]

Such attacks on immigrants served a dual purpose. They tapped into concerns about crime while concurrently stoking, just as Nixon had, white fears of the dark-skinned "other." Trump made this especially obvious in a 2018 television commercial that made Nixon's 1968 "vote like your whole world depended on it" ad seem like a model of enlightened discourse. Against the backdrop of a migrant caravan from Central America and acontextual footage of hundreds of people rushing across the border – which one was not really clear – the ad featured a twice-deported undocumented Mexican chuckling about his murder of two California sheriff's deputies while ruing his failure to kill more. "Who else would Democrats let in?" it asked. Political historian Kevin Kruse called the commercial "a whole lot worse" than George Bush's exploitation of "Willie" Horton.[10] Indeed, the ad was so misleading – not to mention racially incendiary – that even the right-wing cable network Fox News, whose primetime pundits essentially served as hagiographers of Donald Trump, refused to air it.[11]

Such responses only heightened the president's animosity for the press. This was a sentiment he shared with his Republican predecessor fifty years earlier. The Nixon administration had placed journalists on its list of "political enemies" that, according to White House Counsel John Dean, they intended to "screw" using "the available federal machinery," such as tax audits and other repressive measures.[12]

The Watergate Scandal

What began with a bumbling break-in ended with the only resignation of a president in American history.

In the early morning hours of June 17, 1972, five men acting at the direction of Nixon administration officials broke into the headquarters of the Democratic National Committee in the Watergate complex in Washington, D.C. The men, who were part of the same Plumbers group that had earlier broken into the

Beverly Hills office of Dr. Lewis Fielding, the psychiatrist of the Pentagon Papers leaker Daniel Ellsberg, were caught and arrested. The administration immediately worked to cover up its connection to the burglars.

The cover-up slowly unraveled, however. By July 1974, following months of law-enforcement investigations, dogged media reporting (especially by Bob Woodward and Carl Bernstein of the *Washington Post*), and congressional hearings, the House Judiciary Committee recommended three articles of impeachment against President Nixon. Days later, the release of a "smoking gun" tape – Nixon had surreptitiously set up a recording system in the Oval Office – revealed that, just days after the Watergate break-in, Nixon ordered the CIA to obstruct the FBI's investigation of it. It was clear evidence that the president had attempted to hide the administration's campaign to illegally spy on the Democratic Party.

The little remaining support that Nixon enjoyed in Congress all but dissipated. Told by the Republican congressional leadership that the full House would soon vote to impeach him and that the Senate was sure to convict, Nixon, on August 9, 1974, resigned from office in disgrace. The Nixon presidency was done.

Members of the administration also conspired – their plans were cut short by the Watergate scandal – to assassinate the journalist Jack Anderson.[13] Decades later, Trump expressed similar disdain for the Fourth Estate. He regularly denounced unfavorable coverage as "fake news," he revoked the press pass of CNN chief White House correspondent Jim Acosta on fabricated grounds, and he repeatedly declared the media the "enemy of the American people" and the "true Enemy of the People."[14] At least one of Trump's supporters took his charge as a directive, mailing pipe bombs to CNN's offices in Atlanta and New York (as well as to a number of high-profile critics of the president).[15]

Both Trump and Nixon demonstrated a persistent disrespect for the law. Nixon was of course undone by the illegalities of his administration, and three years after leaving the White House he notoriously proclaimed that "[i]f the president does it, that means it's not illegal."[16] Trump, whose presidency was engulfed by a special counsel investigation of his campaign's possible collusion with Russia, nominated to the Supreme Court a right-wing jurist, Brett Kavanaugh, who asserted that it was a "traditional exercise" of presidential power to disregard laws that the White House believed unconstitutional.[17] Both presidents saw members of their administrations convicted or plead guilty to criminal offenses.

And if Nixon frequently misled the public and was ultimately driven from office because he lied about his knowledge of the Watergate break-in, Trump built his presidency on a demonstrable disregard for the truth. Just over a year-and-a-half into his administration, the fact checkers for the *Washington Post* found that Trump had already made over 4,000 false or misleading claims.[18] That worked out to, on average, about seven false or misleading statements per day. Even Nixon, who demonstrated little appreciation for the importance of honest discourse, did not lie that regularly.

It is not without reason that numerous analysts saw shades of Nixon in the figure of Trump. Yet Richard Nixon was no Donald Trump. Nixon was far more knowledgeable than his twenty-first-century Republican successor, and he oversaw a number of significant policy achievements. Not only did he open the door to the normalization of relations with China, but he negotiated the Anti-Ballistic Missile Treaty and an interim arms limitation agreement, contributing to the growing détente between the United States and the Soviet Union. Domestically, he supported the creation of the Environmental Protection Agency (EPA) and the Occupational Safety and Health Administration (OSHA), and he signed the Title IX civil rights law, the Clean Air Act, and the Marine Mammal Protection Act.

Yet whatever his accomplishments, Nixon's presidency is best remembered today for its ignominious end. That would include the Watergate scandal, of course, but also the tragedy in Southeast Asia. Nixon may have ultimately overseen the withdrawal of U.S. military forces from Vietnam, but he set the stage for the collapse of America's longtime ally in Saigon. His policies in Cambodia, moreover, destabilized that country, ushering in a brutal revolution under the Khmer Rouge that claimed approximately 1.7 million lives. And in Laos (as well as in Cambodia and Vietnam), which the United States turned into the most heavily bombed country per capita in history, unexploded U.S. ordnance continued to kill and maim innocent civilians – at least 20,000 people since 1973 – for decades following the war.[19] These are among Nixon's legacies.

The November 3, 1969, speech by the president proved a critical moment in American history. Before millions of viewers and listeners, Nixon broadly presented his Vietnamization policy, justified continued warfare as essential to preventing a bloodbath, and introduced the world to the "silent majority." U.S. foreign policy and American political culture would never be the same. This became apparent in the decades that followed. The basic premise of Vietnamization – withdraw U.S. ground troops, increase support for a local regime, and escalate or at least continue the air war – would be replicated in Iraq in the twenty-first century. George W. Bush, in defending his warmaking in the Middle East, would hearken the bloodbath theory.[20] And while Nixon was neither the first nor the last to appeal to a silent majority, he would forever be associated with the term, which Donald Trump so effectively resurrected in 2015.

Whether they liked it or not, Americans in the twenty-first century continued to live under Richard Nixon's shadow.

NOTES

1 Nicholas Fandos, "Trump Defiantly Rallies a New 'Silent Majority' in a Visit to a Border State," *New York Times*, July 11, 2015. For video of the speech, see Charlie Redden, "Trump Mentions the 'Silent Majority,'" YouTube, July 19, 2015, at www.youtube.com/watch?v=zmhiju9SB_Q (accessed December 5, 2018).

2 Franklin D. Roosevelt, "Radio Address from Albany, New York: 'The "Forgotten Man" Speech,'" April 7, 1932, *The American Presidency Project*, at www. presidency.ucsb.edu/documents/radio-address-from-albany-new-york-the-forgotten-man-speech (accessed December 5, 2018).

3 Donald Critchlow, "Politicians Have Long Used the 'Forgotten Man' to Win Elections," *The Conversation*, October 1, 2018, at https://theconversation.com/politicians-have-long-used-the-forgotten-man-to-win-elections-103570 (accessed on October 5, 2018).

4 Richard Nixon, "Address Accepting the Presidential Nomination at the Republican National Convention in Miami Beach, Florida," August 8, 1968, *The American Presidency Project*, at <www.presidency.ucsb.edu/documents/address-accepting-the-presidential-nomination-the-republican-national-convention-miami> (accessed December 5, 2018).

5 Bill Clinton, "A New Covenant: Responsibility and Rebuilding the American Community," October 23, 1991, in Stephen A. Smith, ed., *Preface to the Presidency: Selected Speeches of Bill Clinton, 1974–1992* (Fayetteville: University of Arkansas Press, 1996), 89.

6 Tom Porter, "Trump Confused the Baltics with Balkans – And Accused Confused Leaders of Starting Yugoslav Wars: Report," *Newsweek*, November 18, 2018, at www.newsweek.com/trump-confused-baltics-balkans-and-accused-confused-leaders-starting-yugoslav-1210939 (accessed November 15, 2018); Cleve R. Wootson, Jr., "Trump Implied Frederick Douglass Was Alive. The Abolitionist's Family Offered a 'History Lesson,'" *Washington Post*, February 2, 2017, at www.washingtonpost.com/news/post-nation/wp/2017/02/02/trump-implied-frederick-douglass-was-alive-the-abolitionists-family-offered-a-history-lesson/ (accessed November 15, 2018); Jonah Engel Bromwich, "Trump on the Civil War: 'Why Could That One Not Have Been Worked Out?'" *New York Times*,

May 1, 2017, at www.nytimes.com/2017/05/01/us/politics/trump-andrew-jackson-fact-check.html (accessed November 15, 2018); and Jim Acosta and Paula Newton, "Exclusive: Trump Invokes War of 1812 in Testy Call with Trudeau Over Tariffs," *CNN*, June 6, 2018, at www.cnn.com/2018/06/06/politics/war-of-1812-donald-trump-justin-trudeau-tariff/index.html (accessed November 15, 2018).

7   In fact, studies showed that immigrants committed crimes at lower rates than people born in the United States. Meg Kelly, "Fact-Checking President Trump's Numbers on the 'Human Toll of Illegal Immigration,'" *Washington Post*, July 6, 2018, at www.washingtonpost.com/news/fact-checker/wp/2018/07/06/trump-falsely-claims-the-human-toll-of-illegal-immigration (accessed November 27, 2018).

8   Julie Hirschfeld Davis, "Trump Calls Some Unauthorized Immigrants 'Animals' in Rant," *New York Times*, May 16, 2018.

9   Glenn Kessler, "President Trump's Consistent Misrepresentation of How the Diversity Visa Lottery Works," *Washington Post*, February 26, 2018, at www.washingtonpost.com/news/fact-checker/wp/2018/02/26/president-trumps-consistent-misrepresentation-of-how-the-diversity-visa-lottery-works/ (accessed July 27, 2018); Josh Dawsey, "Trump Derides Protections for Immigrants from 'Shithole' Countries," *Washington Post*, January 12, 2018, at www.washingtonpost.com/politics/trump-attacks-protections-for-immigrants-from-shithole-countries-in-oval-office-meeting/2018/01/11/bfc0725c-f711-11e7-91af-31ac729add94_story.html (accessed on July 27, 2018).

10 Kevin Kruse, "It's Worse Than the Willie Horton Ad," *History News Network*, November 1, 2018, at https://historynewsnetwork.org/article/170383 (accessed November 27, 2018).

11 Michael M. Grynbaum and Niraj Chokshi, "Media Giants Recoil from Caravan Ad Called Racist," *New York Times*, November 5, 2018.

12 Stanley I. Kutler, *The Wars of Watergate: The Last Crisis of Richard Nixon* (New York: Alfred A. Knopf, 1990), 104–105.

13 Gil Troy, "When Nixon's Henchmen Plotted to Assassinate a Journalist with LSD," *The Daily Beast*, January 20, 2017, at www.thedailybeast.com/when-nixons-henchmen-plotted-to-assassinate-a-journalist-with-lsd (accessed January 28, 2017).

14 Michael M. Grynbaum, "Trump Calls Media the 'Enemy of the American People,'" *New York Times*, February 17, 2017; John Wagner, "Trump Renews Attacks on Media as 'the True Enemy of the People,'" *Washington Post*, October 29, 2018, at www.washingtonpost.com/politics/trump-renews-attacks-on-media-as-the-true-enemy-of-the-people/2018/10/29/9ebc62ee-db60-11e8-85df-7a6b4d25cfbb_story.html (accessed December 5, 2018).

15 The New York bombs sent to CNN were reportedly addressed to television commentators (and former intelligence officials) James R. Clapper and John Brennan, though the latter worked for MSNBC, not CNN. Matt Zapotosky, Danielle Paquette, and Devlin Barrett, "Package Bomb Suspect Cesar Sayoc Kept List of More Than 100 Possible Targets, Official Says," *Washington Post*,

October 29, 2018, at www.washingtonpost.com/world/national-security/cnn-says-authorities-have-intercepted-another-suspicious-package-directed-to-the-news-organization/2018/10/29/0bb3ee6e-db87-11e8-b732-3c72cbf131f2_story.html (accessed December 5, 2018).

16   James Reston, Jr., *The Conviction of Richard Nixon: The Untold Story of the Frost/Nixon Interviews* (New York: Three Rivers Press, 2007), 103.

17   Manu Raju, "Trump Supreme Court Pick: Presidents Can Ignore Laws They Think Are Unconstitutional," *CNN*, August 7, 2018, at www.cnn.com/2018/08/06/politics/brett-kavanaugh-president-ignore-laws-unconstitutional/index.html (accessed November 27, 2018).

18   Glenn Kessler, Salvador Rizzo, and Meg Kelly, "As President Digs In, False-hoods Fly," *Washington Post*, August 2, 2018.

19   Legacies of War, "Leftover Unexploded Ordnance," n.d., at http://legaciesof-war.org/about-laos/leftover-unexploded-ordnances-uxo/ (accessed December 5, 2018).

20   See, for example, George W. Bush, "Remarks at the Veterans of Foreign Wars National Convention in Kansas City, Missouri," August 22, 2007, in *Public Papers of the Presidents of the United States: George W. Bush, 2007*, Volume II (Washington, DC: Government Printing Office, 2011), 1103–1104.

Documents

Richard Nixon's "Silent Majority" Speech, November 3, 1969

Below is the transcript of Richard Nixon's thirty-two-minute "silent major-ity" speech, which was broadcast nationally on both television and radio. It was his most significant public statement about the war in Vietnam since be-coming president over nine months earlier. The speech spelled out Nixon's plan for what he called "Vietnamization" while justifying continued U.S. involve-ment in Vietnam on both strategic and moral grounds. The line that made the address famous – Nixon's invocation of the "great silent majority of my fellow Americans" – came near the end, as the president was situating his actions in a longer historical arc and asking for unity and support.

Good evening, my fellow Americans:

Tonight I want to talk to you on a subject of deep concern to all Americans and to many people in all parts of the world—the war in Vietnam.

I believe that one of the reasons for the deep division about Vietnam is that many Americans have lost confidence in what their Govern-ment has told them about our policy. The American people cannot and should not be asked to support a policy which involves the overriding issues of war and peace unless they know the truth about that policy.

Tonight, therefore, I would like to answer some of the questions that I know are on the minds of many of you listening to me.

How and why did America get involved in Vietnam in the first place?

How has this administration changed the policy of the previous administration?

What has really happened in the negotiations in Paris and on the battlefront in Vietnam?

What choices do we have if we are to end the war?

What are the prospects for peace?

Now, let me begin by describing the situation I found when I was inaugurated on January 20.

—The war had been going on for 4 years.
—31,000 Americans had been killed in action.
—The training program for the South Vietnamese was behind schedule.
—540,000 Americans were in Vietnam with no plans to reduce the number.
—No progress had been made at the negotiations in Paris and the United States had not put forth a comprehensive peace proposal.
—The war was causing deep division at home and criticism from many of our friends as well as our enemies abroad.

In view of these circumstances there were some who urged that I end the war at once by ordering the immediate withdrawal of all American forces.

From a political standpoint this would have been a popular and easy course to follow. After all, we became involved in the war while my predecessor was in office. I could blame the defeat which would be the result of my action on him and come out as the peacemaker. Some put it to me quite bluntly: This was the only way to avoid allowing Johnson's war to become Nixon's war.

But I had a greater obligation than to think only of the years of my administration and of the next election. I had to think of the effect of my decision on the next generation and on the future of peace and freedom in America and in the world.

Let us all understand that the question before us is not whether some Americans are for peace and some Americans are against peace. The question at issue is not whether Johnson's war becomes Nixon's war.

The great question is: How can we win America's peace?

Well, let us turn now to the fundamental issue. Why and how did the United States become involved in Vietnam in the first place?

Fifteen years ago North Vietnam, with the logistical support of Communist China and the Soviet Union, launched a campaign to impose a Communist government on South Vietnam by instigating and supporting a revolution.

In response to the request of the Government of South Vietnam, President Eisenhower sent economic aid and military equipment to assist the people of South Vietnam in their efforts to prevent a Communist takeover. Seven years ago, President Kennedy sent 16,000 military personnel to Vietnam as combat advisers. Four years ago, President Johnson sent American combat forces to South Vietnam.

Now, many believe that President Johnson's decision to send American combat forces to South Vietnam was wrong. And many others—I among them—have been strongly critical of the way the war has been conducted.

But the question facing us today is: Now that we are in the war, what is the best way to end it?

In January I could only conclude that the precipitate withdrawal of American forces from Vietnam would be a disaster not only for South Vietnam but for the United States and for the cause of peace.

For the South Vietnamese, our precipitate withdrawal would inevitably allow the Communists to repeat the massacres which followed their takeover in the North 15 years before.

—They then murdered more than 50,000 people and hundreds of thousands more died in slave labor camps.
—We saw a prelude of what would happen in South Vietnam when the Communists entered the city of Hue last year. During their brief rule there, there was a bloody reign of terror in which 3,000 civilians were clubbed, shot to death, and buried in mass graves.
—With the sudden collapse of our support, these atrocities of Hue would become the nightmare of the entire nation—and particularly for the million and a half Catholic refugees who fled to South Vietnam when the Communists took over in the North.

For the United States, this first defeat in our Nation's history would result in a collapse of confidence in American leadership, not only in Asia but throughout the world.

Three American Presidents have recognized the great stakes involved in Vietnam and understood what had to be done.

In 1963, President Kennedy, with his characteristic eloquence and clarity, said: "... we want to see a stable government there, carrying on a struggle to maintain its national independence."

> We believe strongly in that. We are not going to withdraw
> from that effort. In my opinion, for us to withdraw from that
> effort would mean a collapse not only of South Viet-Nam, but
> Southeast Asia. So we are going to stay there.

President Eisenhower and President Johnson expressed the same conclusion during their terms of office.

For the future of peace, precipitate withdrawal would thus be a disaster of immense magnitude.

—A nation cannot remain great if it betrays its allies and lets down its
   friends.
—Our defeat and humiliation in South Vietnam without question
   would promote recklessness in the councils of those great powers
   who have not yet abandoned their goals of world conquest.
—This would spark violence wherever our commitments help maintain the peace—in the Middle East, in Berlin, eventually even in
   the Western Hemisphere.

Ultimately, this would cost more lives.

It would not bring peace; it would bring more war.

For these reasons, I rejected the recommendation that I should end the war by immediately withdrawing all of our forces. I chose instead to change American policy on both the negotiating front and battlefront.

In order to end a war fought on many fronts, I initiated a pursuit for peace on many fronts.

In a television speech on May 14, in a speech before the United Nations, and on a number of other occasions I set forth our peace proposals in great detail.

—We have offered the complete withdrawal of all outside forces within
   1 year.
—We have proposed a cease-fire under international supervision.
—We have offered free elections under international supervision with
   the Communists participating in the organization and conduct of
   the elections as an organized political force. And the Saigon Government has pledged to accept the result of the elections.

We have not put forth our proposals on a take-it-or-leave-it basis. We have indicated that we are willing to discuss the proposals that have been put forth by the other side. We have declared that anything is ne-gotiable except the right of the people of South Vietnam to determine their own future. At the Paris peace conference, Ambassador Lodge has demonstrated our flexibility and good faith in 40 public meetings.

Hanoi has refused even to discuss our proposals. They demand our unconditional acceptance of their terms, which are that we with-draw all American forces immediately and unconditionally and that we overthrow the Government of South Vietnam as we leave.

We have not limited our peace initiatives to public forums and public statements. I recognized, in January, that a long and bitter war like this usually cannot be settled in a public forum. That is why in addition to the public statements and negotiations I have explored every possible private avenue that might lead to a settlement.

Tonight I am taking the unprecedented step of disclosing to you some of our other initiatives for peace—initiatives we undertook privately and secretly because we thought we thereby might open a door which publicly would be closed.

I did not wait for my inauguration to begin my quest for peace.

—Soon after my election, through an individual who is directly in contact on a personal basis with the leaders of North Vietnam, I made two private offers for a rapid, comprehensive settlement. Hanoi's replies called in effect for our surrender before negotiations.

—Since the Soviet Union furnishes most of the military equipment for North Vietnam, Secretary of State Rogers, my Assistant for National Security Affairs, Dr. Kissinger, Ambassador Lodge, and I, personally, have met on a number of occasions with representatives of the Soviet Government to enlist their assistance in getting meaningful negotiations started. In addition, we have had extended discussions directed toward that same end with representatives of other governments which have diplomatic relations with North Vietnam. None of these initiatives have to date produced results.

—In mid-July, I became convinced that it was necessary to make a major move to break the deadlock in the Paris talks. I spoke directly in this office, where I am now sitting, with an individual who had known Ho Chi Minh [President, Democratic Republic of Vietnam] on a personal basis for 25 years. Through him I sent a letter to Ho Chi Minh.

I did this outside of the usual diplomatic channels with the hope that with the necessity of making statements for propaganda removed, there might be constructive progress toward bringing the war to an end.

Let me read from that letter to you now.

Dear Mr. President:

I realize that it is difficult to communicate meaningfully across the gulf of four years of war. But precisely because of this gulf, I wanted to take this opportunity to reaffirm in all solemnity my desire to work for a just peace. I deeply believe that the war in Vietnam has gone on too long and delay in bringing it to an end can benefit no one—least of all the people of Vietnam....

The time has come to move forward at the conference table toward an early resolution of this tragic war. You will find us forthcoming and open-minded in a common effort to bring the blessings of peace to the brave people of Vietnam. Let history record that at this critical juncture, both sides turned their face toward peace rather than toward conflict and war.

I received Ho Chi Minh's reply on August 30, 3 days before his death. It simply reiterated the public position North Vietnam had taken at Paris and flatly rejected my initiative.

The full text of both letters is being released to the press.

—In addition to the public meetings that I have referred to, Ambassador Lodge has met with Vietnam's chief negotiator in Paris in 11 private sessions.

—We have taken other significant initiatives which must remain secret to keep open some channels of communication which may still prove to be productive.

But the effect of all the public, private, and secret negotiations which have been undertaken since the bombing halt a year ago and since this administration came into office on January 20, can be summed up in one sentence: No progress whatever has been made except agreement on the shape of the bargaining table.

Well now, who is at fault?

It has become clear that the obstacle in negotiating an end to the war is not the President of the United States. It is not the South Vietnamese Government.

The obstacle is the other side's absolute refusal to show the least willingness to join us in seeking a just peace. And it will not do so while it is convinced that all it has to do is to wait for our next concession, and our next concession after that one, until it gets everything it wants.

There can now be no longer any question that progress in negotiation depends only on Hanoi's deciding to negotiate, to negotiate seriously.

I realize that this report on our efforts on the diplomatic front is discouraging to the American people, but the American people are entitled to know the truth—the bad news as well as the good news—where the lives of our young men are involved.

Now let me turn, however, to a more encouraging report on another front.

At the time we launched our search for peace I recognized we might not succeed in bringing an end to the war through negotiation. I, therefore, put into effect another plan to bring peace—a plan which will bring the war to an end regardless of what happens on the negotiating front.

It is in line with a major shift in U.S. foreign policy which I described in my press conference at Guam on July 25. Let me briefly explain what has been described as the Nixon Doctrine—a policy which not only will help end the war in Vietnam, but which is an essential element of our program to prevent future Vietnams.

We Americans are a do-it-yourself people. We are an impatient people. Instead of teaching someone else to do a job, we like to do it ourselves. And this trait has been carried over into our foreign policy.

In Korea and again in Vietnam, the United States furnished most of the money, most of the arms, and most of the men to help the people of those countries defend their freedom against Communist aggression.

Before any American troops were committed to Vietnam, a leader of another Asian country expressed this opinion to me when I was traveling in Asia as a private citizen. He said: "When you are trying to assist another nation defend its freedom, U.S. policy should be to help them fight the war but not to fight the war for them."

Well, in accordance with this wise counsel, I laid down in Guam three principles as guidelines for future American policy toward Asia:

—First, the United States will keep all of its treaty commitments.
—Second, we shall provide a shield if a nuclear power threatens the freedom of a nation allied with us or of a nation whose survival we consider vital to our security.
—Third, in cases involving other types of aggression, we shall furnish military and economic assistance when requested in accordance with our treaty commitments. But we shall look to the nation directly threatened to assume the primary responsibility of providing the manpower for its defense.

After I announced this policy, I found that the leaders of the Philippines, Thailand, Vietnam, South Korea, and other nations which might be threatened by Communist aggression, welcomed this new direction in American foreign policy.

The defense of freedom is everybody's business—not just America's business. And it is particularly the responsibility of the people whose freedom is threatened. In the previous administration, we Americanized the war in Vietnam. In this administration, we are Vietnamizing the search for peace.

The policy of the previous administration not only resulted in our assuming the primary responsibility for fighting the war, but even more significantly did not adequately stress the goal of strengthening the South Vietnamese so that they could defend themselves when we left.

The Vietnamization plan was launched following Secretary Laird's visit to Vietnam in March. Under the plan, I ordered first a substantial increase in the training and equipment of South Vietnamese forces.

In July, on my visit to Vietnam, I changed General Abrams' orders so that they were consistent with the objectives of our new policies. Under the new orders, the primary mission of our troops is to enable the South Vietnamese forces to assume the full responsibility for the security of South Vietnam.

Our air operations have been reduced by over 20 percent.

And now we have begun to see the results of this long overdue change in American policy in Vietnam.

—After 5 years of Americans going into Vietnam, we are finally bringing American men home. By December 15, over 60,000 men will have been withdrawn from South Vietnam including 20 percent of all of our combat forces.
—The South Vietnamese have continued to gain in strength. As a result they have been able to take over combat responsibilities from our American troops.

Two other significant developments have occurred since this administration took office.

—Enemy infiltration, infiltration which is essential if they are to launch a major attack, over the last 3 months is less than 20 percent of what it was over the same period last year.
—Most important—United States casualties have declined during the last 2 months to the lowest point in 3 years.

Let me now turn to our program for the future.

We have adopted a plan which we have worked out in cooperation with the South Vietnamese for the complete withdrawal of all U.S. combat ground forces, and their replacement by South Vietnamese forces on an orderly scheduled timetable. This withdrawal will be made from strength and not from weakness. As South Vietnamese forces become stronger, the rate of American withdrawal can become greater.

I have not and do not intend to announce the timetable for our program. And there are obvious reasons for this decision which I am sure you will understand. As I have indicated on several occasions, the rate of withdrawal will depend on developments on three fronts.

One of these is the progress which can be or might be made in the Paris talks. An announcement of a fixed timetable for our withdrawal would completely remove any incentive for the enemy to negotiate an agreement. They would simply wait until our forces had withdrawn and then move in.

The other two factors on which we will base our withdrawal decisions are the level of enemy activity and the progress of the training programs of the South Vietnamese forces. And I am glad to be able to report tonight progress on both of these fronts has been greater than we anticipated when we started the program in June for withdrawal. As a result, our timetable for withdrawal is more optimistic now than when we made our first estimates in June. Now, this clearly demonstrates why it is not wise to be frozen in on a fixed timetable.

We must retain the flexibility to base each withdrawal decision on the situation as it is at that time rather than on estimates that are no longer valid.

Along with this optimistic estimate, I must—in all candor—leave one note of caution.

If the level of enemy activity significantly increases we might have to adjust our timetable accordingly.

However, I want the record to be completely clear on one point.

At the time of the bombing halt just a year ago, there was some confusion as to whether there was an understanding on the part of the enemy that if we stopped the bombing of North Vietnam they would stop the shelling of cities in South Vietnam. I want to be sure that there is no misunderstanding on the part of the enemy with regard to our withdrawal program.

We have noted the reduced level of infiltration, the reduction of our casualties, and are basing our withdrawal decisions partially on those factors.

If the level of infiltration or our casualties increase while we are trying to scale down the fighting, it will be the result of a conscious decision by the enemy.

Hanoi could make no greater mistake than to assume that an increase in violence will be to its advantage. If I conclude that increased enemy action jeopardizes our remaining forces in Vietnam, I shall not hesitate to take strong and effective measures to deal with that situation.

This is not a threat. This is a statement of policy, which as Commander in Chief of our Armed Forces, I am making in meeting my responsibility for the protection of American fighting men wherever they may be.

My fellow Americans, I am sure you can recognize from what I have said that we really only have two choices open to us if we want to end this war.

—I can order an immediate, precipitate withdrawal of all Americans from Vietnam without regard to the effects of that action.
—Or we can persist in our search for a just peace through a negotiated settlement if possible, or through continued implementation of our plan for Vietnamization if necessary--a plan in which we will withdraw all of our forces from Vietnam on a schedule in accordance with our program, as the South Vietnamese become strong enough to defend their own freedom.

I have chosen this second course.

It is not the easy way.

It is the right way.

It is a plan which will end the war and serve the cause of peace—not just in Vietnam but in the Pacific and in the world.

In speaking of the consequences of a precipitate withdrawal, I mentioned that our allies would lose confidence in America.

Far more dangerous, we would lose confidence in ourselves. Oh, the immediate reaction would be a sense of relief that our men were coming home. But as we saw the consequences of what we had done, inevitable remorse and divisive recrimination would scar our spirit as a people.

We have faced other crises in our history and have become stronger by rejecting the easy way out and taking the right way in meeting our challenges. Our greatness as a nation has been our capacity to do what had to be done when we knew our course was right.

I recognize that some of my fellow citizens disagree with the plan for peace I have chosen.

Honest and patriotic Americans have reached different conclusions as to how peace should be achieved.

In San Francisco a few weeks ago, I saw demonstrators carrying signs reading: "Lose in Vietnam, bring the boys home."

Well, one of the strengths of our free society is that any American has a right to reach that conclusion and to advocate that point of view. But as President of the United States, I would be untrue to my oath of office if I allowed the policy of this Nation to be dictated by the minority who hold that point of view and who try to impose it on the Nation by mounting demonstrations in the street.

For almost 200 years, the policy of this Nation has been made under our Constitution by those leaders in the Congress and the White House elected by all of the people. If a vocal minority, however fervent its cause, prevails over reason and the will of the majority, this Nation has no future as a free society.

And now I would like to address a word, if I may, to the young people of this Nation who are particularly concerned, and I understand why they are concerned, about this war.

I respect your idealism.

I share your concern for peace.

I want peace as much as you do.

There are powerful personal reasons I want to end this war. This week I will have to sign 83 letters to mothers, fathers, wives, and loved ones of men who have given their lives for America in Vietnam. It is very little satisfaction to me that this is only one-third as many letters as I signed the first week in office. There is nothing I want more than to see the day come when I do not have to write any of those letters.

—I want to end the war to save the lives of those brave young men in Vietnam.

—But I want to end it in a way which will increase the chance that their younger brothers and their sons will not have to fight in some future Vietnam someplace in the world.

—And I want to end the war for another reason. I want to end it so that the energy and dedication of you, our young people, now too often directed into bitter hatred against those responsible for the war, can be turned to the great challenges of peace, a better life for all Americans, a better life for all people on this earth.

I have chosen a plan for peace. I believe it will succeed.

If it does succeed, what the critics say now won't matter. If it does not succeed, anything I say then won't matter.

I know it may not be fashionable to speak of patriotism or national destiny these days. But I feel it is appropriate to do so on this occasion

Two hundred years ago this Nation was weak and poor. But even then, America was the hope of millions in the world. Today we have become the strongest and richest nation in the world.

And the wheel of destiny has turned so that any hope the world has for the survival of peace and freedom will be determined by whether the American people have the moral stamina and the courage to meet the challenge of free world leadership.

Let historians not record that when America was the most powerful nation in the world we passed on the other side of the road and allowed the last hopes for peace and freedom of millions of people to be suffocated by the forces of totalitarianism.

And so tonight—to you, the great silent majority of my fellow Americans—I ask for your support.

I pledged in my campaign for the Presidency to end the war in a way that we could win the peace. I have initiated a plan of action which will enable me to keep that pledge.

The more support I can have from the American people, the sooner that pledge can be redeemed; for the more divided we are at home, the less likely the enemy is to negotiate at Paris.

Let us be united for peace. Let us also be united against defeat. Because let us understand: North Vietnam cannot defeat or humiliate the United States. Only Americans can do that.

Fifty years ago, in this room and at this very desk, President Woodrow Wilson spoke words which caught the imagination of a war-weary world. He said: "This is the war to end war." His dream for peace after World War I was shattered on the hard realities of great power politics and Woodrow Wilson died a broken man.

Tonight I do not tell you that the war in Vietnam is the war to end wars. But I do say this: I have initiated a plan which will end this war in a way that will bring us closer to that great goal to which Woodrow Wilson and every American President in our history has been dedicated—the goal of a just and lasting peace.

As President I hold the responsibility for choosing the best path to that goal and then leading the Nation along it.

I pledge to you tonight that I shall meet this responsibility with all of the strength and wisdom I can command in accordance with your hopes, mindful of your concerns, sustained by your prayers.

Thank you and goodnight.

Source: Richard Nixon, "Address to the Nation on the War in Vietnam," November 3, 1969, *Public Papers of the Presidents of the United States: Richard Nixon, 1969* (Washington, DC: Government Printing Office, 1971), 901–909.

Letter from Mrs. Dennis W. Harrison to Richard Nixon, November 4, 1969

Nixon's speech stirred countless Americans, who wrote to the White House by the hundreds of thousands. One of these was Mrs. Dennis Harrison, who "decided that I have remained silent long enough." She confessed to the president that she had earlier been opposed to the war. Indeed, after learning a month before the speech that her husband, a lance corporal in the Marine Corps, would be going to Vietnam, "I was upset and immediately bitter." But, following the speech, she changed her mind. "I support your Viet Nam policy," she told Nixon, and "[y]ou can be assured that when anti-war peaceniks try to sway my opinion that I will stand behind you one hundred percent." The president's response must have pleased her. "The confidence and understanding you have shown will do much to strengthen our efforts to achieve the just and lasting peace that all of us desire," he wrote.

Dear Mr. President,

I have just listened to your speech about the war in Viet Nam. I decided that I have remained silent long enough.

Shortly after the first of October, I learned that my husband, a Lance Corporal in the Marine Corps, would be going to Viet Nam in December. Naturally, I was upset and immediately bitter. Even before this, I had been opposed to the war and to your administration. I had not[,] however, ever been involved in any anti-war demonstration. After listening to you speak tonight, I realize that I knew very little of your policy which I had proclaimed to oppose and also very little about why the involvement in the first place.

There may be many things about your policy that I will disagree with in the future, but I support your Viet Nam policy and wanted to tell you that you have two young people behind you. You can be assured that when anti-war peaceniks try to sway my opinion that I will stand behind you one hundred percent. I will spread my opinion in a peaceable manner.

Thank you for enlightening me on this matter. Thank you also for reading this.

Yours very truly,
Mrs. Dennis W. Harrison

Source: Mrs. Dennis W. Harrison to Richard Nixon, November 4, 1969, Folder: SP 3-56/PRO, 11/21/69 (1 of 2), Box 107, Subject Files: Speeches (Ex), White House Central Files, Nixon Presidential Materials Staff, National Archives II, College Park, MD.

Commentary by George Salem on KWGN Television, November 5, 1969

George Salem *worked for KWGN Television in Denver, Colorado. In this commentary broadcast two days after Nixon's speech, Salem argued that the question of whether the United States should get out of Vietnam was the wrong question. Rather, Salem suggested, "[t]he real issue is how to get out. A complete and total withdrawal as demanded by the communists, or a gradual withdrawal, depending on the shape of the South Vietnamese army and the level of communist activity." Amidst Americans "screaming at each other" about pulling out, "the president outlined a middle of the road course of action," Salem said. And the newsman, who assumed that American power was benevolent in an underdeveloped and ignorant Asia, liked it. What the president was doing was "[t]rying to make our huge losses mean something instead of writing them off and still provide a chance for those Asians who wish to be something other than poverty-stricken, hungry, and uneducated."*

Good evening:

The White House was right, there was really nothing new in President Nixon's speech of Monday night. And, the balance of dissent and support has not changed appreciably because of it. Hanoi's rejection of the speech and its obvious tone of desperation in trying to start meaningful negotiations[] was a foregone conclusion. The North Vietnamese and the Viet Cong have nothing to lose by rejecting all overtures and proposals by the United States.

It is just not in the communist book of rules to make concessions when all they have to do is sit back and wait it out, as the other side makes one more concession and then another, and another.

One of the main bones of contention between dissenters and supporters[] keeps showing itself up as a question. "Should we get out of Vietnam or [n]ot?" And, this ridiculous polarization of opinion is

blinding Americans to the real issue. Here are the administration supporters and the dissenters, screaming at each other about getting out
of Vietnam, when a short pause to listen should make it very evident
that *both* sides want to get out of Vietnam. Nobody, including the
President[,] wants to remain involved in this Asian war. The real issue
is *how* to get out.

A complete and total withdrawal as demanded by the communists, or a gradual withdrawal[] depending on the shape of the South
Vietnamese army and the level of communist activity.

From a purely selfish and short[-]range point of view, total withdrawal[,] and right now, would be the logical answer. Pull out, abandon all those we have been allied with[,] and to hell with Asia, the
communists[,] and all their related problems. We could wash our hands
of the entire affair and retreat behind the plush walls of our affluent
society. We could shut out all the news of millions of people coming
under a harsh totalitarian rule with the hunger and bloody purges that
go with it. Maybe we should give up the idea of lifting Asia's millions
out of centuries of poverty and starvation, and, by abandoning them,
sentence them to centuries more of ignorance and darkness.

The other extreme would be to make an all-out military effort and
blast the communists in North Vietnam to oblivion, devastate South
Vietnam in our search for the Viet Cong, and then, when all is destroyed[,] start building up from scratch.

Two extremes. And Monday, the president outlined a middle of the
road course of action. Trying to make our huge losses mean something
instead of writing them off and still provide a chance for those Asians
who wish to be something other than poverty-stricken, hungry[,] and
uneducated.

Your support, dissent[,] or rejection of any of these courses of action depends on what you, as a human being, can live with.

At least that's one man's opinion.

George Salem, KWGN [N]ews.

Source: Commentary by George Salem ["Copy of 11/5/69 Comment"],
KWGN Television, November 5, 1969, Folder: SP 3-56/Con, 11/6/69 –
2/16/70, Box 113, Subject Files: Speeches (Gen), White House Central
Files, Nixon Presidential Materials Staff, National Archives II, College
Park, MD.

Editorial in the *Orlando Sentinel*, November 5, 1969

*T*his Orlando Sentinel *editorial, which was a response to Nixon's speech, applauded the president's Vietnamization policy – other editorials in other newspapers did the same – while pointedly embracing the bloodbath theory. "Nixon's avowal that U.S. troop withdrawal from Vietnam must be gradual and secret" may have disappointed those hoping for a "massive, imminent withdrawal," the editors wrote. "Of course Hanoi would like to know our timetable of troop withdrawal; the Communists would then prepare their own timetable – of intrigue, assault, and takeover." Such a takeover would result in a "blood bath [that] might approach the genocide of Hitler's Germany in the 1940s." The president's Vietnamization policy was sound, the newspaper argued. Yes, the United States must "get out of this undeclared war as quickly as feasible." But in doing so, the editors continued, "we must leave our South Vietnamese allies in a position to defend themselves and to decide what kind of a government they want. This is what Mr. Nixon told the world, and he is right."*

President Nixon didn't come up with anything new in his frustrating efforts to find peace in Vietnam.

But, then, why should he? The President was already on solid ground and could not have made further concessions to the enemy without endangering our fighting men and allies.

The much-publicized Nov. 3 speech may have disappointed some dovish Americans because of Nixon's avowal that U.S. troop withdrawal from Vietnam must be gradual and secret.

Missing from the speech were the developments that had been all but worn out in the rumor mills, such as a unilateral ceasefire and a massive, imminent withdrawal of U.S. servicemen.

But what Mr. Nixon's message lacked in surprise, it more than made up for in substance. Our policy of seeking an honorable peace with self-determination for the people of South Vietnam remains in effect, as it should.

It is absurd to suppose that North Vietnam and the Viet Cong would restrain themselves from taking full and perhaps devastating advantage of any American pull-out that left the [sic] South Vietnam's defenses weak.

Of course Hanoi would like to know our timetable of troop withdrawal; the Communists would then prepare their own timetable – of intrigue, assault[,] and takeover.

And if they could thus destroy the Thieu government and overrun the south, the ensuing blood bath might approach the genocide of Hitler's Germany in the 1940s.

Such a tragedy would, of course, be unthinkable, not only on humane grounds but because it would reflect disastrously on the position of the United States as a world leader and a dependable friend.

We must get out of this undeclared war as quickly as feasible but in so doing we must leave our South Vietnamese allies in a position to defend themselves and to decide what kind of government they want.

This is what Mr. Nixon told the world, and he is right.

Source: Editors, "President on Solid Ground in Search for Vietnam Peace," *Orlando Sentinel*, November 5, 1969, Folder: SP 3-56/Nationwide T.V. and Radio Address re: Vietnam at Wash. Hilton Hotel, November 3, 1969 (1 of 3), Box 106, Subject Files: Speeches (Ex), White House Central Files, Nixon Presidential Materials Staff, National Archives II, College Park, MD.

Letter from Robert T. Park, et al., to Richard Nixon, November 17, 1969

Shortly after the president's November 3 speech, dozens of soldiers at Fort Bliss sent the president a letter stating that "those of us in the 'vocal minority' who have demonstrated for peace ... are neither basicly [sic] anti-American nor even anti-Nixon. Despite the harsh language in your speech," they continued, "we do not seek to 'defeat' or 'humiliate' America. We want our country to be strong. And we believe wholeheartedly that the policies we advocate will benefit America by extricating her from a war which is sapping both her international and domestic strength." Their letter speaks to the growing disillusionment of the men and women who served in the American armed forces during the Vietnam War. The soldiers took issue with Nixon's insistence on the bloodbath theory, pointing to what they saw as an obvious logical shortcoming – the United States was perpetrating a "slaughter" while ostensibly attempting to prevent one – and they questioned U.S. support for the South Vietnamese regime. At its heart, the soldiers' letter speaks to the debates over the meaning of patriotism that the war inspired.

Dear Mr. President:

We take this opportunity to reply to your recent address and to offer some thoughts on your Viet Nam policy.

In your speech of November 3, you referred to the "silent majority" of Americans who back your conduct of the war in Viet Nam. It is undeniable that a majority of people in this country do back you. But we believe it is also true that they support you because you are our President and not because they fully agree with your war policy. In 1968, you made it perfectly clear that the main reason that the Democratic administration should be voted out was because they had failed to end the war. Americans voted for you in the tens of millions because you promised them a "new team," a team that would be able to bring the boys home. The people of this country still want to bring our fighting men home – and bring them home quickly. In October of this year, the Gallup Poll indicated that 57 percent of the American people favor bringing *all* troops home from Viet Nam before January 1971. The people support you – not because they want to endorse the continuation of the war – but because you are the President of our country. The majority of people will be behind you, and back you even more strongly, if you act decisively to end our presence in Viet Nam.

As for those of us in the "vocal minority" who have demonstrated for peace, most of us are neither basicly [sic] anti-American nor even anti-Nixon. Despite the harsh language in your speech, we do not seek to "defeat" or "humiliate" America. We want our country to be strong. And we believe wholeheartedly that the policies we advocate will benefit America by extricating her from a war which is sapping both her international and domestic strength. Furthermore, we support your pledge to change the Johnson administration policies, and we are glad to note your decision to remove 60,000 troops from Viet Nam this year. But 60,000 from 540,000 still leaves 480,000, and a withdrawal at such a rate will take nine years to complete. We don't want our country to "bug out" on her foreign commitments. We wish to affirm American support for free governments and to continue our commitments to aid our allies if they are subject to external aggression. However, we do not see how it is in our national interest to commit U.S. troops for putting down internal rebellions or for supporting corrupt and repressive governments.

No one wants to witness a "blood bath" in Viet Nam. The slaughter which you predict will occur upon our withdrawal is certainly an ugly possibility. But the slaughter in which we are now participating has already cost 40,000 American lives and hundreds of thousands of Vietnamese lives. Also, over a million South Vietnamese have been left homeless by the war and presently live in "refugee camps," a polite term for what we call concentration camps when they are set up by our enemies. Perhaps the killing will continue in Viet Nam after we leave, but it is time for us to end our participation in that killing. From the kill-ratio figures released by our army, it is plain that it is the United States and not the Viet Cong that are doing most of the killing in Viet Nam today. We urge you to end our part in this massacre.

And, Mr. President, we wish to add that those of us who are demonstrating for peace are not an "effete corps of impudent snobs." [*This is how Nixon's vice president, Spiro Agnew, had characterized antiwar intellectuals two weeks before Nixon's November 3 speech.*] Although a good percentage of us are college graduates, many of us have worked as common laborers to help put ourselves through college. We do not advocate "constant carnival." We do believe it is our duty to continue to speak out and demonstrate, not unlike the men who founded our country, until our goal has been achieved.

The government of the Philippines has recently decided that it can no longer allow its men to kill and be killed in Viet Nam, and it is therefore withdrawing all its forces. We urge you to follow this example. The military control of South Viet Nam exercised by the Thieu-Ky regime is not worth one hundred American lives a week. We want to support you; we want to be able to be proud of our country. But we cannot support or be proud of policies which we consider to be disastrous to both America and to the lives of thousands of Americans. Please reconsider. Please end our part of the killing and bring the boys home.

[SIGNED BY ROBERT T. PARK, PFC, AND 31 OTHER MEN AT BIGGS FIELD AT FORT BLISS, TEXAS]

Source: Robert T. Park, et al., to Richard M. Nixon, November 17, 1969, Folder: SP 3-56/Con, 11/6/69 – 2/16/70, Box 113, Subject Files: Speeches (Gen), White House Central Files, Nixon Presidential Materials Staff, National Archives II, College Park, MD.

DOCUMENT 6

Excerpt from Colonel Robert D. Heinl, Jr., "The Collapse of the Armed Forces"

*O*ne of the remarkable phenomena spawned by the Vietnam War – and one *of the presumptive bases for Vietnamization – was the active resistance that emerged within the ranks of those Americans tasked with fighting in Vietnam. Desertion and racial tensions were widespread, drug use was endemic, and troops were periodically "fragging" their superiors and refusing to obey orders. The situation had become so dire, Colonel Robert Heinl argued in a 1971 essay in* the Armed Forces *Journal, that, "[b]y every conceivable indicator, our army that now remains in Vietnam is in a state approaching collapse, with individual units avoiding or having refused combat, murdering their officers and noncommissioned officers, drug-ridden, and dispirited where not near-mutinous."*

Heinl's commentary was a remarkable testimonial to just how hostile to the war the men and women of the nation's military had become. It also indirectly speaks to the postwar myth that the antiwar movement, which is mostly recalled as civilian in composition, treated members of the nation's armed forces with disdain. In fact, as Heinl's piece suggests, GI and veteran dissent rendered the uniformed men and women of that era an essential part of the antiwar movement. This concerned Heinl, a World War II and Korean War Marine Corps veteran alarmed by the breakdown in military discipline. As the below excerpts suggest, he saw hints of communism in some of the dissent.

The morale, discipline[,] and battleworthiness of the U.S. Armed Forces are, with a few salient exceptions, lower and worse than at any time in this century and possibly in the history of the United States.

By every conceivable indicator, our army that now remains in Vietnam is in a state approaching collapse, with individual units avoiding or having refused combat, murdering their officers and noncommissioned officers, drug-ridden, and dispirited where not near-mutinous.

Elsewhere than Vietnam, the situation is nearly as serious.

Intolerably clobbered and buffeted from without and within by social turbulence, pandemic drug addiction, race war, sedition, civilian scapegoatise, draftee recalcitrance and malevolence, barracks theft and common crime, unsupported in their travail by the general government, in Congress as well as the executive branch, distrusted, disliked, and often reviled by the public, the uniformed services today are places of agony for the loyal, silent professionals who doggedly hang on and try to keep the ship afloat.

The responses of the services to these unheard-of conditions, forces[,] and new public attitudes, are confused, resentful, occasional pollyanna-ish, and in some cases even calculated to worsen the malaise that is wracking them.

While no senior officer (especially one on active duty) can openly voice any such assessment, the foregoing conclusions find virtually unanimous support in numerous non-attributable interviews with responsible senior and mid-level officers, as well as career noncommissioned officers and petty officers in all services.

Historical precedents do exist for some of the services' problems, such as desertion, mutiny, unpopularity, seditious attacks, and racial troubles. Others, such as drugs, pose difficulties that are wholly new. Nowhere, however, in the history of the Armed Forces have comparable past troubles presented themselves in such general magnitude, acuteness, or concentrated focus as today.

By several orders of magnitude, the Army seems to be in worst trouble. But the Navy has serious and unprecedented problems, while the Air Force, on the surface at least still clear of the quicksands in which the Army is sinking, is itself facing disquieting difficulties.

Only the Marines – who have made news this year by their hard line against indiscipline and general permissiveness – seem, with their expected staunchness and tough tradition, to be weathering the storm.

BACK TO CAMPUS

To understand the military consequences of what is happening to the U.S. Armed Forces, Vietnam is a good place to start. It is in Vietnam that the rearguard of a 500,000-man army, in its day (and in the observation of the writer) the best army the United States ever put into the field, is numbly extricating itself from a nightmare war the Armed Forces feel they had foisted on them by bright civilians who are now back on campus writing books about the folly of it all.

"They have set up separate companies," writes an American soldier from Cu Chi, quoted in the *New York Times*, "for men who refuse to go out into the field. It is no big thing to refuse to go. If a man is ordered to go to such and such a place[,] he no longer goes through the hassle of refusing; he just packs his shirt and goes to visit some buddies at another base camp. Operations have become incredibly ragtag. Many guys don't even put on their uniforms any more ... The American garrisons on the larger bases are virtually disarmed. The lifers have taken our weapons from us and put them under lock and key ... There have also been quite a few frag incidents in the battalion."

Can all this really be typical or even truthful?

Unfortunately[,] the answer is yes.

"Frag incidents" or just "fragging" is current soldier slang in Vietnam for the murder or attempted murder of strict, unpopular, or just aggressive officers and NCOs. With extreme reluctance (after a young West Pointer from Senator Mike Mansfield's Montana was fragged in his sleep) the Pentagon has now disclosed that fraggings in 1970 (209) have more than doubled those of the previous year (96).

Word of the deaths of officers will bring cheers at troop movies or in bivouacs of certain units.

In one such division – the morale plagued Americal – fraggings during 1971 have been authoritatively estimated to be running about one a week.

Yet fraggings, though hard to document, form part of the ugly lore of every war. The first such verified incident known to have taken place occurred 190 years ago when Pennsylvania soldiers in the Continental Army killed one of their captains during the night of 1 January 1781.

BOUNTIES AND EVASIONS

Bounties, raised by common subscription in amounts running anywhere from $50 to $1,000, have been widely reported put on the heads of leaders whom the privates and Sp4s [specialists] want to rub out.

Shortly after the costly assault on Hamburger Hill in mid-1969, the GI underground newspaper in Vietnam, "G.I. Says," publicly offered a $10,000 bounty on LCol [Lieutenant Colonel] Weldon Honeycutt, the officer who ordered (and led) the attack. Despite several attempts, however, Honeycutt managed to live out his tour and return Stateside.

"Another Hamburger Hill," (i.e., toughly contested assault), conceded a veteran major, "is definitely out."

The issue of "combat refusal," an official euphemism for disobedience of orders to fight – the soldier's gravest crime – has only recently been again precipitated on the frontier of Laos by Troop B, 1st Cavalry's mass refusal to recapture their captain's command vehicle containing communication gear, codes[,] and other secret operation orders.

As early as mid-1969, however, an entire company of the 196th Light Infantry Brigade publicly sat down on the battlefield. Later that year, another rifle company, from the famed 1st Air Cavalry Division, flatly refused – on CBS-TV – to advance down a dangerous trail.

(Yet combat refusals have been heard of before: as early as 1813, a corps of 4,000 Kentucky soldiers declined to engage British Indians who had just sacked and massacred Fort Dearborn (later Chicago).)

While denying further unit refusals, the Air Cav has admitted some 35 individual refusals in 1970 alone. By comparison, only two years earlier in 1968, the entire number of officially recorded refusals for our whole army in Vietnam – from over seven divisions – was 68.

"Search and evade" (meaning tacit avoidance of combat by units in the field) is now virtually a principle of war, vividly expressed by the GI phrase, "CYA (cover your ass) and get home!"

That "search-and-evade" has not gone unnoticed by the enemy is underscored by the Viet Cong delegation's recent statement at the Paris Peace Talks that communist units in Indochina have been ordered not to engage American units which do not molest them. The same statement boasted – not without foundation in fact – that American defectors are in the VC ranks.

Symbolic anti-war fasts (such as the one at Pleiku where an entire medical unit, led by its officers, refused Thanksgiving turkey), peace symbols, "V"-signs not for victory but for peace, booing and cursing of officers and even of hapless entertainers such as Bob Hope, are unhappily commonplace.

As for drugs and race, Vietnam's problems today not only reflect but reinforce those of the Armed Forces as a whole. In April, for example, members of a Congressional investigating subcommittee reported that 10–15 percent of our troops in Vietnam are now using high-grade heroin, and that drug addiction there is "of epidemic proportions."

Only last year an Air Force major and command pilot for Ambassador Bunker was apprehended at Ton Son Nhut air base outside Saigon with $8 million worth of heroin in his aircraft. The major is now in Leavenworth [prison].

Early this year, an Air force regular colonel was court-martialed and cashiered for leading his squadron in pot parties, while, at Cam

Ranh Air Force Base, 43 members of the base security police squadron were recently swept up in dragnet narcotics raids.

All the foregoing facts – and many more dire indicators of the worst kind of military trouble – point to widespread conditions among American forces in Vietnam that have only been exceeded in this century by the French Army's Nivelle mutinies of 1917 and the collapse of the Tsarist armies in 1916 and 1917.

SOCIETY NOTES

It is a truism that national armies closely reflect societies from which they have been raised. It would be strange indeed if the Armed Forces did not today mirror the agonizing divisions and social traumas of American society, and of course they do.

For this very reason, our Armed Forces outside Vietnam not only reflect these conditions but disclose the depths of their troubles in an awful litany of sedition, disaffection, desertion, race, drugs, breakdowns of authority, abandonment of discipline, and, as a cumulative result, the lowest state of military morale in the history of the country.

Sedition – coupled with disaffection within the ranks, and externally fomented with an audacity and intensity previously inconceivable – infests the Armed Services:

- At best count, there appear to be some 144 underground newspapers published on or aimed at U.S. military bases in this country and overseas. Since 1970 the number of such sheets has increased 40% (up from 103 last fall). These journals are not mere gripe-sheets that poke soldier fun in the "Beetle Bailey" tradition, at the brass and the sergeants. "In Vietnam," writes the *Ft Lewis-McChord Free Press*, "the Lifers, the Brass, are the true Enemy, not the enemy." Another West Coast sheet advises readers: "Don't desert. Go to Vietnam and kill your commanding officer."
- At least 14 GI dissent organizations (including two made up exclusively of officers) now operate more or less openly. Ancillary to these are at least six antiwar veterans' groups which strive to influence GIs.
- Three well-established lawyer groups specialize in support of GI dissent. Two (GI Civil Liberties Defense Committee and New York Draft and Military Law

Panel) operate in the open. A third is a semi-underground
network of lawyers who can only be contacted through
the GI Alliance, a Washington, D.C., group which tries
to coordinate seditious antimilitary activities throughout
the country.

One antimilitary legal effort operates right in the theater of war.
A three-man law office, backed by the Lawyers' Military Defense
Committee, of Cambridge, Mass., was set up last fall in Saigon to
provide free civilian legal services for dissident soldiers being court-
martialed in Vietnam.

Besides these lawyers' fronts, the Pacific Counseling Service
(an umbrella organization with Unitarian backing for a prolifery of antimilitary activities) provides legal help and incitement to dissident GIs
through not one but seven branches (Tacoma, Oakland, Los Angeles,
San Diego, Monterey, Tokyo, and Okinawa).

Another of Pacific Counseling's activities is to air-drop planeloads
of sedition literature into Oakland's sprawling Army Base, our major
West Coast staging point for Vietnam.

- On the religious front, a community of turbulent priests
  and clergymen, some unfrocked, calls itself the Order
  of Maximilian. Maximilian is a saint said to have been
  martyred by the Romans for refusing military service as
  un-Christian. Maximilian's present-day followers visit
  military posts, infiltrate brigs and stockades in the guise
  of spiritual counseling, work to recruit military chaplains,
  and hold services of "consecrations" of post chapels in the
  name of their saintly draft-dodger.
- By present count at least 11 (some go as high as 26) off-
  base antiwar "coffee houses" ply GIs with rock music,
  lukewarm coffee, antiwar literature, how-t-do-it tips
  on desertion, and similar disruptive counsels. Among
  the best-known coffee houses are: The Shelter Half
  (Ft Lewis, Wash.); The Home Front (Ft Carson, Colo.);
  and The Oleo Strut (Ft Hood, Tex.).
- Virtually all the coffee houses are or have been supported
  by the U.S. Serviceman's Fund, whose offices are in
  New York City's Bronx. Until May 1970 the Fund was
  recognized as a tax-exempt "charitable corporation," a
  determination which changed when IRS agents found
  that its main function was sowing dissension among GIs

and that it was a satellite of "The New Mobilization Committee," a communist-front organization aimed at disruption of the Armed Forces.

Another "new Mobe" satellite is the G.I. Press Service, based in Washington, which calls itself the Associate Press of military underground newspapers. Robert Wilkinson, G.I. Press's editor, is well known to military intelligence and has been barred from South Vietnam.

- While refusing to divulge names, IRS sources say that the Serviceman's Fund has been largely bankrolled by well-to-do liberals. One example of this kind of liberal support for sedition which did surface identifiably last year was the $8,500 nut channeled from the Philip Stern Family Foundation to underwrite Seaman Roger Priest's underground paper *OM*, which, among other writings, ran do-it-yourself advice for desertion to Canada and advocated assassination of President Nixon.
- The nation-wide campus-radical offensive against ROTC and college officer-training is well known. Events last year at Stanford University, however, demonstrate the extremes to which this campaign (which peaked after Cambodia) has gone. After the Stanford faculty voted to accept a modified, specially restructured ROTC program, the university was subjected to a cyclone of continuing violence which included at least $200,000 in ultimate damage to buildings (highlighted by systematic destruction of 40 twenty-foot stained glass windows in the library). In the end, led by university president Richard W. Lyman, the faculty reversed itself. Lyman was quoted at the time that "ROTC is costing Stanford too much."
- "Entertainment Industry for Peace and Justice," the antiwar show-biz front organized by Jane Fonda, Dick Gregory[,] and Dalton Trumbo, now claims over 800 film, TV, and music names. This organization is backing Miss Fonda's antimilitary road-show that opened outside the gates of Ft Bragg, N.C., in mid-March.

Describing her performances (scripted by Jules Pfeiffer) as the soldiers' alternative to Bob Hope, Miss Fonda says her cast will repeat the Ft Bragg show at or outside 19 more major bases. Although her project reportedly received financial backing from the ubiquitous Serviceman's Fund, Miss Fonda insisted on $1.50 admission from each of her GI audience at Bragg, a factor which, according to soldiers, somewhat limited attendance.

- Freshman Representative Ronald V. Dellums (D–Calif.) runs a somewhat different kind of antimilitary production. As a Congressman, Dellums cannot be barred from military posts and has been taking full advantage of the fact. At Ft Meade, Md., last month, Dellums led a soldier audience as they booed and cursed their commanding officer who was present on–stage in the post theater which the Army had to make available.

Dellums has also used Capitol Hill facilities for his "Ad Hoc hearings" on alleged war crimes in Vietnam, much of which involves repetition of unfounded and often unprovable charges first surfaced in the Detroit "Winter Soldiers" hearings earlier this year. As in the case of the latter, ex-soldier witnesses appearing before Dellums have not always been willing to cooperate with Army war-crimes investigators or even to disclose sufficient evidence to permit independent verification of their charges. Yet the fact that five West Point graduates willingly testified for Dellums suggests the extent to which officer solidarity and traditions against politics have been shattered in today's Armed Forces.

THE ACTION GROUPS

Not unsurprisingly, the end-product of the atmosphere of incitement of unpunished sedition, and of recalcitrant antimilitary malevolence which pervades the world of the draftee (and to an extent the low-ranking men in "volunteer" services, too) is overt action.

One militant West Coast Group, Movement for a Democratic Military (MDM), has specialized in weapons theft from military bases in California. During 1970, large armory thefts were successfully perpetrated against Oakland Army Base, Fts Cronkhite and Ord, and even the Marine Corps Base at Camp Pendleton, where a team wearing Marine uniforms got away with nine M-16 rifles and an M-79 grenade launcher.

Operating in the Middle West, three soldiers from Ft Carson, Colo., home of the Army's permissive experimental unit, the 4th Mechanized Division, were recently indicted by [a] federal grand jury for dynamiting the telephone exchange, power plant[,] and water works of another Army installation, Camp McCoy, Wis., on 26 July 1970.

The Navy, particularly on the West Coast, has also experienced disturbing cases of sabotage in the past two years, mainly directed at ships' engineering and electrical machinery.

It will be surprising, according to informed officers, if further such tangible evidence of disaffection within the ranks does not continue to come to light. Their view is that the situation could become considerably worse before it gets better.

Source: Colonel Robert D. Heinl, Jr., "The Collapse of the Armed Forces," *Armed Forces Journal* 108:19 (June 7, 1971): 30–38

George McT. Kahin's *New York Times* op-ed, "History and the Bloodbath Theory in Vietnam"

George McT. Kahin was the director of the Southeast Asia Program at Cornell University, the co-author, with John Lewis, of the influential The United States in Vietnam (New York: Dial Press, 1967), and a noted critic of the American war. In this op-ed published three days after Nixon's November 3 address, Kahin claimed that Nixon was wrong on the facts buttressing the bloodbath theory and that his argument against withdrawal because of a likely bloodbath "has made it much more difficult for Americans to trust in a negotiated peace settlement."

The Administration's most persistent argument against a rapid or complete withdrawal of American troops from Vietnam has been that a bloodbath would take place if American forces were no longer available to protect President Thieu's regime from the National Liberation Front. Others hold that even if the President's forecast were correct, the number of victims involved would not approach the number of civilians who are certain to be killed during even a few more months of fighting in South Vietnam.

But however one estimates these possibilities, it is essential that a clear distinction be made between battlefield conditions and the situation existing after an armistice. In heat-of-battle conditions both sides in the past—and probably in the future—have carried out reprisals against those identified as working for the enemy....

This was apparently an important factor in the execution of civilians at Hué, and Army spokesmen have alleged that it influenced American conduct in the massacre at Songmy [My Lai]. So long as a particular battle is simply one episode in a continuing series, both sides will be tempted to take punitive measures against "enemy" civilians.

Such actions will probably continue until there is a ceasefire but they should not be taken as an augury of what will happen after a settlement. This is, however, just what President Nixon suggested in his speech Nov 3 when he equated a post-armistice situation with that of Hué in early 1968, where many civilians are reported to have been executed during three weeks of terribly intense fighting.

In asserting that Hué was "a prelude of what would happen" in a South Vietnam suddenly left unprotected by American troops, Mr. Nixon has not only argued against withdrawal but has made it much more difficult for Americans to trust in a negotiated peace settlement.

MR. NIXON'S WRONG FACTS

Even more damaging to this prospect is the President's appalling misunderstanding of what actually happened after the 1954 Geneva armistice. He charges that with the departure of the French army from northern Vietnam, the Vietminh "murdered more than 50,000 people and hundreds of thousands more died in slave labor camps," and that on the basis of this history we must expect a similar bloodbath in the South if American forces are withdrawn before Thieu's Government can stand on its own.

The President's account is contrary to the historical record. If his advisers have studied the reports of the International Control Commission, responsible under the 1954 Geneva armistice for investigating allegations of reprisal, they must know that in the first two years following that armistice a total of nineteen complaints alleging political reprisal in the North were lodged with the Commission, only one of which involved murder. During the same period at least 214 were lodged against Diem's Government in the South, including several reports of massacres.

[...]

SUPPORT – OR SOLUTION?

It was in the fall of 1956, more than two years after the Geneva [a]rmistice, that violence occurred on a significant scale in the North. This was unconnected with the anti-French struggle and was not in reprisal against Vietnamese who had supported France against the Vietminh.

Those concerned with political reprisals might well insist that in any future Vietnam settlement the I.C.C. or its equivalent be made much stronger to insure that it is capable of investigating alleged reprisals effectively.

And any President worried about a future bloodbath in Vietnam who looks to historical precedent for instruction should be as much concerned with the actions of an American-supported regime as with those of a regime we oppose.

Source: George McT. Kahin, "History and the Bloodbath Theory in Vietnam," *New York Times*, December 6, 1969.

Richard Nixon's Address to the Nation on the Invasion of Cambodia, April 30, 1970

The United States was deeply divided when Richard Nixon announced the U.S. "incursion" into Cambodia in late April 1970. Coming just several months after he had led Americans to believe that the war was winding down, the invasion sparked widespread outrage. Millions of Americans registered their opposition. Some of the largest demonstrations against the war came in the weeks following Nixon's announcement, and hundreds of universities ultimately shut down. The invasion of Cambodia destroyed much of the goodwill that Nixon had accrued in the preceding months.

The president recognized that he was speaking to a divided nation. In his address, which was broadcast live on both radio and television, he offered a throaty justification for what seemed to most Americans like an obvious expansion of the war while explaining that the United States must not appear a "pitiful, helpless giant." If it did, he cautioned, "the forces of totalitarianism and anarchy will threaten free nations and free institutions throughout the world."

Good evening my fellow Americans:

Ten days ago, in my report to the Nation on Vietnam, I announced a decision to withdraw an additional 150,000 Americans from Vietnam over the next year. I said then that I was making that decision despite our concern over increased enemy activity in Laos, in Cambodia, and in South Vietnam.

At that time, I warned that if I concluded that increased enemy activity in any of these areas endangered the lives of Americans remaining in Vietnam, I would not hesitate to take strong and effective measures to deal with that situation.

Despite that warning, North Vietnam has increased its military aggression in all these areas, and particularly in Cambodia.

After full consultation with the National Security Council, Ambassador Bunker, General Abrams, and my other advisers, I have concluded that the actions of the enemy in the last 10 days clearly endanger the lives of Americans who are in Vietnam now and would constitute an unacceptable risk to those who will be there after withdrawal of another 150,000.

To protect our men who are in Vietnam and to guarantee the continued success of our withdrawal and Vietnamization programs, I have concluded that the time has come for action.

Tonight, I shall describe the actions of the enemy, the actions I have ordered to deal with that situation, and the reasons for my decision.

Cambodia, a small country of 7 million people, has been a neutral nation since the Geneva agreement of 1954 – an agreement, incidentally, which was signed by the Government of North Vietnam.

American policy since then has been to scrupulously respect the neutrality of the Cambodian people. We have maintained a skeleton diplomatic mission of fewer than 15 in Cambodia's capital, and that only since last August. For the previous 4 years, from 1965 to 1969, we did not have any diplomatic mission whatever in Cambodia. And for the past 5 years, we have provided no military assistance whatever and no economic assistance to Cambodia.

North Vietnam, however, has not respected that neutrality.

For the past 5 years – as indicated on this map that you see here – North Vietnam has occupied military sanctuaries all along the Cambodian frontier with South Vietnam. Some of these extend up to 20 miles into Cambodia. The sanctuaries are in red and, as you note, they are on both sides of the border. They are used for hit and run attacks on American and South Vietnamese forces in South Vietnam.

These Communist occupied territories contain major base camps, training sites, logistics facilities, weapons and ammunition factories, airstrips, and prisoner-of-war compounds.

For 5 years, neither the United States nor South Vietnam has moved against these enemy sanctuaries because we did not wish to violate the territory of a neutral nation. Even after the Vietnamese Communists began to expand these sanctuaries 4 weeks ago, we counseled patience to our South Vietnamese allies and imposed restraints on our own commanders.

In contrast to our policy, the enemy in the past 2 weeks has stepped up his guerrilla actions and he is concentrating his main forces in these sanctuaries that you see on this map where they are building up to launch massive attacks on our forces and those of South Vietnam.

North Vietnam in the last 2 weeks has stripped away all pretense of respecting the sovereignty or the neutrality of Cambodia. Thousands of their soldiers are invading the country from the sanctuaries; they are encircling the capital of Phnom Penh. Coming from these sanctuaries, as you see here, they have moved into Cambodia and are encircling the capital.

Cambodia, as a result of this, has sent out a call to the United States, to a number of other nations, for assistance. Because if this enemy effort succeeds, Cambodia would become a vast enemy staging area and a springboard for attacks on South Vietnam along 600 miles of frontier – a refuge where enemy troops could return from combat without fear of retaliation.

North Vietnamese men and supplies could then be poured into that country, jeopardizing not only the lives of our own men but the people of South Vietnam as well.

Now confronted with this situation, we have three options.

First, we can do nothing. Well, the ultimate result of that course of action is clear. Unless we indulge in wishful thinking, the lives of Americans remaining in Vietnam after our next withdrawal of 150,000 would be gravely threatened.

Let us go to the map again. Here is South Vietnam. Here is North Vietnam. North Vietnam already occupies this part of Laos. If North Vietnam also occupied this whole band in Cambodia, or the entire country, it would mean that South Vietnam was completely outflanked and the forces of Americans in this area, as well as the South Vietnamese, would be in an untenable military position.

Our second choice is to provide massive military assistance to Cambodia itself. Now unfortunately, while we deeply sympathize with the plight of 7 million Cambodians whose country is being invaded, massive amounts of military assistance could not be rapidly and effectively utilized by the small Cambodian Army against the immediate threat. With other nations, we shall do our best to provide the small arms and other equipment which the Cambodian Army of 40,000 needs and can use for its defense. But the aid we will provide will be limited to the purpose of enabling Cambodia to defend its neutrality and not for the purpose of making it an active belligerent on one side or the other.

Our third choice is to go to the heart of the trouble. That means cleaning out major North Vietnamese and Vietcong occupied territories – these sanctuaries which serve as bases for attacks on both Cambodia and American and South Vietnamese forces in South Vietnam. Some of these, incidentally, are as close to Saigon as Baltimore is to Washington. This one, for example [indicating], is called the Parrot's Beak. It is only 33 miles from Saigon.

Now faced with these three options, this is the decision I have made.

In cooperation with the armed forces of South Vietnam, attacks are being launched this week to clean out major enemy sanctuaries on the Cambodian–Vietnam border.

A major responsibility for the ground operations is being assumed by South Vietnamese forces. For example, the attacks in several areas, including the Parrot's Beak that I referred to a moment ago, are exclusively South Vietnamese ground operations under South Vietnamese command with the United States providing air and logistical support.

There is one area, however, immediately above Parrot's Beak, where I have concluded that a combined American and South Vietnamese operation is necessary.

Tonight, American and South Vietnamese units will attack the headquarters for the entire Communist military operation in South Vietnam. This key control center has been occupied by the North Vietnamese and Vietcong for 5 years in blatant violation of Cambodia's neutrality. This is not an invasion of Cambodia. The areas in which these attacks will be launched are completely occupied and controlled by North Vietnamese forces. Our purpose is not to occupy the areas. Once enemy forces are driven out of these sanctuaries and once their military supplies are destroyed, we will withdraw.

These actions are in no way directed to the security interests of any nation. Any government that chooses to use these actions as a pretext for harming relations with the United States will be doing so on its own responsibility, and on its own initiative, and we will draw the appropriate conclusions.

Now let me give you the reasons for my decision.

A majority of the American people, a majority of you listening to me, are for the withdrawal of our forces from Vietnam. The action I have taken tonight is indispensable for the continuing success of that withdrawal program.

A majority of the American people want to end this war rather than to have it drag on interminably. The action I have taken tonight will serve that purpose.

A majority of the American people want to keep the casualties of our brave men in Vietnam at an absolute minimum. The action I take tonight is essential if we are to accomplish that goal.

We take this action not for the purpose of expanding the war into Cambodia but for the purpose of ending the war in Vietnam and winning the just peace we all desire. We have made – we will continue to make every possible effort to end this war through negotiation at the conference table rather than through more fighting on the battlefield.

Let us look again at the record. We have stopped the bombing of North Vietnam. We have cut air operations by over 20 percent. We have announced withdrawal of over 250,000 of our men. We have offered to withdraw all of our men if they will withdraw theirs. We have offered to negotiate all issues with only one condition – and that is that the future of South Vietnam be determined not by North Vietnam, and not by the United States, but by the people of South Vietnam themselves.

The answer of the enemy has been intransigence at the conference table, belligerence in Hanoi, massive military aggression in Laos and Cambodia, and stepped-up attacks in South Vietnam, designed to increase American casualties.

This attitude has become intolerable. We will not react to this threat to American lives merely by plaintive diplomatic protests. If we did, the credibility of the United States would be destroyed in every area of the world where only the power of the United States deters aggression.

Tonight, I again warn the North Vietnamese that if they continue to escalate the fighting when the United States is withdrawing its forces, I shall meet my responsibility as Commander in Chief of our Armed Forces to take the action I consider necessary to defend the security of our American men.

The action that I have announced tonight puts the leaders of North Vietnam on notice that we will be patient in working for peace; we will be conciliatory at the conference table, but we will not be humiliated. We will not be defeated. We will not allow American men by the thousands to be killed by an enemy from privileged sanctuaries.

The time came long ago to end this war through peaceful negotiations. We stand ready for those negotiations. We have made major efforts, many of which must remain secret. I say tonight: All the offers and approaches made previously remain on the conference table whenever Hanoi is ready to negotiate seriously.

But if the enemy response to our most conciliatory offers for peaceful negotiation continues to be to increase its attacks and humiliate and defeat us, we shall react accordingly.

My fellow Americans, we live in an age of anarchy, both abroad and at home. We see mindless attacks on all the great institutions which have been created by free civilizations in the last 500 years. Even here in the United States, great universities are being systematically destroyed. Small nations all over the world find themselves under attack from within and from without.

If, when the chips are down, the world's most powerful nation, the United States of America, acts like a pitiful, helpless giant, the forces of totalitarianism and anarchy will threaten free nations and free institutions throughout the world.

It is not our power but our will and character that is being tested tonight. The question all Americans must ask and answer tonight is this: Does the richest and strongest nation in the history of the world have the character to meet a direct challenge by a group which rejects every effort to win a just peace, ignores our warning, tramples on solemn agreements, violates the neutrality of an unarmed people, and uses our prisoners as hostages?

If we fail to meet this challenge, all other nations will be on notice that despite its overwhelming power the United States, when a real crisis comes, will be found wanting.

During my campaign for the Presidency, I pledged to bring Americans home from Vietnam. They are coming home.

I promised to end this war. I shall keep that promise.

I promised to win a just peace. I shall keep that promise.

We shall avoid a wider war. But we are also determined to put an end to this war.

In this room, Woodrow Wilson made the great decisions which led to victory in World War I. Franklin Roosevelt made the decisions which led to our victory in World War II. Dwight D. Eisenhower made decisions which ended the war in Korea and avoided war in the Middle East. John F. Kennedy, in his finest hour, made the great decision which removed Soviet nuclear missiles from Cuba and the Western Hemisphere.

I have noted that there has been a great deal of discussion with regard to this decision that I have made and I should point out that I do not contend that it is in the same magnitude as these decisions that I have just mentioned. But between those decisions and this decision there is a difference that is very fundamental. In those decisions, the American people were not assailed by counsels of doubt and defeat from some of the most widely known opinion leaders of the Nation.

I have noted, for example, that a Republican Senator has said that this action I have taken means that my party has lost all chance of winning the November elections. And others are saying today that this move against enemy sanctuaries will make me a one-term President.

No one is more aware than I am of the political consequences of the action I have taken. It is tempting to take the easy political path: to blame this war on previous administrations and to bring all of our men home immediately, regardless of the consequences, even though that would mean defeat for the United States; to desert 18 million South Vietnamese people, who have put their trust in us and to expose them to the same slaughter and savagery which the leaders of North Vietnam inflicted on hundreds of thousands of North Vietnamese who chose freedom when the Communists took over North Vietnam in 1954; to get peace at any price now, even though I know that a peace of humiliation for the United States would lead to a bigger war or surrender later.

I have rejected all political considerations in making this decision.

Whether my party gains in November is nothing compared to the lives of 400,000 brave Americans fighting for our country and for the cause of peace and freedom in Vietnam. Whether I may be a one-term President is insignificant compared to whether by our failure to act in this crisis the United States proves itself to be unworthy to lead the forces of freedom in this critical period in world history. I would rather be a one-term President and do what I believe is right than to be a two-term President at the cost of seeing America become a second-rate power and to see this Nation accept the first defeat in its proud 190-year history.

I realize that in this war there are honest and deep differences in this country about whether we should have become involved, that there are differences as to how the war should have been conducted. But the decision I announce tonight transcends those differences.

For the lives of American men are involved. The opportunity for Americans to come home in the next 12 months is involved. The future of 18 million people in South Vietnam and 7 million people in Cambodia is involved. The possibility of winning a just peace in Vietnam and in the Pacific is at stake.

It is customary to conclude a speech from the White House by asking support for the President of the United States. Tonight, I depart from that precedent. What I ask is far more important. I ask for your support for our brave men fighting tonight halfway around the world – not for territory – not for glory – but so that their younger brothers and their sons and your sons can have a chance to grow up in a world of peace and freedom and justice.

Thank you and good night.

Source: Richard Nixon, "Address to the Nation on the Situation in Southeast Asia," April 30, 1970, *Public Papers of the Presidents of the United States: Richard Nixon, 1970* (Washington, DC: Government Printing Office, 1971), 405–410.

Index

Note: Page numbers followed by "n" denote endnotes and *italic* page numbers refer to figures.

and military withdrawal 2, 40–1,
44–5, 49–50, 54–6, 62, 164–70; and
Nixon's secret negotiations 31–2;
opposition to 1, 28, 31, 39, 44–8, 57,
108; as a stalemate 39, 57, 60;
U.S. motives for 2, 6;
see also U.S. military
Vo, Alex-Thai D. 82
"vocal minority." *See* antiwar
movement
Voice of America 83
Voorhis, Jerry 5–7
Voting Rights Act (1965) 97

Wagner, Robert 10
Wallace, George C. 104–6
War of 1812 122
war on drugs 109–10; *see also* dog
whistle politics
War Powers Resolution 64
Washington, George 8–9

Washington Post 124–5
Watergate 59, 64, 80, 123–5
Wayne, John 74
Weaver, Velsa 106–7
Westmoreland, William 27
white flight 99
white resentment 95, 101, 108–9
"Whole Thing Was a Lie, The"
(Duncan) 48
Wicker, Tom 86–7
Wilkinson, Robert 158
Wilson, Woodrow 5–6, 9
Woods, Rose Mary 102
Woodstock music festival 98
Woodward, Bob 124
World War I 5, 75
World War II 6, 9, 16, 75, 147–8

Young, Marilyn B. 82
Young, Neil 98
Young Americans for Freedom 52

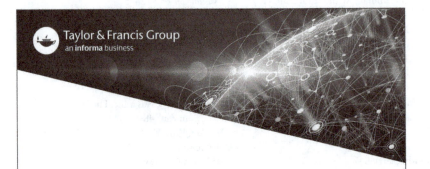